Enlightenment and History

Theory and Praxis in Contemporary Buddhism

Enlightenment and History

Theory and Praxis in Contemporary Buddhism

Bulkwang
Publishing

CONTENTS

It has brought us great pleasure to introduce *Enlightenment and History*, our favorite Korean-language book of Buddhist philosophy of history, to English-speaking societies. As the author Venerable Hyun-Eung writes in his Introduction, this book provides us with new interpretations of Buddhism and a new perspective of life and history that have never been proposed in Korea or anywhere else. We sincerely hope that those who are interested in Buddhism outside Korea also benefit from Ven. Hyun-Eung's insight and wisdom on enlightenment, life and history.

Enlightenment and History was first published in 1990, and this translation is based on its 2nd reprint issued in 2009. The book's 2nd edition was published in 2016 with two more chapters added, the first of which is included in this translation as its 6th chapter. The original Korean-language book has a small number of footnotes. With Ven. Hyun-Eung's permission, we added in, without specific notes on the authorship, several dozens of footnotes to help readers' comprehension. These footnotes are mostly about the definitions of Buddhist terms and the clarifications of their concepts. Some of these terms, which are repeatedly used throughout the book, make entries in the glossary. For the glossary, we have benefited much from A. Charles Muller's *A Korean-English Dictionary of Buddhism* (Unju Books, 2014) and Park Young-eui's *The Practical Dictionary of Korean-English Buddhist Terms* (Joheun Inyeon, 2012). We also used, in appropriate places and contexts, dozens of bracketed words and phrases to add in translators' supplementary explanations.

We thank Ven. Hyangjok, the abbot of Haeinsa Buddhist Monastery, who initiated and supported this translation project. He also invited us to stay at his monastery for three months so that we could, for our work, interact with and learn from Ven. Chong-Mook and Ven. Boihl of Haeinsa Buddhist Seminary. We appreciate the time these monastics generously spared for us. And our three-month stay would not have been possible without the support of Minnesota State University Moorhead for Chang-Seong Hong and the support of Minnesota State University, Mankato, for Sun Kyeong Yu.

We especially thank our twin daughters, Jaehyun Hong and Dahyun Hong, who worked as the copyeditors of this translation, read every single sentence carefully, and gave us very useful comments and suggestions.

Chang-Seong Hong & Sun Kyeong Yu

May 2017

Indian Buddhism started with the Buddha's teaching in his time and unfolded and thrived through the development of Nikaya Buddhism. Sri Lanka, Myanmar, Laos, Thailand and other South Asian countries have preserved, up to the present time, *Theravada Buddhism* that is reputed to have maintained well the Buddha's teaching of Early Buddhism. *Chinese Buddhism* translated into Chinese language all the various Buddhist sutras introduced from India and created the Flower Garland School, the Tientai School, the Pure Land School, the Zen School and other schools that conformed to the Chinese way of thinking and their culture. *Japanese Buddhism* received Buddhism from Korea and China, but they developed their own unique features of Buddhism in the lineage of the Pure Land School and Zen Buddhism. *Tibetan Buddhism* has the doctrinal system of Mahayana Buddhism, but it has the mysterious religious characteristics of Tantric Buddhism that recites mantras and of Transmigration Buddhism symbolized by Rinpoche.

Buddhism has changed, adapted and developed in various

forms for the past 2,600 years in accordance with the ways that peoples in different regions and countries have accepted and responded to it. And we have Korean Buddhism. For the past 1,700 years of its history, Korean Buddhism has maintained its tradition of Mahayana Buddhism, and Pure Land Buddhism and Zen Buddhism have been prevailing. Korean Buddhism has professed, since the 1960's, its stance to combine all branches of Buddhism with Zen Buddhism at its center.

The various forms of Buddhism in many Asian countries, as well as Early Buddhism of the Buddha's time, have been introduced to the West from the 19th Century. Today, not only Asians but also the people in Europe and the American continents have come to be interested in or believe in Buddhism. Be it the East or the West, contemporary humanity has met with the various versions of Buddhism based on the characteristics of many Asian countries. Buddhism has transformed itself in the process of its 2,600 year-old history as it has responded to these countries' cultures, peoples and social problems. That is, the basic teachings of impermanence, non-self, dependent arising, emptiness, wisdom, etc. have been modified and applied with various contents relative to different countries and times. They produced new terms and slogans, and these are the features of Buddhism that we encounter these days. Although we should respect all forms of Buddhism that these countries and peoples accepted and transformed in the past, we do not have to blindly accept them or know all of them in the contemporary time.

These days, when we study natural science, social science and ethics, we do not necessarily need to know everything in the books written 500, 1,000, or 2,000 years ago. It goes the same with the study of Buddhism. We should stop thinking that we must rely unconditionally on the terms and expressions in, and deduce all values from the books authored by the Indian Buddhist monastics 2,000 years ago, the Chinese Buddhist monks 1,500 years ago, and the Tibetan Buddhist monks 1,000 years ago. For the monastics in India, China and Tibet thought and described Buddhism with the social and cultural standards and problems of their own times, and their works cannot directly be applied to contemporary people's lives and historical situations.

It is now the 21st century. I believe that contemporary people should organize and process the Buddhist teaching in a contemporary way following today's culture, standard of knowledge, and identification of problems. It would only be a religious faith to believe that there existed in the past the original form of the teaching of Buddhism and we must derive all teachings from it. This may not be true to all cases. In other words, since Buddhism is not a system of teaching that was created and fixed 2,600 years ago, and since it has incessantly evolved responding to the place, time and people, we need to make Buddhism evolve in such a way that it comes to be appropriate for our time. It would be a misunderstanding on the character of Buddhism to claim that the original Buddhism is the Buddhism of a specific time or country in the past. For Buddhism is a teaching on how to understand life and history and it is a teaching that tells us how to live life and history. Buddhism should be arranged and processed anew as a much nicer and greater teaching in this contemporary time of science and rationality.

My book *Enlightenment and History,* translated from Korean to English in this volume, is a collection of essays that interpret Buddhist doctrines under the new light described above. In particular, this book interprets 'bodhisattva,' which is the initiating subject of the practical life in Mahayana Buddhism, as the combination of bodhi (enlightenment) and sattva (life, history), and defines the life of bodhisattva as 'enlightenment's becoming history' and 'history's becoming enlightenment.' I believe this is the representative of all the new interpretations in this book. Also, I classify the issue of 'fact judgments' on how to understand facts and phenomena as the area of bodhi (enlightenment) and the issue of 'value judgments' on how to live life as the area of sattva (history), and thereby I make their logical differences clear. However, at the same time, I claim that harmonizing these two areas into one area of life is the model of a nice and practical life, which is the bodhisattva that Mahayana Buddhism praises. This is also a new interpretation. And another new interpretation is that I explain the characteristics of 'Sudden Enlightenment' of Zen Buddhism in relation to the series of Thomas Kuhn's and Karl Popper's claims that deny the acceptability of inductive epistemology.

What I need to note, most of all, is that the essays in this book were deeply influenced by the reality of the rapidly changing South Korean society in the 1980's when I was in my thirties. The division of the Korean Peninsula, the undemocratic society under the decades-old military regime, the class strife between haves and have-nots, chronic regionalism, the ideological struggle between the left and the right, etc. – the South Korean society, where all these problems existed being mixed at that time, made a young Buddhist monastic seriously contemplate on how to apply the teaching of Buddhism to the problems of life, society and history. In short, the essays in this book were the attempts to find a way to express the Buddhist teaching in the fiercely heated historical situation of the contemporary time.

I became a Buddhist monastic in my teens and learned Buddhism in the environments of Buddhist monastery and Asian traditions. I did not have a chance to get a systematic modern education. However, monasteries also came to have close mutual exchanges with society due to the development of transportation and communication in the process of Korea's modernization, and, although I was a Buddhist monastic, I spent significant time seriously thinking about the problems of Korean society. Also, from the mid 1980's, I began to actively participate in several Buddhist organizations that were dedicated to the reform movements of society and Buddhism. While I was involved in these activities, I kept reading newspapers, magazines and various publications and published, in the media of the Buddhist society, my essays on the problems of Buddhism, society and history. This book is the collection of these essays.

I have confidence that the problems and claims I raise in this book provide new interpretations and perspectives that have not been discussed in others' writings on Buddhism. However, those Buddhists in Korea who were familiar with the preexisting Buddhist traditions did not really welcome this book of new interpretations that has unfamiliar terminologies and a new system of thinking. The general public dismissed it simply as a discussion of Buddhism and did not pay attention. Only a small number of Buddhist monastics and lay Buddhists gave me kind words of compliment and encouragement.

This book had its first edition published in 1990, its reprint was issued in 2009, and the second edition was published in 2016. Now it comes to be available in English by dint of the affection and support of Ven. Hyangjok, the abbot of Haeinsa Buddhist Monastery,* whom I have always respected. I am curious how the readers of English-speaking societies will respond and pay attention to this book. For this translation project, Dr. Chang-Seong Hong, a professor of philosophy at Minnesota State University Moorhead, and Dr. Sun Kyeong Yu, a professor of philosophy at Minnesota State University, Mankato, visited and stayed at Haeinsa Monastery, a representative traditional Buddhist temple in Korea, in the summer of 2016. Special thanks should go to them.

Bhikshu Hyun-Eung
November 2016

---

* Haeinsa Buddhist Monastery was founded in 802 CE. It is the largest temple in Korea that represents Korean Buddhism. This temple houses *Korean Tripitaka* composed of 81,000 wooden printing blocks made in the 13th Century. UNESCO has officially recognized *Korean Tripitaka* as a World Heritage Site.

1

Twelve Letters for My Dharma Brothers

Each of these letters was published in the monthly Buddhist magazine
Haein from January to December in 1987.

Mahayana and Hinayana

Dear my dharma brothers,[01]

We live in a monastery where we save words as much as possible for our spiritual cultivation. Still, I have found it rather awkward and embarrassing not to share some words of warm greetings when we come across each other on a regular basis. It has been said that scholars must observe each other very carefully after they could not meet for three days or more.[02] Now we need to remember that we are not just scholars but monastics – those renunciant practitioners

---

01 "Dharma brothers" refers to junior monks enrolled at the Buddhist seminary of Haeinsa Monastery.

02 Scholars could come to have serious determinations for their academic, moral and spiritual achievements while we did not meet with them. They could have accordingly improved their virtues significantly in a short period. Therefore, we need to carefully observe and recognize the merits of those who have changed themselves much so that we can pay due respect to them.

who are walking on their path to the truth. We should thereby try to improve ourselves day by day with unassuming but zealous efforts. The Buddha said that the practitioners of his teaching must always try to discuss topics on the truth whenever they get together and should never be lazy in polishing and refining their views. But we are currently deceiving others as well as ourselves as if we were mute. We might in fact be disguising our lack of wisdom and sophistication with 'Vimalakirti's silence.'[03] All this thought makes us tremble and break into a cold sweat.

Oh, I now realize that it has already been several years since you became members of the Sangha.[04] I bet you have read a good number of Buddhist sutras so far. I also believe that by now, you may have established your own vision and resolve as a renunciant[05] monastic. So, what is it like to be a Buddhist monk? Do you find your life as a monastic tolerable? Well, I suppose you might have somewhat developed the stomach to digest such a saying as "You achieve enlightenment at the very moment of your first bodhicitta!"[06] – did I get this right about you? Did you actually

---

03 'The silence of Vimalakirti' is used as a metaphor for 'profound silence' that reveals a deep understanding of the fundamental truth that denies any possibility of verbal description. It is here set in sharp contrast with 'the silence of ignorance.'

04 'Sangha' means 'the Buddhist order or community.'

05 The monks and nuns of this Korean Buddhist Order are required to renounce their family ties, give up personal properties, remain celibate, etc., etc.

06 "Bodhicitta" is a combination of "bodhi(enlightenment)" and "citta(mind)." The idea of bodhicitta is that one should wish (or, 'mind') to achieve enlightenment to save suffering beings of the world. According to the Korean Buddhist tradition, having bodhicitta is as good as achieving enlightenment because the great compassion of practitioners

come to have bodhicitta? There is no advanced levels or beginners' in our quest for truth. Accordingly, my dharma brothers and I should agree to ignore the junior-senior hierarchy[07] and proceed to discuss any topics together with no hesitation or reservations. It is somewhat relieving that we can, in this series of twelve letters, share our stories that we could not normally communicate with each other. Thus, it is truly exciting to choose the topic for the first letter.

It has just occurred to me that you have once tried to explain the distinction between Mahayana and Hinayana to a high school student you met on a trip. But you were frustrated because the student, who asked you the question, was not quite satisfied with your explanation, although you did your best to clarify the difference. Shall we, then, go attempt to discuss the problem of Mahayana and Hinayana for this first letter? I believe this issue of Mahayana and Hinayana involves quite a few important topics that need to be addressed.

What is Mahayana, and what is Hinayana? 'Mahayana' means 'the Greater Vehicle,' and 'Hinayana' is translated to 'the Lesser Vehicle.' Mahayana Buddhism is conventionally understood as the vehicle of teaching that innumerably many people can ride together and reach the state of nirvana in that vehicle. Hinayana

---

helps make their enlightenment easier and faster.

07 In the Buddhist monasteries, it was made clear, though implicitly, that junior monks and nuns were not supposed to challenge the authorities of their seniors in any regards – including the issues of the studies on the Buddha's teaching. Hyun-Eung claims that they should set aside this old tradition and discuss any topics together with no 'obstacles.'

Buddhism is defined, in contrast, as the teaching that can save only one person.[08] It has also been said that the southern traditions of Thailand, Sri Lanka, Myanmar, etc. belong to Hinayana. But the northern traditions of Korea, China, Japan, etc. are Mahayana schools. There are a variety of ways to differentiate Mahayana from Hinayana with their fundamental principles and the history of their orders, but we must admit that none of these typical criteria of distinction can fully satisfy us. On top of this, well, I have been somewhat doubting if Korean Buddhism can really be regarded as belonging to the Mahayana tradition. So, I believe we must now raise fundamental questions about the appropriateness of this criterion on the Mahayana-Hinayana distinction. Then, why don't you give a try and evaluate the following new idea I am suggesting?

Mahayana has upaya-paramita,[09] but Hinayana does not. For example, let me use a bike to clarify my points. Suppose that you understand the mechanics regarding the balance of two wheels and you also learn how to ride the bike. All this still belongs to the way of Hinayana. In contrast, to have a specific goal or clear purpose and ride the bike to go to Seoul, Busan, Daejeon, or other city will

---

08 From the Mahayanist perspective, however, the Hinayana teaching cannot save even one person.

09 Upaya is skillful means or convenient tools. The Buddha and Bodhisattvas use a variety of (innumerably many!) different methods to teach and save suffering beings depending on their aptitudes, temperaments, capabilities, etc. 'Paramita' literally means 'to cross over from this shore (this world of suffering) to the other shore (world) of enlightenment and nirvana.' It also means 'perfection.' Upaya-paramita, which is one of ten-paramitas, is the perfection of (the virtue of) skillful means to lead suffering beings to the other shore and save them.

be a matter of Mahayana's way.

In Mahayana Buddhism, we call the subject of actions and practices[10] 'bodhisattva.' (I believe that "bodhisattva" is a very nicely composed word.) The concept of bodhisattva is, as is well known, a combination of the concepts of bodhi and sattva. Bodhi is the perspective with which we understand the nature of being. In order words, it is to grasp being in terms of its dependent arising (emptiness). So, 'bodhi' means 'enlightenment.' I believe 'sattva' means that the perspective of dependent arising (emptiness) or enlightenment is applied to specific situations in history. Bodhisattvas make judgments and decisions, express their own views, and perform their actions in their own positions when they encounter specific situations in their given times and places. In other words, bodhisattvas are the ones who have the comprehensive criteria of judgments and patterns of action in all the aspects of history – politics, economy, society, culture, etc. However, this concept of bodhisattva may not be attributed to everyone who needs to make judgments and decisions for their actions and thoughts in every instant of their lives. For the unique nature of bodhisattvas is characterized by the way their stances and actions grounded on the perspective of bodhi, that is, enlightenment. Mahayana cannot be anything other than bodhisattvas' specific and historical positions and patterns of action. Now, what do you think of the following story?

---

10 These should include all those moral, social, spiritual, ..., actions and practices that constitute and complete the upaya-paramita of bodhisattvas.

Hinayana eliminates suffering and craving to set you free *from* them. Mahayana liberates you from suffering and craving by having you realize that they arise only dependently on conditions – that is, by having you grasp the emptiness of suffering and craving. To make the point more precise, it needs to be understood that Mahayana in its genuine form teaches freedom to – not *from* but *to* – suffering and craving. In other words, this Mahayanist freedom is not about an escape from suffering and craving; it is rather about the freedom to be obtained *in* suffering and craving.

In light of the foregoing discussion, we can see that suffering and craving never conflict with Mahayana Buddhism – the true Buddhism. To the contrary, Mahayana Buddhists believe that Buddhism is a system of teaching about the way to proactively take advantage of suffering and craving in order to establish our way of life and truly implement it in the midst of suffering and craving. After all, life arises and changes *in* suffering and craving. Don't you find this view surprising and alarming? All in all, I believe in this point so much as to claim that Buddhism should be based on our positive views on suffering and craving. But of course I am well aware that my claim is very different from the traditional and stereotypical view that Buddhism teaches to eliminate suffering and craving.

This is why I find it encouraging that the concept of 'upaya-paramita (the perfection of the virtue of skillful means)' leads us to see a variety of its positive implications. 'Paramita' means practices. We insist on the word "paramita," rather than just "practice," mainly to emphasize that it is the practice based on the worldview of dependent arising. It is just like the way the concept of 'bodhisattva' is a combination of the two concepts 'bodhi' and 'sattva.'[11] Here, we must pay close attention and see how such a significant word like "paramita" is combined with the word "upaya (skillful means)" and comes to bring about the concept of 'upaya-paramita.'

'Upaya' without 'paramita' would only be an ignorant compromise and blind following. Mahayana Buddhism has six-paramitas as its representative practices and virtues: dana-paramita (generosity, charity), sila-paramita (maintaining precepts, the practice of moral rules), kshanti-paramita (forbearance, patience under insult), virya-paramita (exertion, effort), dhyana-paramita (intensive meditation with clear mind) and prajna-paramita (wisdom that sees through the nature of existence).

However, I believe that even these six-paramitas, if they are viewed in light of the foregoing definition of Mahayana, belong to the domain of Hinayana. For these six-paramitas still lack the concept of history (specificity). It is upaya-paramita, which is the seventh paramita, that provides guidance and function for how, where and when to realize those six-paramitas – that is, the guidance and function for how to make them realized in specific historical contexts. I believe that we could attain the title of Mahayana only when we apply and connect the specific upaya-paramita to those universal and abstract efforts of the six-paramitas.

---

11 'Sattva' is about the practice in history based on the view of enlightenment (bodhi). The enlightenment is on the truth of dependent arising (emptiness).

Viewed in this light, the Four Noble Truth,[12] the Noble Eightfold Path,[13] the six-paramitas, the 37-aids to enlightenment,[14] the four winning methods,[15] the four immeasurable states of mind,[16] – all these belong to Hinayana. All these great teachings could become the dharmas (teachings) of Mahayana only when they are combined with the seventh upaya-paramita. If we follow my criterion of Mahayana, how and where do you think that Mahayana manifests itself in our present-day Buddhism?

"Everybody must be good and nice," "Make diligent efforts," "Don't do anything bad," "Be compassionate," "Try to get enlightened and save sentient beings," "Act as a bodhisattva of the Mahayana tradition," "Buddhist practices must be realized in more specific contexts of history" – all these maxims also belong to the domain of Hinayana Buddhism. It is because all these naturally good and impressive statements are nothing but tautologies

---

12 The Buddha's teaching of suffering, craving, elimination and the way: life is full of suffering, its cause is craving, we can eliminate suffering by removing its cause, and there is a way to accomplish this.

13 The Buddha's teaching of right view, right thought, right speech, right action, right livelihood, right effort, right mindfulness and right meditation.

14 They are: the four bases of mindfulness, the four right efforts, the four magical powers, the five faculties of goodness, the five powers, the seven factors of enlightenment and the holy eightfold path.

15 The four leading methods that bodhisattvas employ to approach and save people and other sentient beings: generosity, kind words or speech, beneficial conduct and amicable association.

16 They are: the immeasurable loving-kindness, the immeasurable compassion, the immeasurable mind of joy at the happiness of others and the immeasurable equanimity.

– obvious truths that do not convey any significant or useful meanings – unless they are combined with the specific issues of our real lives. What I mean is that we need to examine what actually is good and what others are bad in the real and specific situations of our time. We should also figure out the realistic way to conduct the acts of compassion. Further, we must apply all the statements of required actions and practices to the specific contexts of our reality and history. We will be able to deserve the title of Mahayana only when we accomplish all these goals. But the ideal of Mahayana would not be anything unexpected or surprising even if it requires all these ends to be met.

Have a good look at those laypeople in the society outside the Buddhist sangha. Take a close look at those monastic practitioners who make all the efforts for their moral and spiritual cultivations and do not even take care of themselves. Observe all of them because Mahayana is not a theory or idea. Perhaps we might always be inadvertently passing by the Mahayanist way of life of innumerably many nameless[17] bodhisattvas. On which level of thoughts do all those bodhisattvas around us have and ponder on these days, what stories do they share with one another, and what actions do they take based on these thoughts and stories? Well, I do not know much about it myself. But this will be understandable if we consider the countlessly many patterns of actions of bodhisattvas that should be as many as the number of bodhisattvas themselves. Furthermore, in this world, I do not think that there

---

17 'Nameless' here means 'unidentified.'

should be any fixed types of bodhisattvas or any collectively standardized patterns of their actions.

I do not myself know clearly why I have come to discuss, among all the available topics, the very issue of Mahayana and Hinayana in this first letter to be sent to my dharma brothers. We might in fact have so many other stories to share. From the trivial matters of everyday life to the difficulties of our studies, subjects to pay attention to, agenda to push forward decisively without hesitation or much contemplation ...

As was the case with the renunciant practitioners of the past, however, the major issue to ponder on for me, has always been the problem of our lives. I have also wanted to find out how to understand and respond to the issues of our society, history, and the world which are the other aspects of our same lives. I have, amid all these efforts, come to have a conviction that the Buddha's teaching itself is nothing but a fundamental clarification and instructions on these problems of our lives. I have even suspected that the Buddhist community came to instill the two different systems of Mahayana and Hinayana mainly to make the Buddha's teaching stand out even more prominently.

These days, I often find it quite boring to understand and discuss Buddhism following the line of this shop-worn classification. How tiring would it be to double-check and reconfirm the most basic principles? Further, what would this routine job be if it is itself not a matter of the Hinayanist manner? However, I believe that the future of our Buddhism – whether it should make us discouraged or hopeful – depends on how we meet these challenges. Perhaps it was this very belief that naturally led me to discuss the topic of Mahayana and Hinayana in this first letter.

Trees have in the end lost all their leaves that were quite thick and luxuriant last summer. The winter is ever more deepening. I guess it is about the time to prepare ourselves for spring.

I hope you make much progress in this year.

No-Mind Is the Way

This mountain monastery has not had as much snow as this for a good while. It feels like tranquility and peace has filled the entire mountain. The smoke occasionally rising from the chimney of the mountain hermitage looks friendly and comforting. The rabbit footprints on the narrow trail seem to be leading us to yearn for endless journeys.

Clouds drifting mindlessly, snow floating casually, tea boiling inside a pot on a hot stove on the warm floor of a cozy little room, a monk dozing off or meditating – perhaps this might be the kind of state that has been called the state of the Way in Buddhism.

A monastic practitioner asked Master Majo (Mazu, Matsu).

"What is the way?"

"No-mind is the Way."

"No-mind is the Way" – How many practitioners have been lost and wandering around in the valley of no-mind from the old times? But now, my dharma brothers, I am going to ask you again.

"Then, what is no-mind?"

I believe that no other system of teaching has been more misunderstood than Buddhism. Most of the Buddha's essential teachings are being understood in their 'bent' and misinterpreted forms. One of these crucial misunderstandings is the view that Buddhism is a 'mindless' religion. Buddhists have been characterized with the image of an aloof hermit who has left behind all the differentiation and judgments of right and wrong. The silence indistinguishable from dozing or sleeping and the attitude of indifference with a seemingly transcendental aloofness often accompanied by a faint smile are being accepted as the states of absolute quietude and nirvana.

In the midst of your studies, my dharma brothers, you must have heard from your senior monks and colleagues countlessly many times that you should not be involved in other people's arguments or disputes and instead you need to exert all your efforts only to obtain the Way of the Buddha. Plug your ears, blindfold your eyes, and keep your mouth shut to all the other 'non-essential' issues and silently make the most sincere efforts for your goals (of enlightenment and nirvana) – all this could look quite admirable on its surface. The Buddhist community has uniformly demanded its practitioners to have no-mind in the contents and circumstances of their studies and practices. But I believe this is where a dangerous trap is set on our way to studies and practices.

In both the Meditation School and the Doctrinal School,[18] 'no-mind' is used as a good expression that describes the state of enlightenment and the Way. But 'no-mind' is a term of rich contents and dynamic meaning that is more than, or in the opposite of, what most people think about it.

No-mind is usually understood as an empty mind. The point of this metaphor is that, as we can store anything in an empty container, we should be prepared to accept and accommodate anything by having our mind empty. But of course this is not a correct understanding of no-mind. On the other hand, no-mind may also be thought of simply as a pure, clean and calm mind compared to a bright mirror and still water. There is actually a method of meditational studies, Silent Illumination Meditation, that aims to keep thoroughly the state of no-thought-no-conceptualization in your meditation by dropping off all thoughts one by one. But wise Zen masters have already pointed out the problem that this method of Silent Illumination Meditation has.

Having no-mind is not a matter of eliminating sufferings and thoughts one after another. Nor is it a name of an advanced state of consciousness which is highly cultivated through gradual learning processes and purification. Not to speak of the state of quietude or

---

18 The names of these two schools manifest their major claims. The Doctrinal School emphasizes the importance of the studies of Buddhist sutras and other texts in their efforts to achieving enlightenment. The Meditation School in contrast focuses on meditation to facilitate the process of enlightenment.

poised silence. To the contrary, and strictly speaking, no-mind is not a mind devoid of everything; no-mind is completely filled [with cognitive activities]. It does not stay with no action; it takes actions proactively. No-mind does not want to stay neutral by choosing a compromised middle point between opposing parties; no-mind comes to be realized as it actively expresses specific views and thoughts.

We take the dictum "No-mind is the Way" at face value erroneously. In the environments of our meditational practices, we sit quietly, control our breathing, fix our postures, and often proceed to the submerged state of consciousness that does not have any perception or other cognitive activities – as if we were rocks or trees. But having no-mind is having active and proactive engagements. No-mind is full of actions and it manifests itself with a specific view and opinion. However, if we want to help the present-day Buddhist community understand and accept these points more easily, we may have to start to interpret Buddhism from a very new perspective.

"Halt everything and rest. Do not be concerned about anything." – Daehye (Dahui), the great master of Zen, criticized this line of erroneous stance for all his life. I also believe that the genuine form of the cultivation of no-mind must be fiercely implemented with a thoroughly critical and intense mind seeking after truth and enlightenment. What is most important is to proceed from the fixed, closed and inactive state (of mind) to the open and active stance (of mind). However, being open-minded and active does not mean that our mind is not able to settle in anywhere, has no stance or perspective, surrenders to relativism and does not find any views or values meaningful. Otherwise, it would also be a matter of falling to the state of nihilistic emptiness which the monastics of the old days warned against. Nihilism would make the vitality of life crushed and we would be alienated from history.

The Way of no-mind might look easy to understand at first glance, but it is not really such a simple matter. For instance, it is to think and act living in the real world but at the same time to have a stance and perspective of non-attachment to worldly affairs. This is the very point of what the Buddha taught in *The Diamond Sutra:* "Raise a mind [of compassion] without being attached [to the objects of compassion]." But the core issue of the problem is to see how these points can be realized in the life of both monastic practitioners and laypeople.

As I wrote in my previous letter, I believe that the true Way of no-mind manifests itself only through the realistic and specific methods of upaya-paramita.[19] In the areas of meditational practices as well, we need to cherish Phrase-Observing Meditation and take it more seriously than any other methods. For Phrase-Observing Meditation is based on the truth-seeking mind, full of intensive determination, faith and methodological doubt,[20] which is as

---

19 As noted in January Letter, 'upaya-paramita' means 'perfection of the practice/virtue of skillful means.'

20 This is about the three basic stances of mind that practitioners must keep in their studies of meditation. "Intensive determination" refers to the mind exploding with willpower. 'Methodological doubt' means the doubt about the propositions of Buddhism, that is, hwadu (key phrase, a single koan). 'Faith' is the belief that studies and meditational practices done by investigating the key phrase will lead to enlightenment.

passionate as an active volcano. In contrast, Silent Illumination Meditation is a dead practice which halts all cognitive activities and make us just like trees and rocks. The everyday life of ordinary Buddhists should also change. They need to stop remaining silent, passive, uncritical and uncreative but instead proceed actively to realize historical upaya-paramita.[21] But the typical way the teaching of no-mind has been received is not just a problem of practitioners of the Buddhist sangha. Laypeople in society have also been 'tamed' and accustomed to this misleading view of no-mind. So, I believe that this is not simply an abstract problem of Buddhist practices; it is something that we must examine fundamentally under the light of the mechanism of history.

My dharma brothers, as you know, our current society is called the post-industrial society. It is the society of advanced science and information technology. It is also divided by capitalism and socialism if classified in terms of political, economic and social system, and it is undergoing changes and modification. On top of all this, we are living in this country [South Korea] a distorted time – the time of divided Korea – which is the byproduct of the complex network of all of it.[22]

Buddhism teaches enlightenment. If getting enlightened is explaining our life and obtaining a correct perspective to see life

---

21 Upaya-paramita should be realized in specific contexts of history.

22 This letter was written in 1987 when the power of the Eastern communist block was still in its full swing. Also, Korea has remained divided as South Korea and North Korea since 1945.

and history, I believe enlightenment is possible by seeing through the relation and change of all beings.

It is not easy or simple to understand the relation and change of things. We need to cool down and get reasonable and rational. Also, we should not be attached to the doctrine of a specific religion or to some social ideology. We now really need our stance of no-mind, but how are we doing in reality? Aren't we letting all sorts of entertainment and decadent culture hurt and paralyze our eyes and ears? The so-called institutionalized media and the voices of established and conservative people have produced arguments and fabricated stories to serve the profits of specific interest groups and upper-classes. We have known this all along. However, media and opinion leaders, whose voices are covering the entire country, are leading the majority people of society to confine themselves to a small scale of ordinary life and live a life without social engagement or opposing opinions. This surely is only one distorted façade of the teaching of 'no-mind.'

To have the genuine form of 'no-mind' is to proceed from me – a small individual – to a new me which is essentially connected to the society, from a distorted me to the life of the entire society which is essentially related to me. So, the true no-mind is a key to make it possible for us to enjoy the freedom of the whole society as well as my individual freedom on the ground of mutual benefits and equality. We cannot simply blame the teachers of Buddhism on their instructions of the distorted no-mind. We should rather give a serious thought on this issue, reflect upon what has happened, and ask ourselves if enormous invisible powers and their intentions have been taming us to live a life without thoughts and criticisms against them.

Oh, my dharma brothers, let us get back to our issues. What is the Buddhist community, and what is a (renunciant) practitioner?

We monastics have left behind the circle of affection and family that make us most fundamentally attached to the secular life. We have also separated ourselves from the interest groups that pursue their own goals. We have tried even more and stepped back, with a calm and clear mind, from our own country, people, the world and human race. Haven't we gone through all these in order to observe and examine the problems of our lives so that we could discuss these difficult problems most objectively and fairly? To make the point rather grandiose, aren't we receiving the offerings and donations from the lay Buddhists (lay society) as a kind of payment for the services that we provide as masters who discuss and investigate all these problems of life comprehensively and objectively, and as authorities who proactively go solve these problems?

Yes, that's right. This stance of ours is the very stance of no-mind. It is the stance of fairness and righteousness, and this is nothing other than the historical stance.

There are various lessons in the teaching of no-mind that we monastic practitioners must keep in mind. Most important of all must be that we should get rid of the four marks[23] – a mark of self,

---

23 *The Diamond Sutra* and other scriptures address the four types of attachments that most people have. (1) The mark of self is about the attachment on the part of self when there is a relation between self and others. (2) The mark of personality addresses the state in which one, being a member of human race, is immersed in the narrow and

a mark of personality, a mark of sentient being and a mark of life
or soul - and at the same time transcend our limited perspectives
that are confined inside the fences of the order of renunciant
practitioners. That is, it is to throw away the mark of renunciant
cultivation.

What is the Way? No-mind is the Way.
What is the Way? The mind is the Way.[24]

This pair of question and answer seem to have the same points,
after all.

My dharma brothers, could you tell me what the Way is if it is
neither no-mind nor the mind?

A passage of an old verse has just occurred to me.

Do not say that no-mind is the Way.
For no-mind is also blocked by one meditative practice...

Snow is still silently piling up outside.

---

limited, very human perception. (3) The mark of sentient being is about the way we
get used to the phenomenon of life and mistake it for a self although life itself comes
into and passes out of existence only in terms of relations and changes. This mark
also refers to the stance that one might assume when he or she comes to have some
inferiority complex when his or her life is compared with the good lives of others. (4)
The mark of soul is a misconception that life is a substance and subsists for a period of
time.

24 This sentence may well be understood as meaning "To have the mind of bodhisattvas
full of compassion is to achieve the Way."

Just Clarify, No Holiness

The three months of the winter meditation retreat is over, and the monks have left for their pilgrimage. The mountain monastery has been immersed in the tranquility of early spring. I walked around the yard enjoying this rarely available free time and also peeked around this room and that. I can feel the last winter's heat of intense truth-seeking endeavors when I come across the sitting-meditation cushions piled up in order at the corner of each room or when I see neatly folded-up leaves of the sutras. I felt a chill as if I had been looking around a battle field. For what did the monks make such great efforts, and what were they looking for when they started their journey?

We usually call renunciant monastics 'travelers looking for the mind' or 'practitioners seeking after enlightenment.' We also call them 'the ones who search for the Buddha and try to make sages.' They regard as worthless what most people desire, say, properties, honor, pleasure and other 'social success'; they instead strive to achieve some 'lofty ideals' in a more noble poverty and a purified lifestyle. 'Lofty ideals' mean 'the state of being a Buddha,' 'the state of being in nirvana,' and 'the state of enlightenment.' Monks are treated in society with respect and prestige because they live a special type of life that most people may not be able to adapt to or easily tolerate.

We monastics live in the space of the temple. It serves us with the most familiar environments. The people we interact with are mostly other monastics or lay Buddhists. All this makes it somewhat likely that we lack a capacity to objectively examine our lives as well as one's own in the context of society and history. Even with regard to the language we use, we are quite accustomed to the Buddhist jargons that have been circulated only among us. The language of the lay society cannot but have certain limits due to its essential dependence on a specific idea or ideology. In contrast, isn't Buddhist terminology a logical language that was created to transcend these limits so that we can examine the problems of life fairly and objectively? Over the past two thousand years, however, I believe that those once-accurate Buddhist terms have gradually turned stagnant and fixed signifying the opposite meaning and that they have even shown the tendency to come to mean something absolute.

People's actions cannot go beyond the scope of their thought, and their thought cannot really escape from the language they adopt. For thought is composed of and carried out by language. We monastics use ordinary language as well, but, if our Buddhist language constitutes the pivot of our thought and logic, we might be using Buddhist terminology with too much ease simply following the traditional way. According to the principle of dependent arising (change and relation), which is the Buddha's core teaching, it is commonsensical that we cannot make anything absolute or fixed including the Buddhist terminology we use. We should not make Buddhist terminology absolute or mysterious, for instance, even such terms like 'the Buddha,' 'enlightenment' and 'truth (dharma)'[25] all of which we cannot dare mention lightheartedly due to the serious and rigid religious atmosphere.

Do you remember Bodhidharma's teaching?

When someone asked him "What is the holiest truth?" he answered "Just clarity, there is no holy truth." My dharma brothers, is there no truth? If there is no such holy truth, why should we go through all the studies and meditational practices, and why have we renounced our lay lives?

My dharma brothers, we need to take a deep breath here and listen to Bodhidharma who is presenting us the genuine form of Buddhism. We may think of his answer as a paradoxical teaching designed to give us a shocking awakening and have us shake off our conventional frame of mind. However, I believe the brilliance and greatness of this teaching actually reveals itself when we take his words at face value.

Numerous belief systems and religions of the world provide

---

25 'Dharma' has a wide range of meaning such as the Buddha's teaching, truth and ontological entity.

us with perspectives to see life and history. Some systems teach us to wear red eyeglasses to see the world. Others make us use blue lenses to observe. There are systems that use yellow glasses or black glasses. They make us view the world with the frame of red, blue or other colors (different belief systems) and claim that we can explain the world from a consistent perspective with the given frame of colored eyeglasses. This means that our cognitive system views things of the world through red (or blue) lenses. At the same time, it means that things come to be (recognized and) ordered in our cognitive system through those eyeglasses (belief systems). All this sounds reasonably plausible. On the other hand, some system claims that eyeglasses with colors (belief systems) cannot provide us with a true vision and that the genuine face of the world can show itself only through colorless transparent glasses. Doesn't this also sound great?

I call this stage of reflection 'a state attached to dharma (truth).' It is in fact a generally received practice to attempt to contemplate on 'some truth' with which we can consistently and thoroughly explain the world and transform the world with the truth. Even monastic practitioners often fall in this view. For instance, they tend to believe that Buddhism has 'the truth (dharma, law, principle),' not available in other belief systems, which lets us see the world most straightly and transparently. However, this is precisely what Bodhidharma criticizes so severely. He makes his point clear that there is no such a dharma, and that there is no such an absolutely true value system, either. That is, even colorless transparent eyeglasses are completely harmful and useless. The frame of eyeglasses should also be abandoned.

We are disposed to pursue some such 'dharmas,' and this disposition is based on a very deeply-rooted delusion. It is not just a problem of monastic practitioners. (But of course we cannot say that this is nothing but bad. Remember that Buddhism also gets started with our mind disposed to seek after such dharmas.) People in society pursue with their own conviction a variety of secular values such as money, pleasure, honor and prestige, ideology and other visions. All these pursuits may not be quite on the same level as the monastic practitioners' inclinations to pursue dharmas, but they show some tendencies of a similar type.

I bet all of you know the story of the search for the ox. It is about the ten stages of ox-herding. The story has been widely known through the mural paintings of temples. This fable tells us a story that if one could find an ox and control it, and when he experiences 'no man on the ox' and 'no ox under the man' and completes the perfectly harmonious unity of the ox and man as he plays a pipe sitting on the ox, and before he knows it, he will be able to get near the state of the Way (enlightenment). However, you must understand that this fable is a basic screening test designed to evaluate practitioners' appreciative eyes. The ox is a metaphor of his mind, temperament or desires. On its surface this story focuses, after one finds the symbolic 'ox,' on the several stages of taming and purifying process which leads to a complete control of the ox. This is where the trap is set.

Let us examine the very first part of the fable. A boy starts his journey to find the ox. Why does he think that it is somewhere out there, and why did he make up his mind to tame it? It is because he heard of the legend: There *is* the ox somewhere, and it will bring him great luck and fortune if he can tame it. If I may tell you of the story's conclusion now, however, the boy does not achieve his Way (enlightenment) by catching and taming the ox. The ox makes him erroneously believe for some while that he has attained the Way, but he achieves the way only after he realizes that the ox is not real and has no substance. He actually realizes this truth while he wanders about to find the ox, catches it, wrestles with it and tames it. 'Realize that neither the 'ox' as an object (of search) nor the boy himself as the searching subject has substance!' – this is the hidden but real message that the fable conveys to us. In this ox-herding story the 'ox' can be said to be what monastic practitioners pursue, but it may also be thought of, without stretch, as those (worldly) things that people in society so strenuously strive for. Accordingly, I think that the more appropriate title of this fable might well be 'A story of a boy who realizes that the ox is not an ox' rather than 'A story of a boy who searches for the ox.'

It is quite difficult to resist the temptation to seek after 'the world of truth' symbolized by 'the ox.' It is a generally observed tendency of virtually everyone, whether they are believers or non-believers of religions, to entertain some thoughts that there must be absolute truth, a transcendental world and the values that last for eternity. Mircia Eliade, a well-known historian of religion, wrote that these beliefs represent the way that primitive people of a very ancient time thought about the world and their lives in it. People tried to understand contingent and localized historical facts or actions (affairs of the secular world) in terms of their view of the transcendental and sacred archetypal world (the domain of holy entities). They attempted to connect with the world of eternity from the impermanence and meaninglessness of their history and thereby tried to escape from the angst on the constantly changing flux of history. I admit, of course, that this view provides a great insight on the steady pattern of human psychology that has lasted from ancient time to present time. It is the stance of Buddhism, however, that such a pattern of our psychology is in fact damaging (to our achievement of the way) and must be straightened out.

All in all, Buddhism makes it clear that we should not postulate the existence of some mysterious realm that is supposed to transcend our lives and history (our space and time). We can find the correct solutions for all the various problems of our lives and history by seeing through the nature of life and history themselves. Buddhism does not recognize or accept any value system based on the existence of God or sacred realms outside the stage of our real lives. In this regard, we may well say that the Buddhist perspective of life and world is in fact identical with the historical perspective of these issues, not with the religious doctrines on them. On the other hand, from the aspect of this historical perspective as well, Buddhism can be said to provide a reasonable (rational) and scientific perspective because it does not recognize the existence of an absolute and complete system of truth.

The Buddhist concept and view of history, which does not presuppose any transcendental or absolute system of values, is crucially different from the other perspectives of history already established and influential. However, the Buddhist historical perspective still remains incomplete and thus it is the task of us Buddhists to implement the Buddhist perspective in history and have its validity confirmed. Since this historical perspective is in a sense relativistic,[26] it must at first be so extraordinary as to make Buddhists quite puzzled. Even the Buddha had to say that it would be rare if there was someone who was not surprised or did not become nervous when he or she listened to 'this teaching (that there is no such thing as the holy truth).'

I believe we can accomplish our monastic practices and engage in historical activities through this rare kind of realization. It is to manage and live our lives in history with no harmful consequences while we do not postulate any transcendental or absolute truth. The Buddhist perspective, which is constituted by the principle of dependent arising, makes it clear that there is no absolute truth. However, this does not mean that there is some kind of logical pathway provided by the perspective of dependent arising which leads us to specific cases of upaya-paramita (specific methodologies and actions suitable in historical contexts). To the contrary, our upaya-paramitas will be available to us only if we observe and investigate all the constantly changing situations and realities of history and apply to them our abundant historical imaginations and practical efforts (bodhisattva practices) with our own convictions.

---

26 It is 'relativistic' in the sense that the Buddhist perspective necessarily considers the historical contexts when we try to solve the problems of our real lives and the world. In other words, Buddhists need to find solutions for life and the world according to, or *relative to*, the contexts of history.

However, aren't we currently wearing black eyeglasses that came up with all the glasses of so many different colors repeatedly overlapped, which is very far from getting rid of even the eyeglasses themselves altogether? But I am not saying that we should throw away our eyeglasses only after we come to have colorless and transparent lenses by peeling off one by one the screen of its red shade, blue shade and other shades of different colors. For we can take off all of them at one fell swoop.

My dharma brothers, you have left for a journey trying to find something. Looking at you from behind, I attach for you the following poem of an old Zen monk.

Live your daily life keeping in your mind the nature of being,
Act considering the relations of the world.
All it takes is to eliminate erroneous views,
There is no reason to seek after the holy truth (dharma).

Transmigration and Liberation

"APRIL is the cruelest month, breeding

Lilacs out of the dead land, mixing

Memory and desire, stirring

Dull roots with spring rain

Winter kept us warm, covering

Earth in forgetful snow, feeding

A little life with dried tubers.

......"

– From T. S. Eliot, "The Water Land"

The season has changed once again. We now stand in front of the prospect of this new spring with the memories of the past year. Although we do not remember exactly when, however, spring has begun to approach us not only as a beautiful sigh of admiration and excitement, but also as a light of sorrow and pain. On one hand, we become completely thrilled with the joy of new life and desires rapidly springing from the excitement for another new year which is currently empty and should be filled [with all our activities]. On the other, the comfortable sleep of the last winter and the rest we took with an excuse of the preparation [for the new season] have by now become an unshakable and familiar temptation we cannot get rid of. At times, this temptation makes us unable to rise up in front of the challenge of a new creative life and has us indefinitely languish in calm and composure.

We have a fear of birth and change. It has settled in our minds, but where has it come from? Our lives are in the process of transmigration which is made of endless chains of 'coming into existence' and 'passing out of it.' This tragedy of our lives has been an essential problem ever since the remote antiquity, and it is also the very starting point of the Buddhist teaching. Many factors cause the tragedy of life, but I believe it is the experiences of frustration and death that are definitely the primary causes of this tragedy. All things surrounding our lives change every instant, which makes them replaced every season and every year. Our lives will likely be over in about 70 years at best, and all the successes and failures, rises and falls, and ups and downs in such a time period are all fleeting and ephemeral.

As my dharma brothers would agree, I do not see transmigration simply as a repeated process of persisting life in which someone lives for about 70 years and dies and then gets reborn as another human, or even as a dog or a bird. A chanting has a line, "Every day and every night, we die and live again tens of thousands of times." We live and die tens of thousands of times even in one day, and we continuously go through this process – is this the true form of transmigration or what? In other words, transmigration means change, and the content of transmigration is the incessant process of 'coming into existence' and 'passing out of existence.'

Sometimes lay Buddhists ask the following question:

"Is it true that we transmigrate? Is it really true that a human dies and gets reborn as another human, or as an animal, too?"

"The Buddha's teaching is so reasonable and scientific that it makes very good sense to contemporary people. However, the issue of transmigration defies our efforts for confirmation and thus allows for lots of questions."

A good number of people have these questions, but I actually believe it is a crucial misunderstanding of the Buddhist teaching that has caused all these problems. The concept of transmigration is not an original or proper idea of Buddhism. It was an idea already widely-discussed among the ancient Indian religious views before the birth of Buddhism. The idea of transmigration was a generally received concept around the 6th Century BCE when the Buddha was living. Its idea was, "You are not finished when you die, you are born again and live and die again, over and over again with no end."

People in the ancient times did not have enough food or other necessities. There was no social system structured and implemented reasonably, and civilization was in its rudimentary stages. Everyday life was full of suffering. Their lives were hard, but they did not think that any more birth would make the situation any better or desirable. People wanted to end their lives peacefully, but in the end they came to wish not to have any further rebirth at all. This belief brought about the concept of 'moksha' meaning the 'liberation' from the shackled life of transmigration. And they thought they could achieve moksha (liberation) through such special religious practices as self-mortification, sacrifices and prayers.

However, the view that life was unsatisfactory and full of suffering was caused not just by the inequality and poverty in the social system and life. It also originated from the religious worldview of their time that claimed that the life of an individual self (atman) is an instance of distorted form of the 'complete whole.' Brahman (the whole self) is the Creator and the origin of all values. The individual life is nothing but a limited form of Brahman when it undergoes delusion in space and time. After all, an individual is an incomplete, impermanent and limited being and thus suffering is unavoidable.

The teaching of Buddhism starts with the total denial of both 'Brahman (the whole self)' as the true foundational substance of the world and 'atman' as the subject of the individual self. The way all beings exist is determined by the changes of and relations to conditions. The domain of the cognizing subject and the domain of the object cognized respond to each other and simultaneously determine the way both domains exist. Therefore, we cannot recognize the existence of any independent or immutable *real* entity.

We can confirm the truth of this view in people, material

entities or any other things in the world. But this truth does not mean 'the non-existence' of beings. In fact, this view repeatedly emphasizes the truth that all beings need to be understood in terms of their mode of existence – that is, in terms of their changes and relations. In light of all this, there can exist in Buddhism neither divine Brahman as the foundational substance nor 'I (atman)' that keeps the identity of individual life.

The Buddha clarifies the features of our lives in a new light with this basic framework of understanding. This framework is the Buddha's teaching of dependent arising, which is about the law of changes and relations, and it lets us accept the preexisting view of transmigration with a new interpretation. This teaching is so innovative as to be quite a surprise not only to the people in his time but also to our contemporaries. We can participate in and contribute to history with an open stance keeping in our minds the truth of changes and relations while not being attached to the subject called 'I.' We are able to incessantly experience life and the world and fulfill our goals without even postulating the subject 'I.' Also, we might very well have a way of life that conforms to the causal laws of morality and science. All in all, the Buddha's teaching opened up a new horizon for the entire humanity.

However, the Buddha's new interpretation of transmigration has not always been easily understood by people. Even Buddhists, not to speak of the general public, often have fears about the impermanence of all the matters of our lives and get attached to the issue of death (attachment to the matter of life and death). Wouldn't it be rather strange if Buddhists, who believe in the truth of changes and relations, are afraid of changes?

There are two kinds of suffering caused by changes and impermanence. The first of these two is the suffering about our real lives in which nothing we cherish lasts for eternity although we wish otherwise. However, we can overcome this problem rather easily because every one of us comes to realize the inevitability of the changes of all things as we grow older and wiser. The problem is the suffering that keeps troubling us even after we understand the truth that everything changes sooner or later, one way or another. This kind of suffering is caused by our ongoing and persistent attachment to the idea of real-being.[27] This is the case in which we are trapped by the erroneous system of beliefs that there exists a certain [immutable] subject and it is this subject that undergoes changes. If we could thoroughly understand the truth of changes and relations, we will come to realize that there can exist neither a subjective real-being (I, atman) nor suffering and joy that accompany it.

Let us recollect what the Sixth Patriarch Huineng awakened us to. It happened when a monastic student asked Huineng for a teaching with an arrogant attitude.

"Where on earth are you from, as you are showing off such an attitude?"

"Our real lives are impermanent and thus cannot wait for any

---

27 This 'real-being' is a being that satisfies the definition of atman. That is, it is something that exists independently with its own essence.

moment to be met and handled. Then, isn't the problem of life, which is nothing other than the issue of birth and death, all the more important?"

"Why don't you realize that life is that which 'has never been born' to begin with?"

This really is a thunderous teaching. Yes, it is. We live the process of our lives in such a way that we transmigrate everyday as we are born and die tens of thousands of times a day. So, we must understand correctly, above all, what birth is, and also what death is. As there is no beginning point or ending point in a circle, so is there no start or end in the continuous process of life which is explained in Buddhism with the twelve links of dependent arising. Necessarily, no being has been born. To understand this truth is to realize the law of no-birth[28] of all phenomena. A candle light keeps burning all night although each flame of each instant is different from any other flame of any other instant. Likewise, we need to understand that a birthless being exists as an endless chain of continuous changes although there is no subject of transmigration. However, it is not the case that there is no law of causality even if there exists no such a subject. Our current names and features connect to other names and features of ours at other time as the result of our experiences and practices.[29] An analogy will help

---

28 'No-birth' means 'birthlessness.'

29 The three occurrences of "our" in this sentence are used only as a convenient tool to make a clearer sense. It does not imply the existence of persistent selves.

clarify this point. A seed of a rice plant transforms, with rain, sunlight and water, to a sprout, flowers, and ripen grains and gets different names and features, but there is here some identifiable process of causal relations and continuity.

Then, what is it that the concept of transmigration truly implies in Buddhism? Of course Buddhists also teach goals such as 'to get out of transmigration and achieve nirvana' and 'to be liberated.' Even in these cases, however, what they mean is different from the goals of Hinduism such as 'to end the phenomenon of transmigration (changes)' and 'to enter the world of silent stillness and death.' There was a time when Buddhists also believed that nirvana or liberation could be achieved through the elimination of suffering and craving, or the elimination of experiences and practices. But this was a case of total misunderstanding. What is correct is never to end or reduce the phenomena of the external world,[30] or to give up experiences or practices. It is just to be liberated from the belief of the really-existing 'I' immanent in our lives. If we are liberated from 'I,' we can accept the actual phenomenon of transmigration itself as the bona fide mysterious world of liberation. The suffering that Buddhism teaches us to eliminate, actually, means nothing but the belief of the really-existing 'I.'

There was a Zen monk who once believed erroneously that the core of [meditational] practices is to end and reduce all the external phenomena, that is, all the various actions and mental states. After

---

30 'The external world' is in contrast with one's internal world.

he finally realized the true meaning of liberation, he confessed as follows.

The poverty of past days was not true poverty,
Today's poverty is genuine poverty.
In the past days I tried not to leave even a spot of land to stick in an awl,
Today I have finally thrown away the awl itself.

My dharma brothers, it seems that those azaleas which have completely reddened this spring, may well be rather the symbol of liberation and nirvana. For they show us the exciting true picture of transmigration which makes us refuse to languish in the status quo or frustration. My dharma brothers, shouldn't we accept as our resolve what we have discussed today with the story of transmigration and then vow to live the lives of Mahayana bodhisattvas in the following way: Buddhists need to abandon the negative view on transmigration they used to have. They should shake off everything that makes them stagnate or abandon history. Also, they must see through, and make use of, the changes of history with their creative resolutions.

Form Is Emptiness, Emptiness Is Form

I am concerned that those several unexceptional letters of the past months might have caused unintended confusion to you in your studies. My dharma brothers, as you must have intensely experienced on your journeys between meditational retreats, sentient beings in the world are suffering in dangerous fires. The sky is filled with their cries calling for bodhisattvas' swift actions and decisive vows (the resolve for historical practices and participation). Our hasty and feeble minds may make us feel the need to get something done immediately, but we cannot solve the problems with just our compassionate minds that feel the suffering of people together. We need the eyes of wisdom that read our lives and see through history.

The moral failure of our contemporary society that has so tragically divided the people in civilizations is rooted in the collapse of the studies of humanities.

This statement of an America journalist is quite full of sharp insight and wisdom. I believe it can help us if we apply the wisdom of this statement to illuminate our situations. All the situations regarding the rapidly unfolding contemporary civilization, politics and economics are driving many people into the belief in trend that social sciences can solve all our problems. However, even capitalism, which we can at first glance effortlessly understand simply from an economic point of view, assumes, deep down, Cartesian dualistic epistemology that differentiates the cognizing subject from the object [of cognition]. It is also widely known to people that such socialism as Marxism is based on the (object-oriented) materialistic worldview.

As we saw above, all the laws of social sciences also naturally presuppose as a backdrop certain worldviews and specific forms of epistemology. So, we will have to face a lot of problems if we accept the entire system of a theory with no critical examination only because some part of it is useful and applied to limited specific cases. Therefore, although the problems of politics and economic policies are much responsible for all the various negative phenomena of our current lives, I believe that the lack of understanding our worldview and realizing its nature – that is, the lack of epistemology and ontology – is also quite accountable for the advent of all these difficulties. All these call for, I feel, the great efforts of us Buddhist monastics.

Today, I suppose I am going to talk about the Buddhist

ontology or epistemology – although these two cannot in fact be separated in Buddhism.

The core teaching of Buddhism which could be found consistently from its early sutras through Mahayana sutras was how to understand beings[31] such as material entities, mental states, languages and value systems like laws and morality. Early sutras say, "He who sees beings (dharmas) comes to see dependent arising (changes and relations), and he who understands dependent arising comes to understand beings." Also, *The Prajnaparamita Sutras* teach, "The five aggregates (a material basis and four types of mental states that constitute a human being) are all empty."[32] Both these traditions provided their points to clarify the core teaching of Buddhism: How to understand beings. 'The teaching of dependent arising,' which views all beings in terms of their changes and relations, is the universal logic of a cosmic scale. It should also become a foundation of the methodology and knowledge of natural science. Further, the teaching of dependent arising needs to be thoroughly and deeply understood so that it can evolve enough to make itself a theory of society and history based on specific facts of history. This teaching of dependent arising obtained more enriched contents when Mahayana Buddhism emerged and the new term 'emptiness' was introduced. "Emptiness" was a word coined as the result of progress for an era and of the accumulation

---

31 What is meant by 'beings' is dharmas.

32 'Empty' here is often translated as 'emptiness.' Hyun-Eung's comments on this will follow shortly.

of our historical experiences. It was a part of the language of life, the historical language. Unfortunately, however, these days the original teaching of emptiness is not being correctly understood by us or transmitted to others. It is actually even seriously distorted, especially in those Buddhist traditions using Chinese texts.

Let us discuss this issue with the famous phrase from *The Heart Sutra*, "Form is emptiness, emptiness is form." It is not hard at all to understand it. Firstly, we focus on 'Form is emptiness' and translate it to "The material world[33] is empty." If we are to explain this point further and understand it in terms of a teaching of dependent arising, it will become *"There is no purely independent domain in the material world. Everything originally relates to, and overlaps with, each other. Above all, all of them are subject to undergoing the process of changes."* Therefore, the sentence "Form is emptiness" replaces all the several italicized sentences with an abridged expression, that is, with one agreed-upon word "empty." In short, "Form is emptiness, emptiness is form" means that 'the material world is composed of changes and relations,' and, conversely, 'what is made of changes and relations is the material world.'

But we have come to have troublesome issues because we have tried to understand this teaching, which is in fact not so difficult to comprehend, as if it had some profound and unfathomable points. Let us examine a number of misunderstandings on emptiness.

---

33 'The material world' originally meant 'the material basis of a human being.' However, its meaning was extended to include as much as the entire material world.

Firstly, it is to think of emptiness as nothingness. Emptiness is here understood as a denial of existence. So, 'Form is emptiness, emptiness is form' should mean, on this erroneous view, 'what exists does not exist, what does not exist exists.' This is to explain the teaching of emptiness in quite a puzzling and groundless way of nihilism.

Secondly, it is an interpretation that the concept of emptiness is the opposite of the concept of matter and that emptiness is something mental. So, they think, 'Matter is mind, mind is matter.'

Another misconception is to believe that emptiness is the immutable substance of things, and that form is its external phenomena which undergo changes. It seems this misunderstanding was caused by the negative influence of Laozi and Zhuangzi's Daoism that had already existed in China when Buddhism was first introduced there and translated into Chinese. There are many mistakes in the translation and interpretation of 'emptiness' among the sutras interpreted during the time when the Chinese tried to understand Buddhism in light of the terms of their preexisting religions and systems of beliefs. We can see that *The Treatise of Zhao,* written by the preeminent Buddhist thinker Sengzhao, also has the Daoist dualistic view of substance and its function.

Su Dongpo's *Ode to the Red Cliffs* has the following passage.

Do you understand [the nature of] that water and the moon?
The water flows as it does but it has never flown away,
The moon may appear full or crescentic but it never changes its size.

Things of the world never stop changing even for an instant from
the perspective of change, but
Everything lasts for eternity from the viewpoint of immutability...

This poem, which more or less has naturalistic romanticism
as its backdrop, shows us the unique pattern of Chinese belief
systems that sees things of the world in terms of their dualistic
viewpoint of substance and phenomena. The problem is that many
Buddhists easily follow this trend of thought in an unexpected
way. Zen masters occasionally use such paradoxical expressions
as "The bridge flows but the water stands still" or "Mountain flows
and water stands still." But we must understand that these cases
also manifest various analyses and insights on the changes and
impermanence of beings, not the dualist view of substance and
phenomena.

Therefore, we should get rid of the dualistic thought of
substance and phenomena when we examine beings, but we
must also stop thinking of 'emptiness' as something separate that
belongs to a different world than the world of 'form.' After all,
we introduced the concept of emptiness primarily as a convenient
tool to shake off dualistic thoughts. In other words, it is not the
case that we bump into emptiness only at the end stage of our
investigation after we thoroughly analyze various states of affairs
of the phenomenal world and discard non-essential elements from
them one by one. We must understand that all the myriad things of
the phenomenal world exist in the mode of emptiness (changes and
relations), and that emptiness is nothing other than the very mode of

existence of the phenomenal world. Form surely is emptiness, and emptiness itself is form.

Now we need to pay attention to the crucial mistake that we are still prone to make even when we understand the features of beings in terms of changes and relations. We usually describe the teaching of dependent arising (the teaching of emptiness) as 'the teaching of changes and relations.' But the gist of this teaching is actually not that there exist some 'things' – whether they are things or concepts – and they change in relation to other 'things,' but that there exist, to begin with, no such 'things' that we give names to and substantivize. This is because all beings change and relate to other beings. This point that we cannot recognize the existence of some 'things' in the phenomenal world starts Buddhist epistemology and provides its representative proposition "No being has substance (atman)."

What this means is, if I may borrow some philosophical jargons, we should always refuse to accept any form of realism. But of course this nonrealist stance should not be confused with nihilism. Buddhists claim with this nonrealism, "There is no purely independent domain in the realm of beings, no form of being is self-caused,[34] and everything comes to existence and changes in relation to other cause and conditions." But the Buddhists' nonrealist stance does not imply that there exists no being at all. What it means is, therefore, that the feature of all beings is such that they exist in the process of changes while being overlapped with one another.

---

34 There exists no such self-caused God, for instance.

There are cases in which some people comprehend the features of beings in terms of their changes and relations but their basic perspective still cannot go beyond the scope of realism. This is a problem. Let me sort out the subsets of this problem as follows.

Firstly, their perspective is grounded on pluralistic realism. According to this view, there are in this world innumerably many people A, B, C, D, ... and their thoughts, and there also are many things a, b, c, d, ... and other entities. All of them go through changes in terms of mutual influences. We may regard this view as a kind of elementalism.

Secondly, their view is based on dualistic realism. This seems somewhat like an abridged form of the first case. They divide this world on a large scale with the cognizing subject and the object of cognition, and then they try to understand our lives and history in terms of the interactions and progress of these two domains. The problem of this dichotomy between the cognizing subject and the object of cognition is that we cannot recognize at all the existence of temporal priority between these two domains, or the existence of any part as a purely independent domain of each, due to the laws of relations regarding their mutual determination and formation. This is the fundamental stance of Buddhism, and the problem of this second view has been already overcome by such theories of general disciplines as dialectical logic or phenomenology.

Thirdly, their view is founded on monistic realism. Brahmanism, the monotheistic Christian belief system, or materialistic Marxism, etc., will belong to this case of the view. (Perhaps Marxism might belong to all three of these subsets of the problem.)

Due to the limited space I cannot here discuss all the related issues, but I must note that it is interesting to observe that all these views are being classified as versions of the realist worldview although each of them is based on a different worldview. Anyhow, it is quite puzzling for the beginners of Buddhist studies to find out that there are many various branches and deep-rooted classifications in 'the realist way of thoughts' that Buddhism steps forward to deny more than anything and before everything else. However, we must be awakened to the message that it is simple but crucially important to understand correctly the principal Buddhist proposition, 'Form is emptiness, emptiness is form.' For only through this fundamental perspective can we shake off agitated and nervous minds and finally achieve nirvana, and Bodhisattvas are able to obtain skillful means to save sentient beings from their suffering.

> Form is emptiness, so, with great wisdom, do not be attached to life and death,[35]
> Emptiness is form, so, with great compassion, do not be attached to remaining in nirvana, either.

I believe this is a lesson practitioners must naturally keep in their minds.

I hope you always take care of your health.

---

35 The choice of words in the text literally means 'birth and death.' I believe that 'life and death' is more appropriate interpretation in this context.

Sudden Enlightenment, for the Revolutionary Enlightenment
- The Twofold Structure of Emptiness

My dharma brothers, today I would like to move onto the principal
issue of Buddhism for our talk. We may well accept that no issue
is unimportant in itself and any issue is a principal problem of
Buddhism. However, I am going to address, among all those
important issues, what Buddhists intend to achieve with their most
fundamental attention.

In Buddhism, we call the conscious efforts to turn to and
achieve a goal 'turning to set a direction to go in' (setting a direction,
hereafter). These days we use this concept to signify 'transferring
to neighbors and society the merits and meaning of Buddhist
ceremonies and events after we carry them out.' However, I believe
it will be correct to see that the true meaning of this concept is
not about what should be done after actions are completed, but
about the goal-oriented intentionality that precedes actions. So, to
have the awareness of 'setting a direction' is to have a consistent

awareness of the goal from the beginning stage of actions till the end.

Buddhists believe that we should direct and converge all our will and actions eventually in the solution of three problems. We call it 'setting directions to three places.'

Firstly, setting a direction to bodhi[36] is [having] the awareness of intention to obtain the correct enlightenment (perspective).

Secondly, setting a direction to actuality means [having] the awareness of intention to make realized the feature of beings revealed by the correct perspective.

Thirdly, setting a direction to sentient beings is [having] the awareness of intention and goals to solve the problems of all sentient beings.

These three issues cannot be separated from one another and they may well be understood to belong to the same dimension. The first reason of this is that all practices and concerns are ultimately for the issues of our lives (setting a direction to sentient beings). The second is that we must first of all correctly understand this world including our lives in order to resolve those issues (setting a direction to actuality). Its third reason is that we must for the same purpose have the correct perspective, that is, the eyes of enlightenment (setting a direction to bodhi). Accordingly, when such a Mahayana scripture as *The Flower Garland Sutra* [*The Huayanjing, The Avatamsaka Sutra*] mentions 'setting a direction to sentient beings,' and when Zen traditions encourage the pursuit of enlightenment (setting a direction

---

36 'Bodhi' means enlightenment.

to bodhi), we must understand that these two traditions are in essence implying 'setting directions to three places' although each of them is emphasizing a different aspect of the same issue.

On this view, all those representative practical endeavors that Buddhism advocates – for instance, the six-paramitas: generosity without hesitation (dana-paramita), putting into practice moral virtues (sila-paramita), patience (kshanti-paramita), exertion (virya-paramita), having a clear mind of concentration (dhyana-paramita), and bright wisdom (prajna-paramita) – should ultimately be directed to the aforementioned three places: bodhi, actuality and sentient beings. Furthermore, each and every move of our life and all the efforts we make in our social activities regarding jobs, environments and patterns of behaviors must also be directed in the end toward these three issues.

These three issues may be said to be three different parts of the same spectrum, but if we carefully examine their contents, we come to realize that we must first complete 'setting a direction to bodhi,' which is a part of the same task, in order to accomplish the final goal of 'setting a direction to sentient beings.' This 'setting a direction to bodhi' is about the very problem of 'enlightenment' which all monastic practitioners pursue and exert themselves to, day and night, giving up desires, pleasure, honors and prestige, and even sleep. It is the primary goal of all studies and meditational practices. Then, what truly is 'enlightenment,' and how do you think we can attain it?

'Getting enlightened' is, as I discussed several times in my previous letters, to learn and internalize in ourselves the points of 'the teaching of emptiness,' that is, 'the teaching of dependent arising.' A good number of scholars and Buddhists understand and explain to others in their own ways what emptiness is, what is the teaching of dependent arising which is the law of changes and relations. With this achievement only, however, neither oneself nor others can have an unbreakable confidence that they have obtained 'the great awakening.' The reason of this lack of conviction is simple and obvious. It is because they have not clearly realized the law of dependent arising or emptiness. We seem to understand 'emptiness' or 'dependent arising' to some degree. At closer and repeated examinations, however, we come to suspect that we lack something in our understanding. This suspicion gives us no choice but to reflect on sutras yet again or keep exerting ourselves with hwadu.[37] Why is all this happening? Is 'the teaching of emptiness' such a difficult topic to understand? Anyone who has learned some level of Buddhism can explain theoretical aspects of 'the world of emptiness' in a grandiose way. But, then, how can we learn and internalize in ourselves 'the world of emptiness' as 'definitely my world of enlightenment'?

Many people are not able to learn by experience 'the world of emptiness.' I believe this is due to the dualistic approach and thoughts that divide the world into the domain of cognition and the domain of beings respectively. Anyone can easily get used to the habitual attachment to this pattern of thoughts, even without the influence of the Western worldview. I am confident that the

---

37 A single koan, a key-word.

Buddha's teaching was designed to help us shake off this most severely impaired pattern of thoughts which has been generally accepted by people.

Let us first examine what cognition is in order to show that 'the cognizing subject' and 'being as the object' do not belong to separate domains.

1) Cognition does not exist as pure cognition itself. It can exist as cognition only when it holds being as the object, that is, only when it has contents.

2) When this happens, cognition is 'being itself,' and cognition is formed and determined by being.

With regard to being as the object, on the other hand,

1) Being exists only as much as it is cognized.

2) That being which is not cognized does not exist.

3) Being is tainted by cognition (being is determined by cognition).

As we saw above, 'cognition' and 'being' do not have their own independent and separate domains; they come to share the same domain as they determine and constitute each other. If I use the terminology of emptiness, cognition is empty and being is also empty. Cognition is incessantly formed by being(s) as the object and it changes constantly, and at the same time it grasps and determines being(s) as the object. Unless we thoroughly understand this point, we will be inclined to the sort of psychologism that tells us, 'Everything depends on how we think of it' or 'All will be fine as long as we train and control our mentality' when we try to solve the problems of the world. Or, we will grasp the problems merely as issues that exist in the world of objects and end up with the kind of objectivism that drives us only to materialistic or institutional aspects of the problems.

Now the most important point to remember is as follows. Objects are empty[38] as objects themselves, and cognition is empty as cognition itself. But when objects are cognized, and when cognition is about the objects, we must understand that objects and cognition have a dynamic structure which makes each other empty. Accordingly, the problem of 'cognition' and the problem of 'being' are not separate issues; they are one problem. Let us pay attention to this point. Usually we seem to get, from the terminology of 'emptiness,' some monotonous impression that it describes objective entities, which gives us some feeling of complication and pedantry. However, I understand 'emptiness' in terms of its two kinds of complex constitution. The one is the feature of 'epistemological emptiness,' and the other the feature of 'ontological emptiness.' I used the concept 'epistemological emptiness' because cognition is empty in its relation to being, and also I used 'ontological emptiness' because being is empty in its relation to cognition. This way, I made stand out the point that 'cognition' and 'being' are not separate, but, on the contrary, they completely relate to and interpenetrate each other.

---

38 'Emptiness' needs to be understood as changes and relations.

If we take this point of view, we can easily derive the following conclusion. We need to normalize the domain of beings to normalize the domain of cognition; likewise, we should normalize the domain of cognition in order to normalize the domain of beings. Namely, the liberation of cognition and the liberation of beings make the necessary and sufficient condition for each other. So, the issue of cognition and the issue of beings should not be handled successively in a temporal order; they are the task that requires a simultaneous solution. To see through and learn by experience this kind of twofold and dynamic structure is nothing other than 'enlightenment.' This 'enlightenment' cannot be achieved by a gradual process in a temporal order. It is completed instantaneously. It is a 'revolutionary situation' that transcends gradual causal processes.

I believe that the aforementioned point is what is implied by the word "sudden enlightenment" that the Zen School uses to refer to 'enlightenment.' I translate 'sudden enlightenment' to 'revolutionary enlightenment.' Since the Buddha and patriarchs have had the same teaching, naturally their enlightenment should also be the same one. I believe that the choice of the word "sudden enlightenment' the Zen School made to describe enlightenment is quite suggestive. It reveals to us not only that it surely shows us the teaching of emptiness in a more pointed way, but also that it clarifies more the key point on the contents and method of studies and meditational practices to learn and internalize in oneself the teaching of emptiness. I see that the concept of 'sudden' is truly significant and wonderful. To understand this concept is to understand the Buddhist world of enlightenment from its core.

The concept of 'sudden' should not be understood literally or only in its temporal sense as 'suddenly,' 'instantaneously' or 'all at once.' 'Sudden' also means 'the instantaneous advent of enlightenment.' What is more important to us is, however, 'sudden' means not only the simultaneous dissolution of the twofold interrelatedness of cognition and being, but it also, in its contents, signifies symbolically the total transformation of the worldview between before and after enlightenment. This view of sudden enlightenment teaches that we do not arrive at enlightenment as a result of training and purifying our efforts remaining in the preexisting perspective or awareness; it teaches that enlightenment is a matter of having a totally new worldview of a different level than the preexisting one. Regardless of the length of time spent in the process of one's efforts to achieve enlightenment, enlightenment takes place not through some gradual process but through a revolutionary transformation. So, the word "sudden enlightenment" has served to declare the guiding principle that we must not understand Buddhist practices and enlightenment as a gradual process of making efforts.

Sudden Enlightenment, for the Revolutionary Enlightenment
– The Great Way Is Gateless[39]

My dharma brothers, we need unusual thoughts and actions in unusual times. No matter how much we elevate the preexisting ideas themselves, we can never reach new ideas. New ideas and new actions are never the consequences of the progress of old ideas and old actions; they are the results of revolutionary creation and transformation. What I need to emphasize repeatedly is that we should not understand enlightenment (sudden enlightenment) as some subjective mental state to be obtained by apprehending a certain world or realm of objects. For this is another dualistic stance and it is a mistake that reduces enlightenment to the common level of cognition. To get enlightened is to learn and internalize in oneself the inseparable and dynamic structure of being and cognition. It is

---

39 As Hyun-Eung clarifies this point in this letter, this sentence means 'There is no special point of access to the Buddhist Way or enlightenment.'

not a gradual procedure; it is a revolutionary transformation. Also, enlightenment is not just about the level of beings as objects or only about the level of cognizing subjects; to get enlightened is to meet the synthesized world of both. Also, this means that the unity of wisdom and its associated practices need to be embodied in oneself; it does not mean that there is a temporal order of before and after in the matters of wisdom and actions. I believe it will be good to refer to the teaching of the Sixth Patriarch Huineng (AD 638-713) in order to understand the revolutionary nature of enlightenment. Huineng Sunim[40] was the *de facto* founder of the current Zen School, and he was the one who made the revolutionary character of enlightenment more specific. It has been said that Huineng had his enlightenment approved by his teacher when Huineng presented a poem and refuted the poem of his fellow Sunim Shenxiu who claimed that practices [leading to enlightenment] should be made of gradual efforts. The contents of their poems are as follows.

The body is the Bodhi Tree,
The mind is like a clear mirror standing.
Take care to wipe it diligently,
Keep it free from all dust.

– Shenxiu (gradual)

Bodhi has no tree to begin with,
The clear mirror is nowhere standing.

---

40 "Sunim" is a transliteration of the Korean word for 'Buddhist monastic.'

Originally there is not a thing (there is no real being),

Where can there be any dust?

– Huineng (revolutionary)

Shenxiu sees enlightenment as the resulting product of gradual efforts. But Huineng does not even postulate any fixed system of cognition or criterion of truth which is symbolized by 'clear mirror' and 'bodhi.' He stands solidly and thoroughly by the position of emptiness and shows that the path to enlightenment is not made of gradual procedure. In other words, it is only superfluous to note that the dust itself is not a real being, and we must realize that even the base to which the dust gets stuck does not really exist. Then, claims Huineng, the problem of dust that appears on the surface of the base is naturally solved. As one might say, "What is the point of cleaning the color or the dust on your eyeglasses so hard? Even the colorless and transparent glasses are unnecessary. Why do you think we should ever wear glasses, in other words, why do you think that we should see things in light of 'some criterion' or 'a certain logical system'? Let us take off any eyeglasses, smash them." This is the very gist of Huineng's sentence "Originally there is not a thing."

The revolutionary nature that Huineng instilled in his School underwent a clear interpretation of his junior Monk Huihae (AD 541-609) that 'sudden' means 'eliminating every erroneous view all at once' and 'enlightenment' means 'not accepting a real being of any logic or contents.' Furthermore, Huineng's tradition of revolutionary enlightenment reached its climax when Haegyeo Sunim (AD 518-568) presented such a paradoxical proposition as

"There is no gate that opens up to the truth."[41]

This statement, "There is no gate that opens up to the truth," claims that there is no 'method [way]' to enter the truth. It professes that no efforts or practices may make a direct cause to let us enter the realm of truth. If we think of the realm of truth as the state of liberated mind that knows the emptiness of all beings and is thus not attached to anything, all the efforts and practices, which are made before we arrive at this state, are directed by an awareness tainted by something. For whether they are attached to an epistemic level, to an ontological level, or to something that combines both the levels, they are all captured by the erroneous awareness of real being.

No matter how much we have controlled and purified our mental states and awareness, as long as they are founded on the view of real being, they have, from a logical point of view, nothing to do with the world of emptiness that transcends the level of the awareness of real being. No matter how much and how deeply we have continuously made our efforts to liberate ourselves from the bondage of cognition, we cannot achieve it unless we are liberated from the world of being. Conversely, we are not able to liberate ourselves from the constraints of being, however hard we try it, unless we are free from the bondage of cognition. As all this signifies, the statement "There is no gate that opens up to the truth" reveals to us, in a paradoxical way, the point that all thoughts and

---

41 The original Chinese sentence literally means 'The Great Way is gateless.' 'The Great Way' signifies 'enlightenment' or 'truth.'

actions before the realization of the world of emptiness, no matter how much they get accumulated and ordered, do not in essence have any necessary relations to the world of enlightenment.

'Enlightenment' is not a result of thoughts and actions piled up before the enlightenment; it is that which belongs to a totally new level. If I may borrow the terminology of logic, it will be: "Enlightenment may not be achieved in the way that a conclusion is derived in inductive logic."

The negative criticisms and unfavorable stance on the scientific methods provided by inductive logic have also become a general trend in Western philosophy since the 18th Century. For instance, David Hume denied the validity of the classical view of causation and claimed that no matter how many individual observational statements are collected they do not derive a general statement that implies an infinite number of observational statements. Karl Popper also thought that a new scientific theory or law does not come to appear as a consequence of the inductive method of investigation. As in the case of arts, according to him, there is in science no fixed logic of methodology that leads to a new scientific theory. Every scientific discovery involves 'irrational elements' or 'creative intuitions' in Bergson's sense. Einstein also said that he had searched for the most fundamental and general law that could be derived with the methods of pure deduction and should be able to draw the way the world exists as its conclusion. However, he admitted that there was no law of logic that led to such a law. He also believed that a theory cannot be produced from the results of observations; for him, it can only be originally created. The views of these philosophers of science give many messages and inspirations to Buddhist practitioners.

If we see from the perspective we must take in our pursuit of enlightenment, we will understand that even our efforts to get out of some specific views, as long as they are made before our realization of the truth of emptiness, have nothing to do with the open world of emptiness because those efforts are made while we still are captured by the erroneous background awareness [view] of real being. However, this new perspective does not imply that studies and meditational practices themselves are meaningless or should be given up. Of course not. We do not ignore or take less important the point that these efforts provide crucial opportunities that serve as momentums for enlightenment, although we do not obtain enlightenment as a result of causal relation when we view the process from a logical point of view.

Accordingly, when we achieve sudden enlightenment through a single koan [hwadu, a key phrase], a learning experience in our ordinary day to day life, an illuminating consideration of a phrase in a sutra, or our own insight into the world, all of these make important opportunities and momentums for enlightenment although they are not necessarily preceding conditions if viewed from the stance of causality. This is why Huihae Sunim presented his second proposition "There is a way everywhere" right after he suggested the first "The Great Way is gateless." As we can see from the history of the Zen School, there was a great variety in the way that so many Zen masters achieved their enlightenment and that all the individually unique experiences of their own constituted the opportunities and momentums for their enlightenment – all this confirms my point.

If we pay attention to this point, we need to realize that it is important, especially for meditational practices in Zen traditions, to exert ourselves to advance to enlightenment as we try not to make the following two types of mistakes. One is the distraction of thinking and actions that we come to have with our thoughts to seek after enlightenment; the other is a kind of nihilistic state of mind (a state of slumber of confused mind) that negates and eliminates any action, thought and efforts. What I mean is that pursuing enlightenment itself is also an outcome of the idea of real being which is constrained by 'truth' or 'enlightenment,' etc. and accordingly it should also be avoided. On the other hand, the actions of our conscious minds could be directed to eliminating pointlessly even the consciousness or awareness itself if our conscious minds lose the targets of their mental activities. Then, these actions of our minds will eventually lead only to enervation and bottomless darkness. So, we must reject them. There is a method of harmonious practices called 'equal maintenance of alertness and quiescence' that was designed to overcome the defects of these two types. It is a way of practices that keeps up 'alert tension' and the mental state liberated from the awareness of real being. Zen masters have always emphasized the importance of this method for ages. With this practice of 'equal maintenance of alertness and quiescence,' therefore, we can escape from the shallowness and narrow-mindedness of empiricism, and we can also protect ourselves from the ahistoricism and antihistoricism that skepticism begets.

If you, my dharma brothers, are suspicious of the revolutionary characteristics of enlightenment, perhaps you may well recollect the story of the ten stages of ox-herding. We usually explain this fable, made up of paintings that show the ten stages of ox-searching, as a metaphor for the process of gradual practices [that leads to enlightenment], but this is a very misguided interpretation. This fable purports to show its core teaching that the point is not to find and tame the ox but to realize that the ox is not an ox. The eighth stage of this fable, 'the disappearance of both the man and ox,' makes the very state of sudden enlightenment, that is, the stage of revolutionary enlightenment.

In this stage, the disappearance of the ox signifies the disappearance of the concept of being; the disappearance of the man symbolizes the removal of the cognizing subject that has been reified and become a real being. Accordingly, 'the disappearance of both the man and ox' is about the mode of 'revolutionary enlightenment' that has simultaneously accomplished the liberation from both cognition and being. It is also to leap into the world of emptiness that has the twofold structure of epistemological emptiness and ontological emptiness.

This is the kind of state in which we make a complete change in history from the stage of delusion to the new stage of enlightenment. Also, this kind of situation is not achieved step by step in a temporal order; it is the new stage of enlightenment made possible only through a revolutionary situation. This is why this situation belongs to a new level which is differentiated from its previous state.

The man makes all efforts and achievements through the stages up to the seventh in order to tame and train the ox so that the man and ox should reach a harmonious unity. At the eighth stage, however, we realize that neither the man nor the ox is a real being. The eighth stage does not have any logical connection with any stage up to the seventh; and there is a deep logical gap. What this means is that all the efforts and actions made before the simultaneous disappearance of both the man and ox, that is, before the state of enlightenment, are not the direct cause that brings about enlightenment. But, of course, although the actions and efforts accumulated in the state of delusion are not the direct cause that leads to enlightenment, this does not make meaningless or useless all the efforts that have been made so far. In spite of this acknowledgement, however, we need to pay attention to and clearly recognize the logical gap between the efforts before enlightenment and the enlightenment itself. For this is the key point to understand the revolutionary character of enlightenment.

So, enlightenment is not an issue that can be settled in terms of the length of time or the amount of efforts invested in its pursuit. Enlightenment is a matter of whether we can transform our perspectives and make them belong to a new level or not. The following passage of Huangbo Sunim helps us have confidence in our understanding of this point.

"If those who learn the Way cannot reach the realm of no-mind at one instant, they are not able to achieve the Way no matter how long they continue their practices. For they cannot obtain liberation because they are constrained by their determination and efforts to achieve the Way. However, depending on individuals, it takes a longer or shorter time to arrive at the realm of no-mind. Some directly reach this realm of no-mind at the spot right away – where and when they listen to the teaching of the Way. Others reach the state of no-mind in the process of their believing, following and practicing the teaching (ten stages of faith, ten abodes, and ten dedications).[42] Yet another group of people achieve the state of no-mind only after they go through the ten grounds of sages,[43] the completion of which enables them to get free from

---

42 The following explanations are extracted from A. Charles Muller's *A Korean-English Dictionary of Buddhism* (2014).
Ten stages of faith: Faith is the entry of Buddhist practice. They are (1) the stage of faith, (2) the stage of mindfulness, (3) the stage of making efforts, (4) the state of mental stability, (5) the stage of the wisdom, (6) the stage of self-restraint, (7) the stage of directing to goals, (8) the stage of maintaining the dharma, (9) the stage of detachment and (10) the stage of aspiration.
Ten abodes: What it means is that the mind dwells peacefully in the principle of emptiness. They are (1) the abode of awakening operation, (2) the abode of nurturing, (3) the abode of practice, (4) the abode of producing virtues, (5) the abode of being replete with skillful means, (6) the abode of correct mind, (7) the abode of no-backsliding, (8) the abode of the true child, (9) the abode of the dharma-prince and (10) the abode of lustration.
Ten dedications (ten kinds of directing): They are (1) dedication to saving all sentient beings without any mental image of sentient beings, (2) indestructible dedication, (3) dedication equal to all Buddhas, (4) dedication reaching all places, (5) dedication of inexhaustible treasuries of merit, (6) dedication causing all roots of goodness to endure, (7) dedication equally adapting to all sentient beings, (8) dedication with the character of true thusness, (9) unbound liberated dedication and (10) boundless dedication equal to the cosmos.

43 The ten grounds of bodhisattva development in the Flower Garland system are (1) the ground of joy, (2) the ground of freedom from defilement, (3) the ground of emission of light, (4) the ground of glowing wisdom, (5) the ground of overcoming the difficult,

the domains of matter and mind.

Accordingly, the process of practices may be long or short depending on individuals. However, we can achieve the Way only when we reach the realm of no-mind and the efforts themselves made during the process of practices are not essentially related to the Way. Reaching the realm of no-mind does not imply that we understand or obtain some contents in this realm. What it means is only that, although we do not even assume any fixed stance or perspective, we come to have a genuine angle of view that functions soundly when we see things. In this realm of no-mind, regardless of whether it has been reached at one instant or through the efforts made for an indefinitely long period of time, there is no difference in its capacity if viewed from the standpoint of enlightenment."

From *Dharma Essentials for Mental Transmission*

(Record of the Transmission of the Lamp, Book 9)

---

(6) the ground of manifestation of reality, (7) the ground of far-reaching, (8) the ground of being unperturbed, (9) the ground of wondrous wisdom and (10) the ground of the dharma-cloud. This exposition is extracted from A. Charles Muller's *A Korean-English Dictionary of Buddhism* (2014).

Sudden Enlightenment, for the Revolutionary Enlightenment
– Enlightenment and History

We now must address another important issue in our discussion of enlightenment.

It has already been several years, but I remember this story of two monks. One was a monk of the Zen order who practiced meditations, and the other was doing Buddhist missionary works on the front line. The Zen monk asked the following question.

"Why are those enlightened ones of our time inferior to the enlightened ones in the distant past? Why is it impossible for our current enlightened ones to exercise their supernatural powers? They even get sick. Why can't they transcend the limit of ordinary human beings? Does this mean that the studies and meditational practices of these days are misguided and ineffective? How can we attain the great enlightenment and capacities as the good teachers in the distant past did?"

Then, the other missionary monk responded as follows.

"I do not think that our enlightenment is something of abstract and idealistic achievement or an issue of a person's individual matters. Of course a person as an individual should be able to keep a revered personality and engage in practical actions. Further, he or she must proceed to embrace and solve all sorts of social problems and build a Pure Land society.[44] We can achieve enlightenment and become Buddhas only when we accomplish all these. Therefore, my missionary work is not a volunteer work being done after my enlightenment; it is my social engagements and activities that make up the process of spiritual path-finding to attain enlightenment."

Both stories of these two monks show us an equally genuine and serious truth-seeking stance resulting from a pure religious zeal. But I cannot but point out a misunderstanding of enlightenment which is involved in each monk's thoughts.

The two monks' stories might be misleading us about the true meaning of enlightenment. Getting enlightened does not mean that an enlightened person comes to have many capacities for individual purposes. It does not indicate, either, that he has solved all social problems. I renounced the secular life and became a monk when I was young, and I also believed at one time that enlightened ones get supernatural powers to see through the events of the past, present, and future, to walk on water and to fly. As I came to be interested in the issues of history and society, I believed that Buddhism has principles, laws and methods of practices that can solve socially all the problems of society and people in the nation, etc. as well as

---

44 'The Pure Land' is an ideal world of Buddhism.

the problems of life in an individual. I just thought that I was still ignorant, so I could not find the principles, laws and methods of practices, or redefine them in a new way following the change of time.

Many Buddhists, including myself, may well have had this kind of view at least once. Those progressive Buddhists who devote themselves to the problems of society with more acute attentions are rather concerned in their mind about, and reflect upon, whether their efforts should be based more on Buddhist doctrines and spirits. So, while they are running on the front line of the field of social practices to their fullest, they at times withdraw themselves to the framework of 'Buddhism' or hesitate to act looking backward to Buddhism, like a stretched-out rubber band snapping back. On the contrary, those conservative Buddhists who try to maintain the traditional stance tend to criticize social engagements and activities of these progressive Buddhists claiming that they are not the way of Buddhists.

However, my dharma brothers, from sometime in the past I have come to realize that all these various types of thoughts have resulted from the confusion about the problems of 'enlightenment' and 'history.' First of all, I would like to tell you that 'the world of enlightenment' and the problem of 'changes and development in history' are the issues which belong to different levels. (This is about a very subtle issue.)

'Enlightenment' is to see life in terms of the law of changes and relation, that is, with the perspective of emptiness. It is thus to take off the screen of the view of real being from life and beings. This is to grasp all lives and beings non-substantially; it is to understand all beings as hypothetical entities or illusory entities in the process of changes. Further, it is needless to say that the subject who realizes all this is also non-substantial and illusory. Accordingly, the world of enlightenment is not a level of so-called Western epistemology in which some subjective frame of cognition exists and it understands being as the object in one way or another. To get enlightened is to realize that the domain of being as the object and the domain of cognizing subject generate, connect to, influence and determine each other, which is to simultaneously realize the mutual connection and reciprocity of the domain of cognition and the domain of being and see through, at the same time, their non-substantiality[45] (non-self, anatman).

Therefore, 'enlightenment' is to realize that the domain of lives is emptiness (the world of changes and relations non-real) non-self, hypothetical and illusory. Unlike all this, on the other hand, 'the cultivation of virtues and the expansion of capacities in an individual's life' or 'the process of changes and development in society' may well be altogether called 'the domain of history' in a broad sense. In the world of history, we recognize the reality of being provisionally or definitely, and, based on this, we pursue the changes and development of being.

We will then come to find a subtle logical gap between the stance of 'enlightenment,' which is about the non-substantiality [non-real-ness] of being, and the stance of 'history,' which is directed

---

45 The literal translation of Hyun-Eung's Korean word is 'non-real-ness.'

towards our ordinary lives of, say, building shelters and houses, running farms, etc. all of which are based on some definite belief of real being. It is just like that each of whiteness and hardness of a stone in Go game belongs to a different level. Consequently, we cannot solve the various problems of history with our enlightenment on emptiness; on the other hand, we can easily understand that no matter how great achievements we may have accomplished historically we are not automatically able to understand that being, that is, history is not real.

All this leads to the point that the two monks in our previous case can never reach enlightenment in spite of their great efforts and pure motivation. For how to establish and take care of individuals and society and how to realize their non-substantial [non-real] feature are different matters. However, the two monks did not have an accurate understanding in differentiating the level of 'history,' which changes and improves various problems of individuals and society, from the level of 'enlightenment,' which sees through the illusoriness of everything in history. So, they roughly mixed these two levels and aroused confusion in themselves.

My dharma brothers, I believe that it is now the time we need to point out, revisiting the same issue from a different angle, that the worlds of 'enlightenment' and 'history' can never be dualistic or have nothing to do with each other. For instance, we must note that, as whiteness and hardness are unified in a Go stone although each of them belongs to a different level of issue, 'the world of enlightenment' and 'the world of history' are unified as one inseparable feature of life.

This unified feature of life consists in the close connection and overlapping of bodhi (enlightenment) and sattva (history); this life is nothing other than the historical life of 'bodhisattva,' which is a dialectically[46] synthesized concept of the concepts of 'bodhi' and 'sattva.' The dialectically unified structure of 'enlightenment' and 'history' has it that Bodhisattvas work out the problems of life on the basis of their realization that life is illusory, and that they solve various social problems through upaya-paramitas derived from the confirmed cases of these social issues which have been successfully handled in historical situations.

I want to emphasize here especially that we must solve the problems of various areas of 'sattva,' that is, the problems of history with creatively applied solutions which are reached with the results of our historical efforts and the accumulated experiences in each of their areas. In other words, the issues of arts should be handled by aesthetical efforts and creative artists, the laws of nature by the efforts we make in natural sciences, the problems of economy with the efforts of economists and policies of government officials specialized in the area, and the problems of society on the level of sociology. And of course we must admit that since all these matters of various areas are organically connected to each other it is important for us to understand them as a whole, in an integrated way, and to make our efforts to solve their problems in a comprehensive way.

However, I do not think that we can ever solve these problems

---

46 Hyun-Eung's dialectical logic follows the line of Hegelian dialectics.

through the enlightenment of Buddhism. But of course I admit that it is true that the Buddhist insight on changes and relations, which constitutes the structure of Buddhism, not only leads us to enlightenment as it helps us shake off the awareness of real being, but it also helps illuminate the comprehensive and dynamic structure of relations of beings as it gives us a perspective of dialectical thoughts when we view the problems of individuals and society.

The perspective of enlightenment based on changes and relations, which is broadly applied to our lives in general, should become the base and ground of our standpoint to view beings. However, we cannot solve, with such a diachronic and universal method of observation, the problems that unfold on the level of various changes, experiences and accumulated facts of history. While we keep having our point of view based on the perspective of emptiness, we will be able to solve historical problems only if we can read the historical relations of characteristic movements of each domain and its surrounding areas in the history of specific space and time. These appropriate efforts in history are what we call 'upaya-paramita.' So, the harmonious life is characterized as the combination of bodhi and sattva, the latter of which is appropriate historical activities based on bodhi (enlightenment).

On the other hand, although those many people who lack bodhi (enlightenment) also come to make historical successes and failures in their own joy and anger together with sorrow and pleasure, if they do not realize that this life and history are all illusory and proceed only through changes and relations, they will have to manage their lives and history with the seed of primordial suffering caused by their ignorance. The Buddha and patriarchs of Zen traditions have already proclaimed that the origin of suffering in the lives of sentient beings lies in accepting their lives with the idea of real being.

If Buddhists, especially Buddhist monastics, have proper historical duties as Buddhists, as each of various areas of society has its own properly characteristic role, it must be to help historical people recollect the truth that all historical beings are illusions, and to call their attention to the point that they need to carry out their historical lives based on the realization of this truth. Therefore, this perspective of illusory history makes [our understanding of] history more elastic and enriched, and it helps us live our lives with a happy and healthy attitude regardless of our historical successes or failures.

Finally, we can tell that the very way of the harmonious life of 'enlightenment' and 'history' is the life of open[47] bodhisattvas, and that this life is a life lived in such a way that an illusory life (bodhisattva) realizes an illusory world (the Pure Land, the world of sentient beings) with illusory efforts (compassion directed to illusory sentient beings).

Now the Buddhists on asphalt-covered streets must not get timid or daunted by 'enlightenment,' but they should become confident about themselves. The Buddhists in high mountains should also be able to properly stand tall in front of 'history.'

---

47 'Open' in the sense of 'open-minded,' 'flexible,' 'advanced,' 'open to new interpretations,' etc.

Sudden Enlightenment, for the Revolutionary Enlightenment

– On the Doctrine of Sudden Enlightenment and Gradual Cultivation and the Doctrine of Sudden Enlightenment and Sudden Cultivation

I now would like to address the doctrine of Sudden Enlightenment and Gradual Cultivation and the doctrine of Sudden Enlightenment and Sudden Cultivation which seem to arouse a very serious confusion in the process of studies and meditational practices. I especially hope that those dharma brothers who still are at the beginning stage of practices pay close attention.

As you will see at a closer look, the story of this letter is in its context of contents a continuation of the previous letter 'Enlightenment and History.' In my previous letter I discussed primarily the relations between the feature of practical life in society and history and the Buddhist way of enlightenment. The story I am presenting in this letter is about the level of 'truth-seeking,'[48] that is, it is about the search for enlightenment and 'the cultivation

---

48 The original Korean word signifies 'seeking after the Way.'

of virtues.'[49]

From sometime in the past, 'the doctrine of Sudden Enlightenment and Gradual Cultivation' has emerged as the most important topic of debates in our Buddhist practices. I believe that my dharma brothers also came to know about this well in the curriculum of their academic courses or regular meditational practices.

Let us start our discussion, first of all, by pointing out that 'the doctrine of Sudden Enlightenment and Gradual Cultivation' is a method of practices that does not take into account the logical gap between 'enlightenment (bodhi)' and 'history (sattva).' As I mentioned repeatedly in my previous letters, if I describe this logical gap with a simple analogy, 'the domain of history' is the level where something is red, it is blue, or we must make it red, we must make it blue, otherwise we should do it this or that way, while 'the domain of enlightenment' is where we see through that the 'thing,' which is a reified form of this 'something,' is not a real being and that it is a hypothetical and illusory entity subject to changes and relations. The issue of 'enlightenment' which is to understand that the 'thing' is not real, and the historical (phenomenal) issue which is to change something and fill in its contents, are the problems that clearly belong to different levels.

Now let us see. The following is 'the gist of the doctrine of Sudden Enlightenment and Gradual Cultivation' that I have roughly summarized.

---

49 The original Korean word means 'the cultivation of the Way.'

When an infant is born it is not different from adults in that it has all the organs, but it begins to function as an adult only after a good number of years because it does not have enough strength. The issue of enlightenment is not different from this. At first, even after we realize the true nature of life, we still have subtle forms of suffering and bad habits and are not able to exercise supernatural powers yet. Therefore, we must make efforts and continue our practices for a long time in order to complete 'the perfect enlightenment' or become 'a sage of the highest level.'

This view focuses primarily on the issues of an individual's personal matters. I cannot but criticize its Hinayanist stance, but let us set aside this problem for now.

First of all, this view has it that we take as the goal of our practices the completion of external capacities and perfect personal character with our continuous efforts after we realize the true nature. But I suspect that the defect which might be lurking inside this view is that it does not understand that getting enlightened is not to accept certain contents or real being and thus this view interprets the realization of true nature as understanding and accepting some form of real being (dharma). If this is the case, it is to downgrade enlightenment from the level of understanding with which to break down the reality and substantiality of some 'thing' – which is described as the true nature – to the level of understanding the thing (the true nature) as 'blue thing' or 'red thing.' Also, on this downgraded level of understanding, the ensuing gradual practices are not different from such activities like building a three-story red house or a two-story red house, and they will result in such issues as constructing a three-story blue house or a two-story pavilion.

I believe, therefore, that 'the doctrine of Sudden Enlightenment and Gradual Cultivation' has basically resulted from the lack of clear understanding of what enlightenment is, and this doctrine has thus made a mistake of handling the domain of 'enlightenment' and the domain of 'history (phenomena)' as if they were connected issues belonging to the same level. In other words, although the issue of accomplishing an individual person's abilities, not to mention the agenda of social tasks, is also an issue of external phenomena and thus belongs to the domain of history, this doctrine understood the issue of the history level as the topic extended from and connected to the issue of enlightenment, and [this doctrine] mistook the external abilities and accomplishments of capacities for the expansion and completion of enlightenment. We can find this point once more in the passage of *The Suramgama Sutra* that people supporting the doctrine of Sudden Enlightenment and Gradual Cultivation like to cite:

> One gets enlightened of principle all at once,
> Suffering (the awareness of real being) is broken down through enlightenment.
> On the other hand, the problems of phenomena are not eliminated all of a sudden,
> They are gradually removed.

One may at first glance think of this passage as stating that the problem of enlightenment and the problem of phenomena belong to different parts on one spectrum of the same level. However, this passage actually reveals that there is a logical gap between the domain of enlightenment (bodhi) as principle, and the domain of history (sattva) as phenomena. All in all, those who claim for the doctrine of Sudden Enlightenment and Gradual Cultivation misunderstood *The Suramgama Sutra* and misinterpreted this passage in the way that supports their view.

Explaining the mutual relation between 'enlightenment' and 'history' in terms of the frame of understanding 'principle and phenomena' came to have, in the Flower Garland studies, a standardized form of theory on 'the world of principle' and 'the world of phenomena.' The Flower Garland studies call the dialectically synthesized state of these two levels [the two worlds of principle and phenomena] 'the world of non-obstruction between principle and phenomena' and further proceeds to 'the world of non-obstruction between phenomena themselves' and portrays this realm as the unified and desirable state. Even in this case, however, it does not view principle and phenomena as belonging to different parts of one spectrum on the same level, unlike the way the doctrine of Sudden Enlightenment and Gradual Cultivation sees them. We can understand, through this very teaching, that our studies and practices should not follow the way of 'Sudden Enlightenment and Gradual Cultivation' which is the concept on the different parts of one extended entity on the same level, but that we should follow the way of bodhisattva (enlightenment/principle + history/phenomena) which is a dialectically unifying combination of the issues of two different levels.

Therefore, we must above all try to have an insight on dependent arising (bodhi) with which we realize that our lives are not real. And, then, with the background of this enlightenment, we should go solve the problems of historical level through upaya-paramita which is a hypothesis based on the verifications and practices in history and historical imagination, although we are well aware that the problems of historical level are all illusory.

Let us examine another claim, the so-called doctrine of 'Sudden Enlightenment and Sudden Cultivation,' in addition to 'the doctrine of Sudden Enlightenment and Gradual Cultivation.' 'The doctrine of Sudden Enlightenment and Sudden Cultivation' has been presented as a refutation to 'the doctrine of Sudden Enlightenment and Gradual Cultivation.' Its gist is as follows:

It is preposterous to claim that we need to gradually practice for perfection even after our enlightenment. Enlightenment is a state in which there is no agitation in our ordinary lives of coming and going and it remains the same even in dreams. On top of this, it is a state that has severed and eliminated even the subtlest delusions in alayavijnana [the store consciousness].[50] Thusness – the true feature of being – comes to reveal itself only in this realm. We call it 'seeing the [Buddha-, or true] nature' and 'the perfect and ultimate enlightenment.'

---

50 The store consciousness is, in Yogacara Schools, the deepest level of consciousness.

If my dharma brothers agree with the points I made in my previous letters on the characteristics of enlightenment and the issues of historical level, I believe you can easily figure out the problem of this doctrine of 'Sudden Enlightenment and Sudden Cultivation.' First of all, if 'the doctrine of Sudden Enlightenment and Sudden Cultivation,' as has just been noted above, claims for the severing and elimination of subtle suffering and [also claims for] obtaining some capacities when it discusses the issue of enlightenment, I must point out that the supporters of this doctrine are also confused, as those who support 'the doctrine of Sudden Enlightenment and Gradual Cultivation' are, about the domains of 'enlightenment' and 'history.' They emphasize 'Sudden Enlightenment,' but if you closely examine the contents of their view, it in fact becomes a case of 'Gradual Cultivation,' which may well be said to be a modified claim of 'Gradual Cultivation and Sudden Enlightenment.'

Let me talk about the statement "One eliminates suffering and eventually arrives at liberation." Such expressions as "One eliminates suffering" and "One sends suffering far away" that you can find in sutras should never be literally accepted. We need to understand them as showing some pattern and law of teaching. "One eliminates suffering" does not mean that one's mental phenomena or suffering itself is eliminated, or that one must literally eliminate suffering. Otherwise, the statement would mean that one should become a rock or a tree. What this statement truly means is that mental phenomena and external processes remain the same but the stance we maintain to accept them is free from 'the awareness of real being.' The same structure of understanding can be found in the interpretation of "One gets out of transmigration (or, one severs the bondage of transmigration)." What this statement means is not that the phenomenon of transmigration (the phenomenon of arising and ceasing, of coming into existence and passing out of existence) disappears. It means that one gets rid of the arising and ceasing mind (the life and death mind),[51] that is, the awareness of real being and he or she comes to accept the phenomenon of arising and ceasing. A Zen monk in the distant past gave us the following metaphor, "A fish does not change its scales even after it becomes a dragon, and an ordinary man does not change his face when he becomes a sage."

We have already pointed out the problem of the doctrine of Sudden Enlightenment and Gradual Cultivation. This doctrine claims that we need to experience and obtain Sudden Enlightenment, cultivate six-paramitas, realize directly the emptiness of self and dharmas, and then finally reach the ultimate enlightenment. Likewise, 'the doctrine of Sudden Enlightenment and Sudden Cultivation,' which claims that we can reach the Great Way only after we pass the gate of gradual cultivation and realization, rapidly comes to have a mystical tendency in its actual practices. All these erroneous views result from the lack of accurate understanding on the relation between sudden enlightenment (revolutionary enlightenment) and the domain of history.

But I do not repudiate or disparage the stance of serious and

---

51 The mind that is subject to the view that something real arises and ceases, lives and dies.

sincere practices that these two doctrines brought about. As Neo-Confucianism played an important role for Confucianism in its efforts to manage our sincere lives that are directed to securing the life of morality and to becoming a sage, these two doctrines also contributed to establishing our tradition of sincere and conscientious practices that practitioners do not give in to the pride of their spiritual superiority (conceit, arrogance) and that they should constantly look back and examine themselves. In spite of all this, however, the logical misunderstanding and confusion about the nature of enlightenment have caused an obstruction in the way to achieving enlightenment and also brought about a distortion in living our historical (social) lives.

Perhaps I can try to summarize and organize what I have so far discussed about enlightenment and historical life with the following statement of a monk in the past:

> "We should not tolerate even a single speck of dust in the actual domain of principle, but we do not discard even one dharma in our manifold practices on our journey."

No reality [real existence as substance] can be established if we illuminate and view our lives with the eyes of enlightenment, but on the level of history we use upaya-paramita, which is just like illusions, and decorate with dignity the limitless world of dharmas. We may well advocate all this with the model of 'bodhisattva (enlightenment + history)' who lives an awakened and enriched life.

Now, our methodology of practices and way of lives should

be about 'the realization [embodiment, materialization] of the way of bodhisattvas' which is neither the one-dimensional 'Sudden Enlightenment and Gradual Cultivation' nor the one-dimensional 'Sudden Enlightenment and Sudden Cultivation,' but a combination of the two dimensions of sudden enlightenment (bodhi) and history (sattva).

Mind • The Buddha • Sentient Beings

It is already autumn. Chilly wind is blowing along the bottom edges of the mountain colored with autumn foliage, and it is shaking leaves off the trees. Streams in the valley are replete with the color of a cobalt-blue sky. It now seems to me that those flowers that bloomed and faded last spring, and the green leaves that stood tall in the heat and under the sun, are all only aspects of a changing life. I talked about 'enlightenment' quite extensively throughout the last summer, but I feel something is missing because it seems that the really important point has not yet been properly addressed as if it had slipped through a net.

Buddhism has come to make its doctrines enriched and sophisticated in the process of its propagation made to various cultures. But in this process, it has also accepted heterogeneous elements that are not compatible with the orthodox stance. The most serious problem of all these is that Buddhism, as it has been introduced to Chinese culture, has made its original, transparent and persisting worldview of dependent arising melted in the Chinese worldview which has excessively naturalistic colors. For instance, the following is Dharma Master Sengchao's passage that the Zen School often cites:

Heaven and earth[52] and I have the same ground,
Everything and I make one body.

Depending on the way we understand this, we can get the impression that his teaching is reminiscent of Chinese Daoist thoughts. The context of this passage is also similar to the passage in Zhuangzi's *On the Equality of Things:*

Heaven and earth and I were born together,
Everything and I are one.

It has been well known that Sengchao Sunim was being deeply influenced by the Daoist view that has the framework of dualist thoughts of substance and phenomenon.

Buddhism influenced preexisting Chinese thoughts significantly as it was translated into the Chinese language. On the other hand, Chinese people accepted Buddhism in a rather distorted way as they interpreted it with their preexisting methods of thinking, which became a factor that continuously gave negative influences to later

---

52 'Heaven and earth' means the (natural) world or the universe.

generations of people as well. However, the real problem is that this issue has never been thoroughly examined and properly criticized; to the contrary, the negative factor has been surreptitiously planted in Buddhism and it is still exerting enormous negative effects on the Buddhist way of cultivation and practices. It was especially the Daoist thoughts that caused most confusion to Chinese Buddhism. According to Daoism, the existence of all things in nature originates from nothingness or voidness. In other words, Daoism claims that, although the features of the phenomenal world manifest various changes and differences, all their bases are thoroughly penetrated by the universal voidness. So, Daoists believe that we need to return to this realm of nothingness in order to establish our subjective existence in the free and liberated stance not constrained or captured by the various features of the phenomenal world. They encourage us to go deep down and reach the abyss of nothingness and, from there, see through the true meaning of phenomena. Wang Bi, a great scholar in orthodox Daoism, wrote as follows.

"Heaven and earth are wide and huge, but its mind is nothingness... Accordingly, if we reflect on this and give it thoughts in depth day by day, the mind of heaven and earth gets clear... If you discard your own interests and yourself, you will be able to rule the world smoothly and people will come and follow you even from afar. But if you come to set yourself at the head and have prejudices, you cannot even protect yourself alright... Everything is precious, but it is in the end completed by nothingness, and we cannot even figure out its form if we ignore nothingness."

As shown above, Daoism assumes, when it observes being, the existence of both the external phenomenal function and the substance as the basis that makes all the phenomenal function possible. This way, the Daoist view necessarily came to postulate two parts, substance and phenomena [function]. This classification of 'substance and function' was imprudently introduced to the Chinese interpretation of Buddhism and resulted in many negative consequences.

The best example is that, with regard to the Buddhist teaching "All dharmas take place in terms of 'innumerably many relations and changes (emptiness)," Chinese Buddhists did not understand the concept of emptiness as 'relations and changes' and they mistook it for the Daoist 'nothingness' and thought of it in a distorted way as something like a womb that works as the origin of all the phenomenal world. In other words, they did not comprehend the concept of emptiness as the feature of elastic and dynamic relations, and they instead defined it as some essential and profound domain on which the phenomenal world is based.

As this tendency permeated (Chinese) Buddhism, Buddhists also came to have in their mind some implicit thought on both the domain of substance and the domain of phenomena when they observed beings, and they conceived of such views that there should exist the essential 'Way' inside all things in nature, or that the genuine feature of truth would be realized if we once removed their ugly and negative features that were only external appearances.

It was also thought that the features of all phenomena were various manifestations of the essential 'Way' or 'truth.' Further, people thought as much as that if they could see through, from the various and distinctive characteristics of phenomena, the 'Way' or 'truth' which is their essence, they would be able to accept the phenomena themselves as the features of truth. Such a rather pantheistic way of expressions as "The silhouette of the mountain is the form of the Buddha, and the sound of streams is the Buddha's dharma talk" or "There is nothing that is not truth" derived from the extension of the same kind of thoughts. Of course, however, there might well be a lot of controversies about this, and these statements themselves might not necessarily be presupposing the Daoist worldview.

Further, if all this story is viewed from a different angle, it could be interpreted as having described the features of being that are seen from the Buddhist, open worldview that has eliminated the awareness of real being. Strictly speaking, however, I believe that Buddhism only requires of us the removal of suffering and attachment (the awareness of real being) but it does not describe what happens after the complete removal as it says such as 'The world that appears after the removal is the world of essence,' 'It is holy,' 'It is true,' etc. For believing that there exists the domain of the holy, the world of truth and the parts of essence is itself a very erroneous way of thinking.

Anyway, this view of 'substance and phenomena' is a dualistic form of thoughts, and it is partly true that this view is shared commonly among Confucianism, Buddhism and Daoism. For in Confucianism as well, the Neo-Confucians who were influenced by Buddhism and Daoism tried to understand the world with another similar framework of thoughts characterized by principle and material force. It was the primary task of Confucian scholars of morality to learn by experience the principle as the powerful and universal foundation that transcends the features of individual entities.

On the other hand, we can find this view not only in China but also in Indian Brahmanism. This system of beliefs explains the world in terms of the relations between Brahman and atman. If I make the point simple, this is the view that every individual (atman) of the universe is a case of a spatiotemporally limited manifestation of Brahman which is the creator and essence of all things in the universe. This limitation is Maya which is called delusion or illusion. For instance, an individual is like the air inside a bottle. If we just break the bottle, the air inside the bottle will return to vast empty space. So, although the air inside the bottle is surrounded and confined by the bottle, it is essentially the same as the empty space outside the bottle. This is the idea of the unity [oneness] of Brahman and atman. An individual (atman) becomes one with Brahman as long as it breaks delusions, that is, Maya.

The descriptions they used might be a little different from each other, but didn't the Chinese and Indians have similar ideas? This kind of worldview shows a tendency to come to emphasize the cultivation of meditation [meditative concentration], that is, it tends to become meditation-cultivationism. Breaking the bottle, that is, taking off Maya (delusion), giving prayers and practicing yoga, forgetting oneself (the elimination of self-interest and self in Daoism), a profound study of self-elimination, Neo-Confucian scholars' method of practices such as their cultivation method of mind and body that promotes our observation and investigation of all things to find their fundamental principles – all these show the same tendency.

Reflecting on these views, on the other hand, I regard them as 'naturalistic ways of thoughts' because they are much too primitive and naïve forms of thinking. However, since the Buddhists influenced by these thoughts understand the world of emptiness as nothingness, the Way, principle, essence [substance], etc., they regard emptiness as some mysterious gemstone or a mirror that is hidden and ready to be discovered somewhere in the world or in themselves. And they believe that the world of emptiness is the profound realm that we must manifest by cleaning the dirt off and eliminating and purifying craving or feelings like joy and anger together with sorrow and pleasure.

The teaching of emptiness is the teaching of changes and relations, and it is a teaching on how to understand and accept all beings in the world. This is also the very content of 'enlightenment' that the seekers of truth pursue. Due to the impressions that the concept of 'enlightenment' gives us, however, we often assume *a priori* the existence of our own subjective domains and then get inclined to being preoccupied with our concerns on the objects that come to us immediately after this assumption. So, we regard 'enlightenment' as some understanding on beings as the objects, that is, we place 'enlightenment' on the level of epistemology where we accept enlightenment as 'cognition of ...' Then how should we understand all beings in the world (dharmas)?

What is clear is that in the world of all beings, 'the domain of cognition' and 'the domain of being' are not determined *a priori*. These two simultaneously generate, and determine the characteristics of each other. It is only the convention of our consciousness that divides all beings into these two domains. Strictly speaking, however, they can never be differentiated from each other. So, all beings in Buddhism are not just beings as objects, but they do not exist only in the *a priori* system of cognition, either. They mean the field of dimension in which even the subjective stance, that is, even 'I' is melted in the world of all beings, and the cognizing subject and the objects in the world – cognition and being – are grasped at the same time. This dynamic character of relations signifies the world of emptiness, and learning this world of emptiness by experience and participating in it with all mind and heart is 'revolutionary enlightenment.'

Accordingly, 'beings in general,' which have gone through the refining process of enlightenment as hot as a smelting furnace, are never unilateral or naturalistic beings as objects that stand in front of the framework of cognition as seen in Daoism or Hinduism. All beings born anew this way – all beings that have returned to their origins – are now called 'mind,' 'the Buddha,' 'all sentient beings,' etc. And this world is not reached through the gradual efforts of meditational cultivation and elimination; we must get enlightened with a revolutionary transformation that embraces and transcends both cognition and being at one fell swoop.

I can never agree with the view that only the bare branches of autumn, which are left after flowers were picked and leaves have fallen, or the tenacious roots of winter show us the true features of the tree.

I hope you keep making efforts...

The Journey of Bodhisattva

Covered with sands, rocks and young pines, this meditation cave in Mt. Gwanak is dark and depressing. I occasionally stand on a rocky hill where I can look down on the city, and I find close by the scenes of the busy city in the early morning fog and the lights of the factory buildings that never turn off.

Humans act [practice] as much as they know, and they come to know as much as they practice. Or, we measure the forms of practices through the contents of knowledge and reveal straightforwardly the magnitude of knowledge through practices. Needless to say, knowing and practices are neither separated nor in a temporal order of before and after, and this is about the unity of knowledge and its associated practices. If I consider that this nameless end part of the corner of this mountain skirts might also be where bodhisattvas devoted themselves for all sentient beings a long time ago, I cannot control these deep emotions arising.

My dharma brothers, with the modernization of society, today's monastic bodhisattvas have come to locate themselves in the middle of all living being's lives. Nowadays, mountains, plains and cities have all become bases of our lives, and neighbors, the world, each of the social classes and every area of lives are all functioning holistically related to each other. The Buddhist worldview based on dependent arising has come to stand out even more specifically and in more various and complex ways in the contemporary time due to the advancement of natural and social sciences. I believe Buddhists should have examined and verified these points earlier with their more advanced wills to [contribute to] history and [engage in] practices.

The theoretical gambit of Buddhism ranges from here in this place over to the cosmic scale. The scope of its compassion and practices covers from the life of our neighbors to all unnamed life forms. However, due to historical limitations that took place, it may well be said that Buddhism has always remained on the abstract level of idealism. It is rather by dint of all sentient beings' [all people's] efforts and the accumulation of history that the relations between the whole and its parts, and between this and that, seem to appear clearly on the surface.

There is a lesson [an episode] about a Buddhist monastic who had to be born as a fox for five hundred lifetimes because he had an erroneous understanding of the problem of history. "Not falling into the pit of cause and effect." This was the understanding that he at first had about being and history. He thought that enlightened ones did not come into conflicts with the law of causation and that they were free from it. For this misunderstanding, he had to suffer miserably for five hundred lifetimes until he could finally learn by experience the precious truth that a true life is a life not ignoring the law of causation.

My dharma brothers, how should we think about various problems of history that constitute the very naked reality in our world of sentient beings? How does the teaching of 'dependent arising' or 'emptiness,' which we address so often, explain these problems? Is it not the case that, still these days, many Buddhists drive the world of emptiness away from this world to a paradise? Or, isn't it the case that they misunderstand the world of emptiness as something that exists in this land and all lives but is nevertheless a transcendental system of values that is free from the world and lives? If this is the case, these people are making a mistake that will make them born as a fox for five hundred lifetimes.

Enlightenment is nothing other than the understanding of life and the history of reality. It is the insight on the changes and relationships of beings. Through this enlightenment, we can come to show the mutually directed relations (dependent arising) of consciousness and being which are not manifest while being hidden in our naturalistic stance. We also come to understand that, be it consciousness, being, form or concept, none of them has an independent real being. And at the very moment we arrive at this awakening, we will be fundamentally liberated from all conditions of history we are embedded in – the conditions that make us laugh and cry. For these conditions can no longer restrain us as something absolute or real. And we can overcome the passive and distorted state of alienation in which we do not realize ourselves as the active agents in the structure of our own lives. So, no matter what kind of situation we have to face, we can have the ability to secure our autonomous subjectivity based on stability and freedom. This is an art of life greater than anything else for human beings who are forced to stand in front of harsh and capricious social conditions. I call this liberated free human an 'arhat' of Hinayana.

On the other hand, the features of being, even if it is not real, still are to be continuously placed in front of us as the states in progress going on in terms of their changes and relations. From a realist point of view, provisional or permanent autonomous causal relations and normativity, which are presupposed and regulated by the view of 'existence as real being,' are functioning in this world as objects (nature, society). These points, accumulated with the experiences and facts ever since generations of lives have passed down, become issues of our historical and social problems.

In Buddhism, these issues belong to the domain of 'sattva (history).' They are the problems of a level where a simple understanding of 'bodhi' (enlightenment), which is an understanding that 'all beings are nonreal entities manifested in terms of changes and relations,' is not able to solve. We need to solve these problems through specific upaya-paramitas combined with 'bodhi.' We should not try to establish actual economic policy, criticize ideological issues, compose poems, cure diseases, or fix a TV set with bodhi's enlightenment. Rather, we must solve these problems through the relevant science of each area and their knowledge obtained in history. For historical problems originate through historical experiences and thus should be worked out only through their nomological characteristics or relationships.

In this regard, 'bodhi (enlightenment)' provides us with a perspective to see through humans, and 'sattva' is upaya-paramita that secures practical solutions for major historical problems. They are 'basic value' and 'primary value' in life, respectively, and they may well be said to be the twofold factor of life that cannot be separated.

On this understanding, we come to require a life [lifestyle] which is an ideal combination of enlightenment (bodhi) and appropriate historical and social practices. We call such a life 'bodhisattva.' And we describe as 'the journey of bodhisattva' the embodied form of zealous and fiery life in which bodhi and sattva are dialectically synthesized and practiced.

When I consider and compare the life of 'arhat' and the life of 'bodhisattva,' I sometimes remind myself of the expressions 'freedom from ~' and 'freedom to ~.' Of course the former is for 'arhat' and the latter for 'bodhisattva.' These two phrases may sound almost the same, but I believe there is a crucial difference. The stance of 'arhat' may be described with the following analogy:

"An untainted perspective is the most important when we see the world of beings. To see the world through red or blue eyeglasses is not the correct way to see the world of beings. Colorless and transparent lenses are also redundant, and we can see the things correctly only when we do not place any kind of eyeglasses in front of our eyes."

However, the stance of bodhisattva is rather different.

"What you say is basically true. Realistically, however, if you have a poor eyesight or the sun is too bright, prescription lenses and sunglasses give you a much better vision. It does not hurt us at all to develop various eyeglasses and use them conforming to our needs."

Arhats seek after freedom by removing eyeglasses. However, bodhisattvas are free as they proactively make use of glasses. Also, since bodhisattvas clearly know the very nature of eyeglasses themselves and use them, they do not misunderstand the world even if they see the world through lenses. For instance, they do not mistake the world for a world painted brown or get attached to it when they are wearing brown sunglasses.

My dharma brothers, if there still exists in the Buddhist society the stance of 'arhat' that regards our practices in history as something wrong or our concerns on society as something against Buddhism, don't you think that we must correct it with the bodhisattva's perspective of history? Suppose that we have reached this much so far, in other words, that we affirm our active participations in the history of society. However, in the bodhisattva's practices of these days, it seems to have become an important issue to draw a line between this being a Buddhist way and that not being a Buddhist way, and between this action following a Buddhist way and that action not following it. What this means is, for instance, the kind of attitude that --ism is fine because it is Buddhist but that ++ism is problematic because it is not Buddhist. Straightforwardly speaking, however, isn't it in fact the case that we cannot really admit that a unique domain or value system of Buddhism exists separately? If there exists something that may be regarded as uniquely Buddhist, it will be the domain of 'bodhi.'

So, I must note that it cannot but be a logical confusion to try to divide various problems in history, which belongs to the domain of 'sattva,' by something that is Buddhist and something that is not. In other words, various isms and claims and all the variety of the features of society belong to the domain of sattva's upaya [skillful means], and they can never be of such a nature as to be divided by being Buddhist and not being Buddhist. It is true that, due to the nature of 'sattva,' various isms and claims derived from it are based on a variety of realisms. However, this is not a problem as long as the fundamentally open perspective of 'bodhi' is behind all this, and as long as this perspective makes sure that these isms and claims do not fall into the lives of upaya fixed and stuck to realism but that they can shine as upaya-paramitas that secure fundamental liberation.

After all, bodhisattvas' appropriate historical imagination and introduction of hypotheses are boldly open to any ism or claim. The viewpoint of 'bodhi' provides a basic ground to realize the 'non-real-ness [non-substantiality]' of being. In addition to this, although bodhisattvas assume that they provisionally admit the existence of real being on the level of 'sattva,' they should not overlook the point that the system of dialectical logic that they use becomes a basic tool greater than anything else when they investigate social problems.

The fundamental perspective of bodhi (enlightenment) helps a bodhisattva get liberated from attachments and beings in status quo and stand fearlessly in front of history with the stance as open and flexible as flowing water. The rich historical paramitas will be blooming through sacrifice, devotion and patience. As we have the word 'Flower Garland,' my heart comes to be filled with excitement by simply imagining how all bodhisattvas beautify this world of sentient beings and make it the Buddha-Land with their own hues and scents through their respective efforts and practices.

My dharma brothers, which upaya-paramitas should you and I use in this land to manifest the journeys of bodhisattvas who accept the law of causality so that we may avoid the consequence of being born as foxes for five hundred lifetimes?

I hope our minds get more clear and determined as much as the wind gets colder.

I encourage you to make ardent efforts…

The Buddha's Pure Land

My dharma brothers, I believe that what is emerging these days as the most important problem of our Buddhism is the concerns about 'history.' This means that Buddhism itself needs to be transformed into history. This is because our Buddhism has kept distance from history.

Many people have said that we should establish a well-written history of Buddhism (history of Korean Buddhism). This is not just because we need a book of history of Buddhism as a course material for schools or Buddhist seminaries. Of course it is not the case that there is no literature or texts that may be regarded as books of the history of Buddhism. However, almost all of them are about the history of Buddhist orders that recorded how the orders developed or what their denominations and schools were like. Or, they were the records of the process of the transmission of dharma [the Buddha's teaching] organized from the perspective of the transmission history of the lamp [in Zen traditions].

I do not think that these kinds of records represent the history of Buddhism. We should proceed further from here, or better, we need to change our perspectives and must organize and describe comprehensively the historical acts and their achievements of innumerably many nameless sentient beings that proceeded under the name of Buddhism. The history of Buddhism should transcend the level of 'the history of orders' or 'the history of the transmission of the lamp [in Zen traditions]' and needs to be written again from the perspective of 'the history of all sentient beings,' 'the history of the people.' This demand of the new history of Buddhism implies a new Buddhist understanding that Buddhism should go beyond the framework of the orders or a group of monastic practitioners and have the view of the entire history and collect data from it. Now Buddhism must develop itself as a historical philosophy so that it can be transformed into history in its doctrinal aspect, and, in its practical aspect as well, its thoughts need to be fulfilled specifically in history. Viewed from this level, the People's Buddhism movement and the Pure Land Realization movement, which have been actively developing these days although they are still in the early stages, may well be regarded as attempts to deny kept-back and distorted features of Buddhism and instead jump right into the original central tasks of Buddhism.

When most people of our time, as well as in the past, think of Buddhism, they do not really get an impression that Buddhism is a system of scholarly doctrines logically organized. Rather, it seems that they receive strong impressions from its religious aspects such as 'the statues of the Buddha(s)' in dharma halls,[53] names and titles of the Buddhas and bodhisattvas like "I faithfully take refuge in Amitabha Buddha[54] and the Bodhisattva of Great Compassion," 'the world of ultimate bliss [the Pure Land],' 'resonant chanting recited to the sounds of the wooden gong,' 'practicing Sunim' and 'warm Buddhist neighbors practicing compassionate actions.' From a realistic point of view, that which may be said to be the traces of Buddhism in history – such as artistic heritage like paintings, architecture, sculpture, Buddhist elements incorporated in ordinary life and customs, and those features manifested in social movement and motions of political changes – were directly related to the Buddhist faith, practices and meditations. This point straightforwardly shows us that the very practices and meditations backed up by faith are all the more realistic, historical and cultural.

From the viewpoint of 'the history of all sentient beings,' the history of Buddhism is the history of the accumulated hopes and efforts of numerous bodhisattvas who have wished for the Buddha's Pure Land. We may be able to find the social and historical meaning of Buddhism by giving a new and positive evaluation on its religious and practical features. I believe that the historical practices of Buddhists developing these days will make more powerful and realistic movements when it is connected to, and united with, preexisting faith and practices.

---

53 'Dharma halls' are buildings or halls where the statues of the Buddhas (and bodhisattvas) are housed.

54 Amitabha Buddha is the Buddha of the Pure Land.

Practices for the Pure Land represent the faith and practices in Buddhism. The Pure Land is inhabited by people of exalted characters who do not have hunger, diseases or quarrels. It is the refuge for sentient beings who have gone through so much suffering and unhappiness. But it has been said that we can reach the Pure Land only through traveling millions of lands to the west, and it has also been claimed that the very spot where you change your mindset is the Pure Land. And, other people have said that this land is the Pure Land if you make it a pleasant place abundant in goods and services.

What do you think, my dharma brothers? What does 'the Pure Land' mean to us, and where is it? How can we accept and accommodate it as ours? The scriptures wrote, "If you recite the name of Amitabha Buddha at least ten times with all your heart, you will be born in the paradise of the Pure Land no matter how much of a bad life you have lived" – but, then, what is Amitabha Buddha and what is rebirth in the other world?

Let us talk about the Pure Land first. Wonhyo Sunim [Korean Buddhist Monk Wonhyo] wrote in his *The Way the Mind Wanders Freely* and *The Key Points of the Sutra of Immeasurable Life* as follows.

"The nature of the mind of sentient beings is free without any obstacle – just like empty space. So, the ground of the mind is equal and its features cannot be defined in any way. Then, how can there be a differentiation of, say, the Pure Land and the Defiled Land? Sentient beings themselves are deluded and they suffer being drowned in various murky streams, and at times they obtain good capacities, reach the realm of nirvana and escape from suffering and bondage, but all these are no more than an extravagant scale of a dream. When we awake out of this dream, we will come to realize that the distinction of this place and that place disappears, things like the Defiled Land and the Pure Land also belong to the One Mind, and life-and-death [the realm of transmigration] and nirvana cannot be differentiated from each other."

Also, many sutras in Mahayana traditions such as *The Vimalakirti Sutra* and *The Flower Garland Sutra* uniformly teach that the Pure Land is in fact the very world of sentient beings and that this world of sentient beings is just like illusions. Then what meaning does the Buddhist practices for the Pure Land, which we believe with faith and practice, come to have? Let us listen to what Wonhyo Sunim added:

"... It was only because many sages wanted us to wake up from such a long dream that they taught the Pure Land as a skillful means. For instance, Skakyamuni the World-Honored One warns against the five evil activities[55] and encourages the ten wholesome behaviors,[56] and Amitabha Thus-Come [Tathagata, Buddha]

---

55 They are killing, stealing, adultery, lying and drinking intoxicants.

56 They are not killing, not stealing, not committing adultery, not lying, not speaking harshly, not speaking divisively, not speaking idly, not being greedy, not being angry,

accepts sentient beings in the paradise of the Pure Land."

That's right. The gist of the practices for the Pure Land is to help the illusion of sentient beings realize the illusion of the world through the illusion of skillful means. Whether it is the Pure Land of the West or the Pure Land of the Freely-Wandering Mind, I believe that they mean the same Pure Land although their expressions are different. And we must understand that the idea of the Pure Land is only a large scale of historical skillful means that helps us realize the actual features of the world of sentient beings.

In order to save sentient beings from their unfortunate reality caused by the attachments based on various kinds of realism, bodhisattvas use skillful means such that they presuppose the same kinds of real beings, and they proclaim to stand for the Pure Land or postulate a desirable ideal society and try to approach it. This is the act of getting smeared with mud and drenched with water[57] and it is actually to volunteer to be fettered in history, but it is never to be buried or attached and drifted away in history. For it can be secured as a fundamentally liberated historical act by dint of the essentially illusory nature of practices for the Pure Land. I believe what is written in *The Vimalakirti Sutra* as follows indicates the very same point: "Although we know that many Buddha-lands

---

and not having wrong views.

57 "Smeared with mud and drenched with water" means 'In order to save one drowning in water, one must be thrown into the water and be covered with the mud and water. An enlightened person who wants to teach others must be willing to go to their level.' [A. Charles Miller, *A Korean-English Dictionary of Buddhism*, Unju Books, 2014, p. 1557]

and sentient beings are empty, we always cultivate the Pure Land and edify sentient beings" and "If you rely on the earth when you build a house, you can accomplish your goal and have no obstacle, but you will not be able to achieve your goal if you rely on empty space."

Then, when we say 'reborn in the Pure Land,' what does 'rebirth in the other world' mean? Great Master Tiantai's *Ten Questions on the Pure Land* explains this in a plain way as follows.

"**Questions** : All dharmas themselves are empty. Originally nothing is born and everything is equal, tranquil and extinguished. But then isn't it irrational to discard this place and want to be born in the other place?
Answer : If you say that wanting to be born in the Pure Land is discarding this place and wanting to be born in that place, and that it thus does not make sense, it is because you are attached to this place and do not want to go find the Pure Land. However, discarding the other place and being attached to this place does not make sense, either. If you proceed further and think that one should not want to be born in the other place but he or she must not want to be born in this place either, this falls in the view of 'nothing exists [nihilism].' Unlike all this, true bodhisattvas, although they try constantly to be born in the Pure Land, conform to the true notion of non-birth because they do not obtain any rebirth itself."

After all, 'rebirth in the other world' is another name of 'non-

birth.' I have thought of this kind of a liberated life, which we obtain
after removing the awareness of real being, with the expression of 'new
birth.' To be reborn in the other world is to live a life of non-birth,
and I suppose it can be nothing other than 'a new life.'

My dharma brothers, we have so far gradually noticed that to be
reborn in the other land is to accept history and engage in it with an
open worldview which is not fixed with the awareness of real being.
The life of bodhisattva who wishes for rebirth in the Pure Land and
engages in practices is a life of realizing the Pure Land in history.

Actually, then, how is the realization of the Pure Land possible?
Let us now examine the method of the Pure Land realization.

First of all, we need 'vow' as the most important method.
To vow is to set a goal in life and try to achieve it. And, on a
grand scale, it may be said to be a historical goal based on rich
historical imagination. This kind of vow is supported by the
positive perspective of beings (perspective of history) grounded on
enlightenment, and at the same time it is realized by the loving-
kindness and compassion for beings. The historical practice of
Buddhism (the realization of the Pure Land) truly becomes possible
by dint of loving-kindness and compassion for history (beings).
Accordingly, we may well say that the essence of the will to realize
the Pure Land in Buddhism, that is, the essence of the will to
history is 'loving-kindness and compassion [hereafter, compassion
in short].' And this compassion is realized only with a specific goal
in history (vow), the power of an indomitable resolve to pursue it
(power), a realistic method to materialize the vow (skillful means),
and realistic and historical wisdom and viewpoint that make it

possible (wisdom).

Skillful means, vow, power and wisdom are different names of realized [embodied, materialized] compassion. Combined with six-paramitas, they make ten-paramitas. So, these ten-paramitas are the very method of the realization of, and the rebirth in, the Pure Land. Also, these ten-paramitas are the core of the practices of ten abodes, ten practices,[58] ten dedications (ten kinds of being directed), and ten grounds in *The Flower Garland Sutra* and make the basic guidance of practices in bodhisattvas' journeys.

On the other hand, according to Wonhyo Sunim, in order to be reborn in the Pure Land, "we should generate bodhicitta, eliminate all suffering, act on good deeds, and save all sentient beings. These are the basic factors. Based on them, we need to have such auxiliary practices as the ten kinds of mindfulness,[59] the sixteen

---

58 Ten practices are (1) the practice of giving joy, (2) the practice of benefit, (3) the practice of non-opposition, (4) the practice of indomitability, (5) the practice of non-confusion, (6) the practice of skillful manifestation, (7) the practice of non-attachment, (8) the practice of that which is difficult to attain, (9) the practice of good teachings and (10) the practice of truth. [A. Charles Muller, *A Korean-English Dictionary of Buddhism*, Unju Books, 2014, pp. 993-994]

59 The ten kinds of mindfulness are (1) mindfulness of the Buddha, (2) mindfulness of the dharma, (3) mindfulness of the sangha, (4) mindfulness of the precepts, (5) mindfulness of giving, (6) mindfulness of the gods, (7) mindfulness of cessation of thoughts, (8) mindfulness of breath-counting, (9) mindfulness of the fact that the body is not eternal and (10) mindfulness of death. [A. Charles Muller, *A Korean-English Dictionary of Buddhism*, Unju Books, 2014, pp. 993-994]

meditations,[60] and the five gates of mindfulness.[61]

These basic factors and auxiliary practices are explained in their very original forms, so we need to continuously derive specific methods from them. But their characteristics and methods may well be said, by and large, to conform nicely to Bodhisattva Samantabhadra's Ten Great Vows of Practices in *The Flower Garland Sutra*. As my dharma brothers already know, these ten vows are as follows: to pay homage to all Buddhas, to praise them, to practice generosity, to repent, to rejoice with others for their merits, to ask for dharma teachings, to ask the Buddha to stay in the world for a long time, to learn from the examples of the Buddha, to comply with the intentions of sentient beings and to be dedicated to all sentient beings.

What we need to heed here is that in the world of Flower Garland, the Buddha is nothing other than a different name of countlessly many sentient beings, the land and environments, and

---

60 The sixteen meditations of Amitabha are (1) meditation on the setting sun, (2) meditation on the waters, (3) meditation on the land, (4) meditation on its jeweled trees, (5) meditation on its jeweled pond, (6) meditation on its jeweled palace, (7) meditation on its flower-adorned throne, (8) meditation on Amitabha's true form, (9) meditation on Amitabha's true body, (10) meditation on Avalokitesvara's true form, (11) meditation on Mahasthamaprapta, (12) meditation on one's universal body after rebirth in the Pure Land, (13) meditation on complex concepts, (14) meditation by superior practitioners, (15) meditation by middling practitioners and (16) meditation by inferior practitioners. [A. Charles Muller, *A Korean-English Dictionary of Buddhism,* Unju Books, 2014, p. 975]

61 The five gates of mindfulness are (1) worship of the image of Amitabha, (2) invoking the name of Amitabha (3) vowing to be reborn in the Pure Land, (4) meditating on the glories of the Pure Land and (5) transferring one's own accumulated merit to all sentient beings. [A. Charles Muller, *A Korean-English Dictionary of Buddhism*, Unju Books, 2014, p. 1091]

the actions of karmic rewards and retributions. So, the practice of Bodhisattva Samantabhadra aims, in fact, to realize the world where innumerably many Buddhas (sentient beings) and countlessly many Buddhas respect, cherish and take care of one another. In this regard, it is quite significant to conclude the massive literature on the Mahayana bodhisattvas' teaching with the statement "If you accomplish Bodhisattva Samantabhadra's Ten Great Vows of Practices, you will be able to be reborn, finally, in the Pure Land."

My dharma brothers, ever since Wonhyo of Shilla,[62] people in this country – including little children living in remote mountain valleys – have understood Buddhism with such phrases as 'I take refuge in Amitabha Buddha' and 'The paradise of the Pure Land,' which I find quite reasonable. What is important is, as we should know the meaning of 'Amitabha Buddha' as 'immeasurable life' and 'immeasurable light' rather than simply recite 'Amitabha Buddha' repeatedly, so we must project our historical wills into the 'history of vast space and time.' Therefore, we must fill the life of suffering people with visions and hopes under the phrase of 'the realization of the Pure Land' so that this domain of sentient beings should not simply fall in Hinayana's nihilistic calm and extinction or the mechanistic view of causality that keeps people from any participation or engagement.

At last, the phrase 'I take refuge in Amitabha Buddha' is a hopeful name, ideology and slogan of bodhisattvas who aim for the Pure Land.

---

62 Shilla is the name of an ancient kingdom in Korea where Wonhyo was born and lived.

2

Awakening – Enlightenment

This article "Awakening – Enlightenment" is based on the lecture I gave for the 219th seminar in the Thursday Philosophy Seminar Series of Gyemyung University on November 12, 1992.

覺 – Enlightenment

We need to let philosophy continue even in our busy days

I am pleased to meet you.

I believe I have had a very rare opportunity. The Thursday Philosophy Seminar series of Gyemyung University has already reached its 219th meeting. I find it quite an honor to present my view in this seminar hall replete with great traditions and high standards. On the other hand, I cannot but feel that it is presumptuous of me to stand in front of this lecture hall.

Your vice president and other acquaintances of mine have almost forced me to show up here, but I need to stay attentive and focused to figure out what I can talk about to you.

On my way here, I spotted a variety of events going on inside and outside of the campus. On a larger scale, the presidential election is approaching, and on the smaller scale there is today a campus election to form your student senate. In spite of all this, it seems that philosophy must go on. This seminar is a place to do philosophy, and a place to think, even in our busy days. Thanks again to all of you who have come to attend my seminar.

The moment of enlightenment – peeping and pecking at the same time [63]

The topic of my seminar is in Chinese '覺' [awakening] – enlightenment.

As you are well aware, Buddhism may be said to be a religion in which enlightenment is taught from the beginning to the end. 'Enlightenment' of Buddhism is a translation of the Sanskrit word 'budh.' From this word 'budh,' that has the meaning of 'come to know' and 'awake from sleep,' the word 'Buddha' was derived, which means 'an enlightened one.' Of course 'Buddha' means 'Bucheo,' which is the Korean pronunciation of 'Buddha.' So, in Buddhism where we aim to become a Buddha and faithfully believe in the Buddha's teachings, this word '覺,' which means enlightenment, may well be the most essential and core term.

Philosophers and scholars are, given opportunities, very much willing to talk about and discuss this kind of topic. Ironically, however, our Buddhist society does not really have a culture in which monastics discuss and debate over the concept of enlightenment. In the Buddhist tradition or culture, any discussion

---

63 This is about the simultaneous actions of the peeping of a chick from inside an eggshell and the mother hen pecking on the eggshell from outside when a chick hatches from the egg. [Park Young-eui, *The Practical Dictionary of Korean-English Buddhist Terms*, Joheun Inyeon Publishing, 2012, p. 1022]

of enlightenment is quite a ridiculous thing to do and is only regarded as meaningless. I myself have been a monk in a Buddhist monastery for more than 20 years, but this is the first time I am talking about enlightenment in a public lecture.

In a sense, a discussion of enlightenment may not be too difficult or impossible to do. However, no matter what kind of story I might tell in this or that way, I might not be able to capture the contents of enlightenment – like water slipping away through a net – and there will remain only a phantom of enlightenment. I might just kill enlightenment this way. On the other hand, I might feel like dying if I cannot clearly explain enlightenment and have to keep wandering about with my exposition. So, it seems that today I am really caught in a dilemma.

There was a monastic practitioner who had read many books before he became a monastic. He was a man of impressive erudition who had read comprehensively the Four Books and the Three Classics,[64] many works of All Philosophers and Literary Scholars in ancient China, poetry, letters, history, etc. This man left his household and became a monastic practitioner. One day, he was called to report to the spiritual master of the monastery, and the master examined him on the degree of his studies and achievements.

The old master told the practitioner to say a word about enlightenment. When this practitioner said something, the old

---

64 The Four Books and the Three Classics of ancient China are *Analects of Confucius, Mencius, The Doctrine of the Mean, Great Learning*; and *The Book of Songs, The Book of History*, and *I Ching*.

master responded, "Cut it out, isn't it a story in *The Flower Garland Sutra*?" When the practitioner said something different, the response was, "Your point is found in *The Suramgama Sutra*. Give me a different explanation." When the practitioner said a word again after some good while of pause, the master said, "That's what Monk X said. Tell me your story, not Monk X's, you idiot."

No matter how hard the practitioner tried to give a right answer, it turned out, in the end, to be a story in a book or of some other monk. Exhausting all the alternatives and feeling desperate, he gave in to the old master and asked him for a teaching on enlightenment.

The old master then smiled in a pleasant mood and said, "Of course I can tell you of my story, but then wouldn't it be my enlightenment which would not concern or benefit you?"

This practitioner was perplexed and at the same time, devastated. He returned to his meditation room. He threw himself into sitting meditation, but no matter how hard he attempted, he remained quite confused. His teacher was watching him without saying a word. Being unable to control his mind, the practitioner finally left for a journey of wanderer.

If all the knowledge and thoughts he had learned and experienced up to that time could not help solve the problem of 'enlightenment' which is the core issue of Buddhism, what was it that he had studied and practiced for? With such a devastating mind of reflection, he wandered about without any destination. One day, he came to stay over at a hermitage in a mountain.

He was sweeping a courtyard with a broom after he got up in the morning. It might have been the broom that flew a pebble, but it hit a bamboo in the nearby bamboo grove and made the sound of 'Tak!'

A clear and resonant sound of 'Tak!'

At that very moment, the problem of enlightenment that had never left his mind all that time even for one second cleared up by itself brightly.

"Aha! That was it. I did not know such a simple thing, I didn't."

After spending quite a period of time in absolute ecstasy, he finally came to his senses, gave a bow of prostration facing the direction of where the old master lived, and whispered to himself as follows.

"Oh, if you had expressively taught me this or that on enlightenment at that time, how could I have obtained such bliss as this today? I am paying homage to you not because I admire your great virtues but because I thank you for your kindness for having not explained enlightenment to me for my own benefit."

This was a story in the history of Zen Schools. It teaches us a lesson that any discussion on enlightenment is utterly meaningless and, in fact, harmful. It is possible to theoretically explain and teach truth or enlightenment, but the problem is that it does not really help those who receive these teachings.

This story suddenly occurred to me when I tried to talk about enlightenment today. What do you think about it? However, this story conveys us the additional point that, to obtain enlightenment, we need a sincere awareness of the problem [goal] to pursue enlightenment fiercely and incessantly.

When your vice president introduced me to you a while ago, he briefly told a story of the bookstore 'Sky Drum' in downtown. This bookstore publishes a booklet called *Peeping and Pecking*. The term "peeping and pecking" is widely used in Buddhism. A hen incubates an egg for 21 days with her body heat, and the chick inside the egg begins struggling to get out of the shell and [peeps and] pecks from the inside. This is Peeping [啐]. The hen pecks [and breaks] the shell from the outside, and this is called Pecking [啄]. The very moment, when the persistent efforts of a student and the master's timely and appropriate teaching become one, is in Buddhism called the moment of 'the Simultaneous Peeping and Pecking.' It is said to be a moment of enlightenment [awakening].

In the case of the practitioner introduced above, the master's ingenious guidance and the student's pertinacious efforts came to bear fruit. That is, for enlightenment, a persistent awareness of the [goal and] problem and the correct guidance corresponding to it are both required. A sloppy preach or wordplay is taboo.

The introductory part of this seminar has become too long. But I would like to ask you to understand that I have come forward to give this seminar running the risk of falling in such a trap because Buddhists cherish direct experience, that is, learning by experience.

It has been said that in order to explain enlightenment, the Buddha taught like a bow and the masters of Zen Schools taught like an arrow. A bow is bent and curved, and an arrow is straight. What this means is that the Buddha taught explaining in details and that Zen masters directly revealed the world of enlightenment whether students understood it or not.

The Buddha logically explains what is enlightenment in a consistent and organized way. This is recorded in what we know as *Korean Tripitaka*.[65] In contrast, Zen masters answer, "Willows are green and flowers are red" or "Clouds are in the sky and water is in a bottle," when they are asked "What is enlightenment?" Well, it is difficult to describe, but these are very straightforward expressions and quite a matter of experience. The Buddha was an Indian[66] and was familiar with abstract and conceptual expressions typical of India. But Chinese Zen masters were used to specific and realistic forms of expressions, which made them give the answers they gave.

When I address the issue of enlightenment today, I will follow the Indian style 80% of the talk and the Chinese style 20%. If the seminar is to be too much of the Chinese style, it will not make a philosophy seminar; but if it is too much of the Indian style, it would not only be of a dry and stiff style but also it would not be able to capture at all what enlightenment is.

The stance of enlightenment – having the perspective of dependent arising

Today I am planning to discuss the topic of enlightenment roughly in three ways.

---

65 Korea has their version of *Tripitaka* composed of over 81,000 wooden printing blocks made in the 13th Century.

66 The Buddha was born in a place which is presently a part of Nepal. He taught both in Nepal and India.

The first subtopic is, what is enlightenment? That is, it is to attempt to delineate the contents of enlightenment. The second is, how can we reach enlightenment? It is about the methodology on how to approach the realm of enlightenment and its contents. Finally, the third subtopic is, what is the life of an enlightened one like? I will unfold my discussion of the topic in this order.

First of all, 'What is enlightenment?' 'What is it that we call enlightenment?' (... a pause) It surely is a difficult question. Let us put this matter in order following a textbook style.

"All things in the universe, whether they are material, mental, conceptual, or whatnot, appear in the world following the law of dependent arising (they are not real being). To understand such a state of affairs is 'enlightenment.'"

How is it? Do you think that enlightenment has been explained in this way? (... a pause) We need a more supplemental explanation.

Let me first explain the term 'dependent arising.' 'Dependent arising' is a compound word made of 'dependent' and 'arising,' and it may be said to mean 'conditioned generation.' This is to say that all things in the world come to be formed and change depending on other causes and conditions – is this such a difficult thing to understand correctly?

Some people say that there is a domain that exists prior to some conditions or processes. Or, they believe that this domain exists *a priori* independently of, or ahead of, the existence of those conditions or processes. Whether it is God or some material entity, such a thing exists and all things originate from and are constituted by it.

However, if viewed from the level of Buddhist enlightenment, there is in this world nothing that exists *a priori* and is self-caused without borrowing other cause (without relying on others). Such a substance as the first cause, which is the cause that does not have its own cause and is the cause reached after innumerably many stages of regress, does not exist at all and can never exist. A realization of this principle is the gist of enlightenment that Buddhism talks about. It is a stance to understand that all beings come to exist because conditions tangle with conditions, these conditions interpenetrate one another, they define and get defined by one another, and they form and are formed by one another.

In a sense, it may have to be said that there is nothing new or special in this teaching because it seems quite rational and plausible. However, when the Buddha gave his dharma talk [lecture, seminar] on this point 2,500 years ago, most people did not understand and accept it. These days as well, those who have the worldview based on 'objective real being,' 'ultimate real being,' or believe with faith the realm of 'God' would not agree with or understand it.

People have believed that they must presuppose the presence of ultimate real being, which exists as the first cause or the self-caused entity, in order to explain everything. With no critical evaluation, people have been subject to this faith that has lasted ever since the beginning of human history. The Buddha himself seems to have been much aware of this problem when he gave his dharma talks. As we can find in many places of the sutras, he frequently added the following statements at the end of his talks: "It would be very rare if there is someone who does not get surprised or afraid when he or she listens to my teaching that there is no substance (atman) at all." As much as the Buddha was concerned, it could be quite confusing to people not to presuppose some real being or substance. Breaking such a belief, however, is the very enlightenment. To live a happy and great life without postulating any real being – this is the life of enlightenment.

Buddhism uses a variety of descriptions to explain this world of enlightenment. As I mentioned above, it is explicated in terms of the concept of 'dependent arising,' and 'non-self (anatman)' is also pointed out to explain it. Non-self is a concept used when we approach the world of dependent arising from a different angle. It means 'There is no substance (atman),' and accordingly, dependent arising and non-self teach the same point. Also, Buddhism uses the concept of emptiness. The emptiness in Buddhism is not about the state of something like empty space or void which people would readily associate with. It is a kind of a conventional term agreed upon in Buddhism: that is, in "~~ is called emptiness," we can replace a statement of "~~" part with "That all things in the universe exist following the law of dependent arising."

According to Karl Popper, a philosopher of science, true sentences often need to be read from right to left rather than from left to right. I cannot here extensively introduce his view due to the time limit, but if I relate his view to our topic and summarize his point, he suggests that we should read and understand the following sentences "Enlightenment is ~~" and "Emptiness is ~~" as "~~ is called enlightenment" and "~~ is called emptiness." In other words, these two sentences [the latter two] indicate that enlightenment or emptiness does not describe and explain what exists as an absolute and really existing autonomous realm and value. In contrast,

Popper claims that they need to be understood as sentences that indicate that 'enlightenment' or 'emptiness' is a conventional term[67] that replaces some state, something's long contents and statement. So, claims Popper, we will be better off if we interpret sentences in such a way that the subject part comes at the end of the sentence because, if the subject part comes in at the beginning of a sentence, the contents of the subject tend to make the readers fall in the fallacy of postulating absolute and really existing entities. This is a very useful point in explaining the concept of enlightenment.

It is the point of enlightenment that everything exists arising dependently on one another and there is no substance or real being anywhere in this world full of all various things. Reifying 'enlightenment,' 'emptiness,' etc. and making them absolute entities are, therefore, only self-refuting. In other words, to have a stance of enlightenment is 'to have a perspective of dependent arising,' 'to have a viewpoint of non-self,' and 'to assume a standpoint of emptiness.' Borrowing the popular expressions in fashion, it may be said to 'have a perspective of non-realism.'

'To have a non-realist perspective' does not have anything to do with the claim that beings should be reduced to nothingness. What it means is that we should see and accept beings without presupposing real being. It is to see beings in terms of their changes and relations, to view them as a tentative mode that never stops changing.

Understanding enlightenment as having a passive or nihilistic

---

67 'A conventional term' is here a term defined by stipulation agreed on by the group of people concerned.

worldview is a case of completely preposterous understanding. I believe that the world of enlightenment is a world in which we are not subject to a system of absolute values, that enlightenment is an open proactivity, and that it is dynamism that aims for changes. To understand this is the key point of Buddhism.

As expected, this is a difficult task to accomplish. For we are so used to the way of thinking that requires at least some form of real being. Absolute real being, idealistic[68] real being, ultimate real being, objective real being, transcendental real being… No matter what kind of real being it may be, and whether it is a monistic, dualistic or pluralistic entity, the belief seized by the view of real being is pointed out in Buddhism as non-brightness, that is, ignorance and non-knowing. Also, Buddhism teaches that it is the origin of all unhappiness and suffering. However, people are accustomed to the experiences in which they develop secondary, tertiary, and further thoughts only when they presuppose real being. The history of human civilization is precisely such a history – from the perspective of Buddhism, however, it is a history of ignorance, not of civilization. (laughter)

I am aware that, in our contemporary time, the philosophy of science and more advanced areas of arts (fine arts, architecture, literature) have presented experimental cases of thoughts – so-called post-modern syndrome – that do not presuppose real being. The so-called post-modern syndrome seems to start with the skepticism on 'rational reason' or 'objective real being' upon which our

---

68 'Idealistic' in the sense of being related to idealism.

modern/contemporary time is based. Although the way it has been currently developing seems to be deemed unstable and confusing, I believe that it will be able to successfully accomplish significantly substantial changes with challenging but stable formulations if it meets with the Buddhist worldview… Anyhow, Buddhism defines enlightenment as the stance to understand and accept the world (or beings) without presupposing real being.

Let me stop here the explanation on the first subtopic. Although the explanation was not complete, since we will have some question and answer time, let us move on to 'the second subtopic – how can we enter the world of enlightenment?' The second subtopic is about the issue of methodology.

In the 2,500-year tradition of Buddhist practices, many methods have been suggested about the way to reach enlightenment. As you also know well, they are what even the middle and high school textbooks have: the Noble Eightfold Path, the 37-aids to enlightenment, six-paramitas, etc. These methods of practice are the cardinal points of practice that have been handed down from Early Buddhism. The following is their contents. It is to constantly observe and meditate on my body and feeling (perceptive function) or various thoughts and concepts. It is also to see my bodily constitution and the structure of various beings, and it is to look at the act of breathing, and the act of moving. It is to examine analytically and objectively all the variety of feelings, thoughts and concepts. These methods have been cherished as the most secure and efficient ways to achieve enlightenment.

These days we can easily see in bookstores introductory

books on 'vipassana' among books of Buddhism. These books on vipassana are about the very method of practice I explained above. This method of practice is also the method that the Buddha himself taught to his disciples. I believe it is a very appropriate method of practice for contemporary people as well. The core of this practice method is to train oneself to observe the nature and relations of all things in the universe including oneself. It is to train to grasp the relations of dependent arising about certain things or agenda without being narrowly attached to or buried in them.

If we first look at the method of observing breathing, we need to continuously observe the process of breathing as follows: 'I am breathing, I am pausing for a moment, the breath has begun to go out again, I am breathing out a long breath...' This method of practice is not just about breathing. It is to observe every action in our ordinary lives. When you get up, you observe it as 'I am getting up... I am getting up...' and you observe all the variety of actions as 'I am walking, I am taking a step forward, I am handing something out, etc.'

Following this method, we watch all our actions and we also anatomically observe the structure of our own bodily constitutions. We do the same with various thoughts and concepts. Then the destination we arrive at is to realize the nature of interdependent arising of all things in the world, and to realize the nonexistence of self-nature. No self-nature is the same as non-self, and it is to deny real being, that is, it is to realize the non-real-ness [non-substantiality] of all things. Dependent arising, non-self, emptiness, enlightenment, etc. are the words – conventional terms stipulated by agreements – all of which refer to this non-real-ness of things.

The key of this observation is to trace the changes and relations of the objects of observation. This is very important...

Neo-Confucian scholars also observe things for their studies. *Great Learning,* one of the primary texts of Confucianism, emphasizes it. *Great Learning* teaches eight kinds of practical virtues which scholars refer to in cultivating their mind and body and to exercise for their society and nation. They are called the eight items (the study of things and nature, extension of knowledge, absolute sincerity, rectification of mind, cultivation of one's character, regulation of the household, ruling of a country and the pacification of the world).

The first item of practical virtue is the study of things and nature. It means that we need to approach, investigate and research all things in the world. As we can see here, Neo-Confucians' study method also encourages us to approach things and observe them. It is to select a thing, whether it is a bamboo or a rock, and observe it. They investigated the nature and principle of things with this practice of observation. Someone like Wang Yangming (the founder of Yangmingism) understood this practical virtue rather differently. For him, it was not a matter of 'approaching' and 'researching' but of 'correcting.' He claimed that understanding correctly the distorted features of things was the very study of things and nature. This is how he established the research system of his Mind Study.

All in all, it is widely known that both Zhu Xi's Neo-Confucianism[69] and Wang Yangming's version were deeply influenced by Buddhism, but I believe that neither of them had

---

69 This is the first version of Neo-Confucianism introduced above.

sufficient appreciation of things' changes and mutual relations, which is the key to enlightenment in Buddhism. The core of Buddhist practices has its focus on the realization of the hypothetical and tentative mode of beings that manifests itself as changes and relations – this is what is crucially different from Neo-Confucians' views.

˙Simultaneous Disentanglement˙ – Sudden Enlightenment

Let me also talk about the method of practice that has been respected and performed in both China and Korea. This practice method has been used for over a millennium. It is the method of study that you have known well as meditation. This meditation method has originated from Indian yoga practice or the meditative concentration of six-paramitas and others, but, as it was introduced in Chinese soil, this method changed, developed and made itself a very unique method of practice, and settled in China. We may think of it as the method of practice chosen through various challenges and responses in the long history of its examination process.

Anyhow, today's Korean Buddhism has this meditation at the center of its practices. The name "Jogye Order" of Korean Buddhism originated from the Sixth Patriarch Huineng who lived in Mt. Jogye in China for a long time and taught the method of meditation. It has been said that this Huineng Sunim described the enlightenment of Buddhism as 'Sudden Enlightenment.' I translate it to 'revolutionary enlightenment.' I believe that this word "Sudden Enlightenment" is a very suggestive and pointed expression in explaining the world of enlightenment and describing the features of reaching the world of enlightenment.

Let me explain a little more. I said that Sudden Enlightenment is 'revolutionary enlightenment.' I was inspired to use the expression "revolutionary" as my term by Thomas Kuhn's *The Structure of Scientific Revolutions*. According to Kuhn, the discovery of a scientific law is not a process completed by refining and developing a preexisting scientific law of paradigm. If we compare this to the issue of enlightenment, enlightenment cannot be achieved with forging, purifying and completing preexisting perspectives or thoughts. As there is sociohistorical revolution, scientific revolution is going on in science. And the history of science is that which is interspersed with scientific revolutions.

We may understand Sudden Enlightenment, that is, revolutionary enlightenment as follows. Why do we call enlightenment revolutionary? It is because enlightenment discards the preexisting paradigm based on a realist way of thinking and then establishes a new paradigm with a non-realist perspective. For instance, we may describe as 'revolutionary' the change of a nation made from a monarchy where the monarch presides over everything to a democratic republic. It is revolutionary because the identity of a nation and the government system related to it have been completely replaced with those of utterly different characters. And this revolutionary character means that the process or method to achieve enlightenment should not be approached by grasping the problem only partially or in a temporal order of before and after. 'Simultaneous approach, simultaneous solution and simultaneous disentanglement' are the very features of enlightenment, and we may call this 'Sudden Enlightenment.'

I have mentioned a while ago that all things in the universe can be divided by the subjective world and the objective world. Our shackles [of convention], our delusions, and our prejudice and narrow-minded worldview are making these two domains look as if they existed absolutely as real beings. However, these two realms, which are believed indubitable by the people, actually become only fictions and hallucinations if viewed from the perspective of dependent arising. Everything in the objective world is a reflection of the subject, and the world of subject is also a reflection of the objective world. Each of the two domains defines and forms the other – in this respect, neither can exist as an independent domain or a real being.

In short, whether we call it the subjective domain or the objective domain, all beings exist arising dependently. Therefore, if we want to grasp correctly the way that beings exist dependently on other conditions, it is impossible to comprehend them accurately with the stance of an only partial perspective or of a view of temporal orders. No partial comprehension that does not include the relations with others is going to work or going to be acceptable as correct. And since the stance of dependent arising sees beings as existing in various relations and in the process of continuous changes, we cannot grasp beings as if they were divided as what precedes and what follows. A cause is at the same time an effect, a part is also a whole, this is this but is also related to that. So, to have the perspective of dependent arising that Buddhism advocates, that is, to reach the world of enlightenment is, to have the stance to read correctly all things in the universe in terms of relations and changes. This stance requires a comprehensive and simultaneous viewpoint.

Even the expressions "enlightenment" or "get enlightened [realize]" can, in a sense, invite misunderstandings. To say that we 'get enlightened' tends to make us associate it with phrases like "realize ~" and "understand ~." But, then, there should exist the objects of enlightenment (or the objects of cognition/understanding), and we will have to postulate the subject of enlightenment (or the cognizing subject). As long as things turn out this way, we will have to fall, again, in the dichotomy of subject and object. The goal of Buddhism is to break down this dichotomy, but there is always misunderstanding due to the limit of language.

Accordingly, it is frequently pointed out in Buddhism that saying "I earned enlightenment" or "There is an attainment of enlightenment" is an incorrect description and reflects an erroneous thought. Anyway, we need to use careful expressions in explaining enlightenment, and when we have to use them, we must make sure in advance that we be aware about the limit of language.

I believe that the word "Sudden Enlightenment" has also been coined for the same reason. 'Sudden' here means 'all of a sudden, all at once.' So, 'Sudden Enlightenment' means 'getting enlightened all at once' and it seems to include much temporal element. However, the concept of 'Sudden Enlightenment' includes the spatial element in its contents that the subject and object get disentangled altogether at the same time. If you get enlightened after ten years of meditation, it's Sudden Enlightenment; if enlightenment takes only a day, it is also Sudden Enlightenment; if it takes a hundred years, it is Sudden Enlightenment, too. At the very moment of enlightenment, simultaneous disentanglement and simultaneous solution take place in understanding all things in the universe.

In this respect, the method to approach such enlightenment also embraces both the subject and object at the same time. To realize the world of subject and object simultaneously in this way and participate in the world of dependent arising may well be called 'a revolutionary situation.' To jump into this world of Sudden Enlightenment, the world of enlightenment, is to open a horizon of a new world which is completely different from the preexisting paradigm, preexisting worldview.

The practice methods of Silent Illumination Meditation and Phrase-Observing Meditation

Then, how do we practice meditation and come to meet this revolutionary situation of Sudden Enlightenment? Meditation is also a stance to read life and things in terms of changes and relations, that is, in terms of the law of dependent arising. There are roughly two representative methods of meditation. One is Silent Illumination Meditation, and the other is Phrase-Observing Meditation.

Silent Illumination Meditation may well be said to be about 'silently observing.' But to see and illuminate in Silent Illumination Meditation is different from observing and facing up the reality in Early Buddhism, that is, in vipassana. In vipassana practices, one continuously observes the mode of changes in some acts, things and concepts, but there is no subjective value judgment of good, evil, like or dislike in there. One just keeps observing.

However, Silent Illumination Meditation regards any thought or concept as something negative, distorted, partial and limited. So, it works on eliminating such things. If a thought arises, the practitioner thinks, 'Oh, a thought arose, I must erase it,' and then he or she erases it. Human consciousness cannot but have some thought at any moment, and there is no moment when the same thought stays. Thoughts constantly arise and change. In this Silent Illumination Meditation practice, however, a practitioner finds the flows of consciousness one by one, pursues them to the end, and kills them to make sure that they are absolutely eliminated.

If a thought arises, I realize it.
When I realize it, it disappears.

This teaching is found in Buddhist scriptures, and the practitioners of Silent Illumination Meditation take this as their guidance. Yes, this is the case. Non-Thought and Non-Conceptualization is the realm they want to achieve.

It needs to be admitted that sentient beings' thoughts are at any event the tainted and distorted mind. We cannot grasp the true features of all things in the world with this tainted mind. So, we must start to eliminate some small flows of consciousness and move on to eradicate the worldview itself that these flows are based on. Only when the mind becomes as open as a bright mirror and still water, can we reach enlightenment – this is the practice method of Silent Illumination Meditation. Here, not only trivial flows of consciousness but also philosophical ideas and even such preconceptions as 'Enlightenment is this and Buddhism is that,' etc. are taboos. It is the cardinal point and method of Silent Illumination Meditation to maintain the stance of not arousing any slightest hint of thought.

The other practice method, Phrase-Observing Meditation, is a method of meditation to observe a key phrase.[70] This key phrase may not be understood or approached with our ordinary thoughts. It is made of a word or concept (with no content) that is meaningless but gives us a strong impression. Let me give you some examples.

> Somebody asked Master Zhaozhou the following question:
> "The Buddha said that each of all things in the world has Buddha-Nature (the nature of the Buddha, or a potential to become a Buddha). Then, does a dog have Buddha-nature?"
> Master Zhaozhou answered, "Nothing."
> The practitioner keeps wrestling with this episode of the key phrase "Nothing" wondering 'Why did Master Zhaozhou answer "Nothing" when the Buddha taught that there was Buddha-nature in everything?"
> Another one asked,
> "Why did Master Bodhidharma come here from India, from the west?" Master Zhaozhou answered, "A cypress tree in the yard."
> The practitioner keeps thinking, 'Why did he answer "A cypress

---

70 A critical phrase, a single koan.

tree in the yard" when I asked him about Master Bodhidharma's intention to come from the west?' This is the key phrase 'A cypress tree in the yard.'

When someone asked about the principle of the Buddha's dharma,[71]

"Hairs grow on front teeth" was the answer. This became the key phrase 'Hairs grow on front teeth.'

What do all these mean? They sound like meaningless words coming out of the blue. As people often say, Zen dialogues are obscure and confusing. However, this is also the very secret and gist of Phrase-Observing Meditation.

The Chinese letter "看," which means 'observing' in this Phrase-Observing Meditation, has the shape of having a hand (手) over one eye (目). It has a clearly different nuance from the other Chinese word "觀" that means 'seeing.' 觀 has a strong implication of seeing by way of thinking with the mind, and 看 means primarily 'observing with visual sensation.'

But the key phrase is a concept. Can we observe a concept visually? Furthermore, if the concept is neither verbally explained nor understood with thinking, how would it be possible at all to visually observe it? What Phrase-Observing Meditation really means to teach lies in here. When we come to concentrate everything on the key phrase that can neither be thought about nor make sense, we will be able to eliminate all thoughts and delusions,

---

71 The dharma here is the Buddha's teaching.

as Silent Illumination Meditation aims to do.

This Phrase-Observing Meditation is the method of practice that has been presented after Silent Illumination Meditation was in current. Silent Illumination Meditation's teaching of Non-Thought and Non-Conceptualization is practically difficult to achieve, and in the process of this meditation we often fall in torpidity, slumber and enervation. Phrase-Observing Meditation was suggested as an alternative to overcome all these problems. We use a skillful means called the key phrase and expect to produce the same effect as what Silent Illumination Meditation aimed for. Perhaps Phrase-Observing Meditation is a more developed method of practice.

Anyhow, it is realistically very difficult not to have any thought, but it is relatively much easier to focus on something. The idea is that we can cut off all the thousands and millions of conceptions by concentrating on a key phrase – isn't this convenient? At the same time, if we think of this key phrase as something that thinking cannot reach, something like an iron ball on which even toothmarks cannot be made, Phrase-Observing Meditation can protect us from the fallacies and preconceptions that originate from varied philosophical notions – this is to get two birds with one stone, a hundred birds with one stone.

In Phrase-Observing Meditation, to analyze and think of a key phrase philosophically is regarded as the first taboo on the list. You hold your key phrase just remembering "A monk asked if a dog has Buddha-nature, and Master Zhaozhou answered 'Nothing.'" You throw away not only varied conceptions but also even the words or thoughts of 'enlightenment' and 'the Buddha,' and you simply hold your key phrase. When you practice it, you will be liberated from the thoughts caused by the varied awareness of real being and will enter the dependently arising world, that is, the world of enlightenment.

Let us compare and contrast the methods of practice introduced above. First of all, I am aware that everybody in this seminar room is a philosopher. To assume a stance to conduct thinking with a philosophical proposition may be said to be a case in which we have both 'the content and form.' Practitioners of meditation believe that this stance has a great possibility to fall in errors. For the postulated proposition itself is based on a certain worldview, and both the subjects who think about it and the language used to describe it are also grounded on various stances and views. So, the practice method of Zen rejects such a method that has both 'the content and form.'

The vipassana method of practice may be said to be 'a method that is attached to neither the content nor form.' Suspending all value judgments, the practitioners simply and steadily observe and watch.

Silent Illumination Meditation also denies both 'the content and form.' In vipassana, the practitioners let both remain intact; they simply keep observing the flow, but are not attached to them. In contrast, Silent Illumination Meditation thoroughly eliminates them from the beginning.

Phrase-Observing Meditation has form but no content. 'Form without content' may also signify the characteristics of a key phrase itself that could be described as a concept with no content. Form with content can make us fall in errors which the content leads us to;

in contrast, 'form without content,' since it has no content, blocks errors of thoughts and at the same time makes our concentration easier because the frame of form exists. The practice method of vipassana vaguely observes the flow of consciousness and action without acute awareness. Silent Illumination Meditation tries to achieve Non-Thought and Non-Conceptualization, but it often loses conceptions and falls in torpidity and slumber. The method of Phrase-Observing Meditation is good because it is easier than vipassana and Silent Illumination Meditation and it makes intensive concentration possible. It is said to be an awakened state of tension, and it is also a stance to maintain the state of a delicate touch-and-go situation.

We describe the stance to hold a key phrase as 'Alertness and Calm' or 'Equal Maintenance of Alertness and Calm.' This is to teach that we need to simultaneously achieve both alertness and calm in a balanced way. In other words, 'Alert' means 'staying awake' and 'Calm' means 'tranquility.' 'Alertness' is the state in which the practitioner stays awake holding a key phrase trying to concentrate on the form that does not have content. 'Calm' means the tranquil state of Non-Thought and Non-Conceptualization in which the practitioner simultaneously removes all thoughts and does not associate any thought with the key phrase itself.

The practitioners of Silent Illumination Meditation can easily fall in the torpidity and slumber of consciousness or enervation, and their stance to deny any thoughts may well be regarded as a philosophical relativism. The key phrase [of Phrase-Observing Meditation] is useful as a skillful means to overcome these problems. To be captured by a certain thought such as a philosophical proposition, etc. may be said to fall in absolutism, but the practitioners of Phrase-Observing Meditation can be protected with the meaninglessness of the key phrase.

All in all, Phrase-Observing Meditation proceeds on beyond the issue of meditation practices and makes itself an exquisite skillful means to overcome simultaneously both absolutism and relativism in life. And, I would like to complete my talk about the second subtopic, which has been on the contents of methodology – 'How we should achieve enlightenment' –, as I am telling you that this Phrase-Observing Meditation is the representative method of practice that Korean Buddhism is exercising.

The features of an enlightened person's life

Finally, it is the subtopic of 'What is the life of an enlightened person's life like?' What is the realm of an enlightened person like, and what is the feature of an enlightened person's life like? Can an enlightened person walk on water, fly in the sky, see through the wall blocking his or her eyesight, and read other people's minds? The answer is a straightforward no. All of them have nothing at all to do with the issue of enlightenment.

Does an enlightened person then obtain some special abilities different from others'? No, that is not the case, either. An enlightenment person just understands and lives this world following the law of dependent arising (changes and relations). Then, what does it mean to live a life 'following the law of dependent arising'? As I have said repeatedly, it is the realm in which one lives a life without any awareness of real being. To have no awareness of real being is to realize that there is in the mode of being no real being or substance, which is completely different from the view that there is no existence.

To live a life of an enlightened person is to have a stance to observe things without presupposing real beings, and it is the life to understand the world in terms of its mode of changes and relations. A life [a person] that has reached this enlightenment is called an 'arhat' in Buddhism; in short, a life of arhat is the world of freedom. In Buddhism, it is the world of liberation. For arhats, all the features of history that appear in space and time do not belong to the realm of real being. So, the features of history cannot seriously restrain them. The life of an arhat, the life of an enlightened person is the life that has secured a fundamental freedom from any [fixed] historical forms or values.

This realm of freedom comes from the realization of dependent arising. To recognize real being or not is, in Buddhism, a matter of not getting enlightened or getting enlightened. This is a crucially important point, but it has not been clearly analyzed or understood.

It has often been said as follows. People believe that we can see that all religions, such as Buddhism, Christianity and Confucianism, actually have the same teaching if we once learn their fundamental doctrines. However, I do not agree with this. I believe such a vague and obscure stance does not let us know anything properly. To know properly is not to realize what is common among all; but it is to understand what difference each has from the other(s).

Let me give you an example. This is a story of Popper I

mentioned a while ago. For instance, today is Thursday. But suppose that there is someone who believes that today is Friday. A person who believes correctly that today is Thursday and another one who erroneously thinks of it as Friday can tell the same stories, although they have very different beliefs about what day today is. That is, they can share and present a good number of common propositions such as "Today is not Monday," "Today is not Tuesday," ... This is what Popper claims when he says that we can derive the same propositions even if they are based on different worldviews. Isn't this interesting?

As the foregoing example suggests, even if Buddhism, Christianity and other religions talk about the same points, it is not the case at all that their worldviews are also similar. The enlightenment of Buddhism is especially clearly distinguished from Laozi and Zhuangzi's Daoism or Brahmanism, and also from the currently popular philosophy of meditation of Rajneesh and his ilk. The criterion of this distinction is whether we postulate ultimate real being(s) or we assume a stance of nonrealism as in Buddhism.

As we have seen above, to have a stance which is liberated from any view of real being, to live a life which has thrown away all the awareness of real being is the life of an arhat. An arhat sees through the properties of the features of history that used to restrain and restrict him/her before his/her enlightenment, and realizes that the properties themselves are not real beings. Through this insight and realization, the arhat obtains by experience the enlightenment that these properties cannot fundamentally restrain or restrict him/her. So, he or she finally comes to enjoy a liberated life, a free life. Nothing – from the phenomena and laws of trivial things to those of ideology, culture or anything – can restrain the life of an arhat any more. There was in the old history of Buddhism a martyr who reached the realm of arhat. He composed the following poem in front of a swinging blade.

Our body arises depending on conditions,
All beings are only hypothetical entities.
Cutting through my neck with a blade is
Only as good as cutting through a spring breeze.

Of course there could not have been any immediate difference in his fear or pain. There is an expression that describes the realm of enlightened person: "I sleep when I am sleepy, and I eat when I am hungry." Therefore, in the life of this arhat as well, it could not have meant that he was not hungry or in pain when he did not eat or got hurt. A little child would cry as though he or she had lost the whole world if you took away a toy from the child. But grown-ups behave differently. They would be rather sorry about it, but they are free from the emotions that a little child would have if his or her toy should be taken away. This of course is a story of analogy.

Likewise, in the case of the life of an arhat, he needs to sleep if he is sleepy and he should also eat. Both a loving-kindness and a feeling of hatred might show up in his mind; however, since he knows the very nature of the objects of feeling or thought, that is, since he sees through that they are fundamentally nonreal, he does not suffer from them in the end.

As a Chinese classic had it,

Even when I am sad, I do not get hurt.

Even when I am happy, I do not get dissipated.

Perhaps it would make sense to say that an arhat thinks of life and history as a play or movie. Life is not real, and it is only a phenomenon generated by a rapid and continuous movement of distinct frames of film. An arhat is not, in the end, attached to it. In short, the life of an arhat may be said to be a life free from history (freedom from being and history).

Bodhisattvas' dream toward history

However, there is another kind of an enlightened life. This kind of life is called the life of a 'bodhisattva.' In Korea, women lay Buddhists who attend temples are usually called bodhisattvas. Well, this is a case in which the original meaning of the word has been modified. It seems that people call them bodhisattvas to encourage them to 'live a great life of a bodhisattva.' Then, what is the original meaning of "bodhisattva"? I can tell that the answer is already implied by the name itself.

In "bodhisattva," "bodhi" is a noun form of "budh" which I mentioned at the beginning of this seminar. 'Budh' means 'enlightenment.' This enlightenment may be said to be the enlightenment of understanding beings in terms of dependent arising.

If the life of an arhat, which I discussed a while ago, is a life of enlightenment on dependent arising, the life of an arhat is included as a part of the life of a bodhisattva in its 'bodhi' part. And the bodhi complemented by sattva constitutes the life of a bodhisattva. 'Sattva' means 'sentient beings,' and it actually means all lives and history.

In this realm of sattva are included not just human beings but also lifeforms, even non-lifeforms, and the ecosystem of nature. So, all these various domains, which change and relate to one another, are altogether called 'sattva,' that is, all beings. Personally, I use the word "history" interchangeably with "sattva."

This way, "bodhisattva" turns out to be a compound word made of "enlightenment" and "history." To use popular expressions, I would like to say that it is 'enlightenment's becoming history' and 'history's becoming enlightenment.' However, in the life of a bodhisattva, he or she does not just enjoy the freedom from history which is based on his/her enlightenment. Bodhisattvas proceed a step farther and participate in and project themselves into history so that they can deal with history. I often say that this is a life of freedom from being and history that also has freedom to being and history.

Bodhisattvas have a perspective on history that has shaken off the awareness of real being. However, they do not look at history in a passive way remaining unconcerned about it. They do not just stay enjoying freedom from history that is passing by them, either. On the contrary, they aspire to influence history actively and passionately, and they try to implement specific actions according to their aspirations. However, each of these historical actions cannot always guarantee a success either in its process or in the stage of its completion.

It is just that bodhisattvas have a merit that they have a more flexible and comprehensive worldview than those who are buried in some specific value or real being. Also, bodhisattvas have realized thoroughly the law of dependent arising that constitutes the structural or systematic characteristics of the principles of the world. However, since they have not themselves grasped all the details of the principles of the world, they may have misjudgments, errors and failures. But they will come to enjoy a very satisfying and happy life that consciously pursues a goal consistently regardless of the consequence of success or failure. I think this is a great life. What do you think?

I mentioned a point about 'the awareness of goal' when I talked about the historical life of bodhisattvas a short while ago. In Buddhist terminology, it is also called 'the awareness of setting a direction.' This 'awareness of goal' usually includes a specific historical goal which is appropriate to each bodhisattva's time and situation, and this is also called 'vow [aspiration].' Buddhism introduces innumerably many kinds of bodhisattvas' vows from abstract ones to specific ones, from small ones to great and universal ones. But they usually focus on overcoming sentient beings' unhappiness (poverty, disease, ignorance, loneliness, ugliness, struggle, etc.).

In Buddhism, we usually call the birth of an ignorant sentient being 'a karmic birth' and the birth of a bodhisattva in this world 'a vowed birth.' We may understand this point as follows: Sentient beings face history and participate in it due to their karmas, but bodhisattvas do the same with their vows. 'Karma' means causal actions and thoughts subordinate to something (values and real being). In contrast, vow is about intentional (or hypothetical) actions and thoughts that are, as I said a while ago, liberated from the view of the real-ness [substantiality] of history, but originate from some special awareness of a goal.

On the other hand, however, Buddhist scriptures point it out that bodhisattvas are not attached to the actions and processes that realize a vow, or to the completed form of the vow (for instance, 'the realization of the Pure Land' means the establishment of a desirable society). So, bodhisattvas get liberated from the absolutism of history with the enlightenment of 'bodhi' and at the same time they come to overcome the problems of historical relativism with the practice of sattva which is bodhisattvas' 'vow.'

I often use the analogy of eyeglasses when I explain the lives of arhats and bodhisattvas.

"Eyeglasses, from the fundamental point of view, give us only made perspectives, manipulated perspectives; they do not help us see things as things themselves. So, let us take off any kinds of eyeglasses!" This is about the lives of arhats who have achieved the freedom from eyeglasses (history) which is a metaphor for the awareness of real being or a metaphor for the veil of real-ness.

On the other hand, "It suffices to know the fictitiousness and true characteristics of eyeglasses. We do not get affected by eyeglasses in the end. We do not really have to take them off." Well, bodhisattvas proceed one step further and come to have a stance such as "We proactively select and use eyeglasses if necessary" and "We use brown or blue eyeglasses to protect our eyes from strong sunlight, we get prescription lenses when our visions change, and we wear glasses for fun and fashion, too!" – this is the life of a bodhisattva.

However, although bodhisattvas wear eyeglasses, they do not think of the world as blue or yellow, or see the world bigger or smaller than it is. They wear some specific and special eyeglasses that are based on historical imaginations and visions while they are aware of these possible issues. I call this 'freedom to eyeglasses (being and history).'

In the cases of arhats and bodhisattvas, both show the features and stance of enlightened ones. It may just be each individual's temperament, circumstance and situation that make them different. However, it would not be the case that to live a life of an arhat diminishes his or her world of enlightenment, or to live a life of a bodhisattva expands the world of his or her enlightenment. For, to increase or shrink, to succeed or fail, and to enrich or impoverish – all these belong to the level of history, not to the level of bodhi (enlightenment). The world of enlightenment truly has history (sentient beings' lives, the world of sentient beings) as its content, but it also means that it is liberated (moksha) from the features of history.

Buddhist scriptures describe enlightenment as follows:

Neither birth nor death,
Neither defilement nor purity,
Neither increasing nor decreasing

"It is neither born nor perishes, it is neither defiled nor pure, it neither increases nor decreases" – this also tells us the same teaching. However, Mahayana Buddhism ardently requires us to consistently live the life of a bodhisattva. 'A bodhisattva's dream to history' – this dream is the vow of bodhisattva, but it may be something transparent or invisible. It might be such actions and thoughts that cannot be captured by the net of history.

I like movies. I go to movie theaters with no sense of shame and often rent video tapes. I believe it is the movies that can explain quite appropriately the Buddhist worldview, especially, the life of a bodhisattva. When I explained the life of an arhat a while ago, I said that arhats regarded life and history as plays and the films of movies. Their lives are only movies for them, so, they have a stance to keep an objective distance from life and history and they are not tied down by them.

However, although bodhisattvas know that life and history are only continuous movements of distinct frames of film, they do not discard life or history because of their fictitiousness or the groundlessness of their modes of tentativeness. To the contrary, they plant their dreams, love and passion in that film (history), just like the way that people actively use and develop screens in many useful ways instead of throwing them away because of their fictitiousness.

The world of enlightenment, which is described with the concepts of non-real-ness [non-substantiality], non-self, dependent arising and emptiness, should not turn passive, nihilistic, non-realistic or non-historical. To the contrary, it should develop into proactive historical sports and activities! And this should be the life of a bodhisattva.

"To shake off the awareness of real being," "Not to postulate real being when we face things and the world" – these points may never be understood as long as we are captured by the awareness of real being. However, as the Buddha said, they may bring about 'surprising and frightening' consequences. "If there is no real being, how on earth can reality be established or exist? Where should we have our efforts and passion originate from? Where does the will or motive to history start from? How can we find meaning at all in history?" We may easily come to be worried about the confusion and meaninglessness about history.

However, if we can go through the so-called switchover of ideas and embrace revolutionary enlightenment, we will come to understand how free, comfortable, proactive and active, specific and realistic the world of this enlightenment can be. Bodhisattvas are boldly open to countless tests and hypotheses of reality, and they are the lives of continuously opening themselves.

I am confident that all the various problems, which today's history and civilization have and collide with, might perhaps learn many lessons and suggestions from the lives of arhats and bodhisattvas that keep unfolding the world of enlightenment. I believe enlightenment should be applied to the studies of humanities, social and natural science, arts, ethics and all other thoughts and actions.

Let me finish today's incoherent and lengthy[72] talk of mine with the following phrase: 'History becomes enlightenment, and enlightenment becomes history – this is the very world of enlightenment.'

Thank you.

---

72 Many Asians typically complete their talks in this way to show some modest and humble attitudes. Obviously, Hyun-Eung's talk was neither incoherent nor lengthy.

3

A Stroll for Enlightenment

I completed this article in a hermitage of a monastery in the Southwestern part of South Korea where I was practicing meditation intensively during the summer retreat in 1984. Its six parts were published serially in the monthly magazine *Mahayana Newsletters* from May to October, 1988.

A Stroll for Enlightenment

All phenomena are consciousness

When we say, "All phenomena are consciousness," what is 'all phenomena' and what is 'consciousness'? Let me start this article as I explain these points.

"All phenomena are consciousness" is a literal translation of '萬 法唯識 [All dharmas are only consciousness]' which is the fundamental proposition of the Consciousness-Only [Yogacara] School in Buddhism.

According to this Consciousness-Only School, 'all phenomena' mean all the phenomena of this world. The world may be thought of as having three kinds of domains: the domain of cognition, the material domain, and the domain of concepts such as language, customs, law, religion, arts, etc. that have abstract but objective structures. 'All phenomena' are about the forms that these three domains are organically interconnected to one another, perform actions, and unfold themselves through space and time. In this sense, all 'phenomena' do not have their own pure and separate domains; and they are not simply fixed entities like sensitized papers for photos. To the contrary, they are the ground and field of history that is living and changing. It is the important starting point of this essay to understand that all phenomena overlap one another and get folded by one another, and thus that there cannot exist any independent domain.

The concept of 'phenomenon' is closer to the concept of 'event' rather than that of 'thing' or 'fact.'

When we say "I am watching a flower," this sentence is interpreted as "An individual 'I' is cognizing a thing (fact) 'flower'." However, if we see this sentence from the perspective of 'phenomenon,' "An event 'I' is watching an event 'flower'" is a more accurate interpretation. Also, when we say "I am watching a flower," we cannot accept a view that claims that 'I' as the cognizing subject and 'flower' as the object of cognition exist separately as independent domains. I am starting this article by denying a naïve dualistic distinction (of cognition and being) that this domain of phenomena can be dichotomized by 'the domain of cognition' and 'the domain of object (being).'

Let us first examine 'cognition.'

1) No cognition can exist as pure cognition.

2) Cognition exists as cognition only if being as the object [of cognition] is given (whether the object is a concept or a material thing).

3) Cognition is sustained as it grasps being. In other words, cognition has contents, and this can be expressed as "Cognition is impregnated with being" or "Cognition is tainted by being." The former means that cognition can be cognition only if it presupposes being, and the latter means that cognition is defined by being.

Let us now examine the case of being.

1) Being is not being purely as itself.

2) Being exists only as much as it is cognized. For instance, we say "There is a desk" when its shape that appears to us together with our preconception of its use and function make us believe that there is a desk. However, the present existence of the desk is not completely revealed by these only. If the desk is made of wood, we must consider the following: all component elements of the wood such as its grain, figure, minute particles of wood, etc., other materials like nails and glue, a specific process of some workers that produced the desk, the method of transportation that brought it here in front of us, and the desk's special use or properties. Unless we know all these, the being called 'desk' is not completely revealed to us (but of course there can exist no completely-revealed being). In this regard, the desk exists as much as the observer cognizes it. This point is applied not just to desks but also to all beings in general.

3) Accordingly, we can say, "Being is grasped by cognition" or "Being is tainted by cognition."

From the foregoing discussion on cognition and being, we can conclude as follows: "There is no pure cognition as itself, and there is no pure being as itself."

If we describe this point in Buddhist terminology, it is "Cognition is emptiness, and being is emptiness." Let me explain the meaning of this word "emptiness" so that I can help you understand our upcoming discussion. We will be able to understand 'emptiness' correctly only when we liberate ourselves from the erroneous preconception of emptiness and the [mysterious] feeling surrounding the word "emptiness."

Contrary to what most people believe, 'emptiness' is not at all similar to the concept of 'nothingness.' Also, it does not have such a vague or messy logical structure as to say that (A=B) is equivalent to (If A is B, then B is A), to say this is correct, to say that is also correct, this is that, and that is this, etc. Further, emptiness has nothing to do with a trained, matured and highly purified state, or a mysterious, grandiose and certain completed realm of the mind from which immeasurable values and meanings spring forth.

Then, what is 'emptiness' that has caused such confusion? 'Emptiness' means, in a nutshell, a being that comes into existence in terms of relations, or the non-independence of the being. When we say that a being is composed of relations, it does not mean that the being does not exist or it is devoid of everything. A being composed of relations exists as a form of existence that is sustained in virtue of being linked to many other causes.

So, when we say "All phenomena are emptiness" in Buddhism, it does not mean that phenomena do not exist. It means that no beings are self-caused existence. In other words, no being exists as a purely independent substance; rather, beings overlap and influence one another.

For instance, if we say "Korea is empty," we are stating quite an accurate expression. For, firstly, from a geopolitical point of view, Korea is in a peninsula in Northeast Asia and it is on the western side of the Pacific Ocean – in other words, its location is determined only on the map of the entire globe. Korea's location is not independent of the locations of surrounding areas, its location is determined only by geographical factors of the globe, so, in this respect, Korea is geographically empty in its relation to the globe. As I made clear above, this does not mean that Korea does not exist on the earth. If we proceed a little further with this point, we can see that the earth can have its form of existence and meaning only in the order of the solar system. The earth does not exist outside the system of the universe. In this respect, the earth is empty in its relation to the solar system. Likewise, the solar system is also empty in its relation to a broader level of the order of the universe.

Secondly, Korea is empty on the level of politics as well. This does not mean that there exists no political entity 'Korea.' The international political situation in the process of its foundation as a country, its status as a newly emerging nation, its international recognition and political exchanges with other nations, etc., etc. – from all these historical events up until this moment, Korea has never been out of the order of international politics even for one moment. Like any other country on the globe, Korea was established and stands in the midst of all the entangled political relations of all countries – in this point, Korea is empty in its aspect of international politics.

In its economic or military aspect as well, Korea is empty on the same line of logic. And since Korea is not separate from the structure of the entire human history in its language, culture, customs, and any other area, we can say "Korea is empty."

So far, I have talked about the emptiness of Korea from the external point of view. Let us have a look at Korea itself. It is not the case that Korea is made of a chunk of slippery ice and relates to outside entities in this way or that way. First of all, if we examine the official name of Korea [The Great Democratic Nation of Koreans], we can see immediately that "Koreans" refer to a race and 'Democratic Nation' means that it is a country where the will of the people is respected. Also, if we here dig down deeper on such things as how the concept of democracy emerged, we will have to talk about the entire human history in order to explain the meaning of the word "The Great Democratic Nation of Koreans."

The name 'the Great Democratic Nation of Koreans' is phenomenally not a certain real being; it is just a word conventionally agreed upon because Koreans needed to call their country 'The Great Democratic Nation of Koreans.' As is well known, the inner side of this conventional word is not only related to so many historical meanings but it also includes them. So, the name 'The Great Democratic Nation of Koreans' is also emptiness [empty].[73] In this

---

73 Bryan Magee summarizes Karl Popper's view related to this point as follows: "Another point to be made about good definitions in science is that they are, as Popper puts it, properly to be read from right to left and not from left to right. The sentence 'A di-neutron is an unstable system comprising two neutrons' is the scientists' answer to the question 'What shall we call an unstable system comprising two neutrons?', not

name 'The Great Democratic Nation of Koreans,' which is empty, there are many components that belong to different levels. From natural components like the sky, sea, and land to administrative jurisdictions such as province, country, and city and various interest organizations, innumerably many families and individuals, invisible legal and political binding force, economic order, social customs, religions or ideologies – all these are connected to, overlapped with, and woven with one another in all directions. As the entire net is shaken if you pull one knot of a large net, so, if you pick one of the components of the name 'The Great Democratic Nation of Koreans,' it is connected to all the other components of the name 'The Great Democratic Nation of Koreans.'

That is not all. It is connected to everything on the earth, and further, it will be related to the solar system and as far as to the entire universe. In this regard, the mode of existence and movement of an individual comes to have meaning to the entire universe. A poet's line "When you pick a flower on the earth, stars in the sky get hurt" cannot simply be regarded as a sentimental structure of his or her cognition.

Then, there is no reason that we should be tied to the proposition "The Great Democratic Nation of Koreans is empty." We can instead say "All beings and actions are defined and unfold themselves only by the relations they have to all the other parts." All in all, each and

---

an answer to the question 'What is a di-neutron?'. The word 'di-neutron' is a handy substitute for a long description, that is all..." [Bryan Magee, *Popper*, Frank Cass Publishers, London, 1973, pp. 49-50.]

every part is empty in their relations to the other parts.

"Everything is empty to everything." To make it simpler, "Everything is empty."

'Emptiness' is synonymous with 'relationship,' that is, 'dependent arising (conditioned origination).' We agree and promise to call the state in which beings are related to and overlap with one another as 'emptiness.'

Let us go back to our original point of discussion. Since it is 'cognition defined by being' and 'being defined by cognition,' we borrow the theory of emptiness and say "Cognition is empty and being is also empty." Or, making a noun form of the empty state, we can derive the proposition "Cognition is emptiness and being is also emptiness." Then, since these two (cognition and being) are in the relation of emptiness, cognition is not purely cognition as itself and being is not purely being as itself. It was the mistake of preexisting philosophy and thoughts to think of each of them as an independent domain. Then, can we have a new expression that will help us avoid this mistake? The concept that was suggested as an answer to this question is 'consciousness.' It is the very 'consciousness' in the proposition "All phenomena are consciousness," which is the title of the first subtopic of this article.

Consciousness is a kind of conventional word [of stipulated definition] that refers to phenomena which are sustained as empty states. No phenomenon can exist as a purely independent domain that has nothing to do with other things. No names of the phenomenal world that we can describe with the forms of noun, such as 'cognition,' 'object,' 'mind,' 'thing,' etc., can in fact become the concepts of real being.[74] So, the concept of consciousness was suggested in order to describe the phenomenal world more comprehensively and accurately. That is, cognition is consciousness, and humans and animals are also consciousness. Further, all the mental and material phenomena such as stones, flowers, trees, etc. are consciousness. This word "consciousness" is a term that we can use to call all phenomena from the perspective of emptiness. In other words, this means that we agree to call all empty phenomena 'consciousness.'

If we divide the entire domain of phenomena into the cognizing subject and the object of cognition, 'consciousness' is a concept that includes both being and cognition. So, it is distinguished from the 'cognition' which psychology regards as the cognizing subject.

According to Asvaghosa's *The Awakening of Mahayana Faith*, 'consciousness' has a feedback mode that develops with nine stages of processes.

The first stage: karma consciousness

This may be called 'cognition defined by being' that I mentioned above. It is cognition tainted by being. That is, this is the stage in which being taints cognition. This being is, though, mental or material being determined by preceding cognition. 'Karma' is about 'move,' 'act,' 'think,' etc., and it means all kinds of mental and material intentional actions. Accordingly, karma consciousness

---

74 We should never accept real being only because we have the forms of noun that appear to refer to abstract entities as real being.

means 'the state of cognition being tainted by karma,' and it is not pure consciousness itself. Since being and actions are mixed up with cognition, it is called 'karma consciousness.' Other stages of consciousness to be explained below have the same meaning. This karma consciousness is, figuratively speaking, the stage in which colored eyeglasses are painted with more colors.

The second stage: rotation consciousness

This is the stage in which we see (or act) afresh with 'the cognition defined by being (the karma consciousness of the first stage: eyeglasses painted with colors),' and it is about the autonomous activities of karma consciousness. 'Rotation' is a symbolic description of the way of activities that karma consciousness moves.

The third stage: manifestation consciousness

This is about the new 'mode of mental and material being grasped by cognition,' which is manifested when the newly formed 'cognition defined by being' responds to the mode of being grasped by cognition that went through the reification process of the fourth stage of knowledge[75] consciousness of its previous cycle. This is about the world that appears painted that we see through colored eyeglasses already painted. 'Manifestation' is about 'appear' and

75 The Chinese letter for this is closer to 'wisdom' in its meaning, but 'knowledge consciousness' describes the meaning of the fourth stage better because it is about the differentiating or discriminating activities of consciousness.

'reveal.'

The foregoing three stages are the processes that are almost simultaneously completed to the point of being done 'secretly.' To be more precise, I need to point out that all nine stages of processes, which include the six stages to be explicated below, are always being completed simultaneously. For one process includes in itself the rest of the other eight processes. The process of the world seen as tainted with colors (manifestation consciousness) which is seen through the colored eyeglasses (rotation consciousness) while we are wearing colored eyeglasses (karma consciousness) – this process goes through the next six stages of later processes and then the cyclic processes of continually painting colors on colored eyeglasses. However, this is not a simple cyclic repetition because the colored eyeglasses gradually change.

The fourth stage: knowledge consciousness

It is very important to understand this 'knowledge consciousness.' In short, 'knowledge consciousness' is a stage in which one decisively perceives the state of karma consciousness developing into manifestation consciousness, and performs the reification of the state. That is, the reification of karma consciousness produces the 'awareness of self' that restricts one's viewpoint such that there exists the subject 'I'. The reification of rotation consciousness makes rotation consciousness thought as the cognitive-subjective function of the awareness of self, and it causes to produce the reification of the cognizing subject. The reification of manifestation consciousness realizes the mode of mental and material being. In a broad sense, the awareness of self, which is the reification of karma consciousness, results in this reification of manifestation consciousness.

The fifth stage: continuity consciousness

This is the stage in which the stage of knowledge consciousness deepens and the awareness of real being becomes more and more fixed.

The five stages of the above, from karma consciousness to continuity consciousness, are the basic stages of the structure of phenomena (cognition and being). Everything in the domain of phenomena interacts with one another and develops itself based on these processes. (The Consciousness-Only School regards these processes as belonging to the domains of seventh consciousness and higher.)

The sixth stage: appropriation consciousness

This is a process in which cognition (defined by being) meets being (tainted by cognition) and interacts with it through sensory organs, etc. 'Appropriate' means 'get limited and take.' This means to accept the phenomena of beings that are limited by the awareness of real being through the processes of reification on the fourth stage of knowledge consciousness and the fifth stage of continuity consciousness.

The seventh stage: conceptualization consciousness

This is about what we usually say 'I am conscious' and 'I think.' This is a stage in which we analyze and examine what we accept with appropriation consciousness. We figure out things as salty, spicy, hot, cold, displeased, good, incorrect, correct, etc. The title of this consciousness signifies to 'figure out' or 'differentiate' the 'concepts' of things. This consciousness conceptualizes and differentiates that which are accepted (appropriated).

The eighth stage: to create karma

This is the stage in which specific and active functions are performed in relation to phenomena. This is caused by the previous seven stages. It is about such actions as 'to throw something away if one dislikes it,' 'to pursue it if one likes it,' 'to reject it if it is incorrect,' 'to support it if it is correct,' etc. Here, 'karma' means the same as the 'karma' in karma consciousness. These karmic actions and their consequences taint, again in their turns, karma consciousness.

The ninth stage: to receive consequences

This is about the specified consequences of actions in the eighth stage. Whether it is a conceptualization of a thinking process or it is a necessary mode of existence that physically results from something, it is about the features of the domain of phenomena that has changed. This is the ninth stage – 'the consequence stage.' The features of the phenomenal domain, as the changed consequences, provide yet again empirical information for the first stage of karma consciousness and change karma consciousness in its quality and quantity. This is what Buddhism calls 'permeation' – 'to expose something to, and cook it with odor or smoke and make it tainted.'

The eighth and ninth stages are not named '~ consciousness.'

However, we call them 'consciousness' like other stages in the sense that some comprehensive and holistic things, in which cognition and being cannot be distinguished in the actions and consequences of the eighth and ninth stages, are moving and functioning.

The nine stages of the processes of consciousness show us that all phenomena's mode of existence is such that there is no pure cognition or pure being – unlike the way the claims of realism present to us. Cognition and being are intermingled with each other to the point that one cannot be distinguished from the other. This is the very feature of the domain of phenomena.

The nine stages of processes of consciousness that we discussed above can be summarized as follows.

····→ colored eyeglasses^1 → to see through colored eyeglasses → a world tainted with colors^1
   (karma consciousness)   (rotation consciousness)   (manifestation consciousness)

→to live in a tainted world →to taint eyeglasses again →colored eyeglasses^2 ·····colored eyeglasses^n
(from knowledge consciousness   (permeation)
to actions and consequences)

We could here ask the following question: Where did colored eyeglasses^1 come from? The answer to this question is as follows. They came from the previous nine stages. We could ask further questions. Let us then set aside the colors painted. But how did the eyeglasses themselves come into existence? This question is asking if the pure eyeglasses themselves that are not painted should have originally existed. This kind of thought is the very awareness of self (eyeglasses themselves) that results from the reification of facts [phenomena] in the fourth stage of knowledge consciousness.

Colored eyeglasses come to conduct countlessly many actions as they go through the reification process, and they come to be reborn as new eyeglasses with the consequences of these actions. In other words, eyeglasses taint the world, and the tainted world in its turn taints eyeglasses as it undergoes various interactions. This means that cognition and being define and include each other. Since there exists neither pure cognition nor pure being, we say that cognition is empty and being is also empty.

If cognition (colored eyeglasses) includes in itself being, it is not appropriate to call it simple [pure] 'cognition.' If the domain of beings (the colored world) is restricted [defined] by cognition (colored eyeglasses), we cannot call it simple [pure] being. Cognition defined by being and being restricted by cognition – they are thoroughly related to and define each other. We call this domain 'consciousness.'

Now we can call all beings in the domain of phenomena with the new word "consciousness." This 'consciousness' comes to have the meaning of 'horizon' which appears as cognition and being include, define, and constantly interact and communicate with each other. On this line of thought, 'consciousness' is not only about the state which is not spatially stalled, but it also comprehensively refers to the changes in the temporal aspects of things, events, awareness and actions. So, the concept of 'consciousness' is closer to the concept of 'history' than to the concept of 'cognition' or 'being.'[76]

---

76 Buddhism sees everything as a changing process. However, what is important for us to note is that an individual, conscious phenomena or groups of human society, which

Accordingly, the proposition of the subtopic 'All phenomena are consciousness' may well be replaced by 'All phenomena are history.' 'All phenomena,' 'consciousness' and 'history' are synonymous. So, "history is cognition tainted by being, and it is the collection of forms and (psychological and behavioral) actions that develop responding to beings grasped by cognition."

It now has a significant meaning that this essay, which is a new approach to understanding history in a new and correct way, has come to reach the conclusion that "History is consciousness that includes cognition and being."

Two hidden meanings of emptiness

In Buddhism, the meaning of emptiness is its alpha and omega in that one must first comprehend it and also in that it is the third eye – that is, it is the middle way that avoids both absolutism and relativism – that constitutes the ground of all historical actions. So, we must make it a starting point to have a precise comprehension of emptiness if we want to gain a perspective to see history correctly.

'Emptiness' destroys all forms of the awareness of real being. In fact, however, all this comes down to two kinds of forms of the

---

form organic wholes, maintain their own identities. We can define 'consciousness' as 'history' because 'consciousness' is the accumulation of individuals or groups that continuously sustain their identities. As the Buddhist scriptures say, a flame is an accumulation of constantly changing, different flames but nevertheless it continuously exists as one same flame. In this sense, history is a process in which an organic entity keeps maintaining its own identity, and the truth that this process cannot be permanent is also included in the meaning of the word "history."

awareness of real being. The stage of knowledge consciousness, which was the fourth stage of the nine stages of consciousness that we discussed above, showed us that it could not observe all historical phenomena as empty but instead it got fixed with the awareness of real being and reified all phenomena. To reify phenomena – mental, material and conceptual – is not to correctly grasp history as empty, and it is a primordial error. All errors start with this awareness of real being. So, if we want to make efforts to eliminate this error, we must first start to destroy this awareness of real being.

When I previously explained 'knowledge consciousness' I said that it reified karma consciousness, rotation consciousness and manifestation consciousness. Since the reification of karma consciousness is included in the reification of rotation consciousness and manifestation consciousness, the process of reification may be said to come down to roughly two kinds. One is the reification of the cognizing subject (rotation consciousness), and the other is to reify as object the extant material and mental phenomena. This is to see the cognizing subject and objects of cognition as belonging to separate domains, although they are overlapped with each other and they are not able to be separated. In order to cope with the error of these two types of reification, we need to make sure that the stance of emptiness should not be one-sided or applied only to one level. Accordingly, the perspective of emptiness also usually comes to have the feature of two modes that repudiate and avoid these two forms of reification.

The one is the stance of 'ontological emptiness,' and the other is the stance of 'epistemological emptiness.'

Firstly, the 'ontological emptiness' has it that all beings are fundamentally causally connected to innumerably many conditions through space and time and thus they are not real being (substance). There exists no such real being (substance). If we observe nature from the viewpoint of natural science, ontological emptiness tells us that no phenomenon can exist or come to exist as self-caused. The view of ontological emptiness includes the perspective of social science that any situation of an individual or a part [of a whole] can be interpreted only in organic relations to the whole – society, politics, economics, etc. It also includes the stance of philosophy of language that concepts, languages, names, and explanations and hypotheses (propositions) that unfold themselves on the foundation of these concepts, languages and names, should be accepted not as having substantive or essential meanings but as having uses, that is, their meanings are manifested in their relations or uses. To have a stance of ontological emptiness is not to have all things fall in the state of 'nothingness.' What it means is that beings and phenomena do not have substances. However, it does not deny that they keep their own identities understood in terms of their organic relations. To the contrary, it is to grasp phenomena not from one perspective but from a variety of perspectives, and not as fixed entities but as dynamic entities. It is to see phenomena and things positively and dynamically.

This 'ontological emptiness' may mean to deny the reification of manifestation consciousness in the fourth stage of knowledge consciousness.

Manifestation consciousness is 'cognition defined by a newly formed being – karma consciousness (colored eyeglasses)^n – and it is 'the mode of mental and material being grasped by new cognition' – manifestation consciousness (the world tainted with colors)^n – which is manifested when it responds to the mode of being grasped by cognition – knowledge consciousness (the world tainted with colors)$^{n-1}$ – that went through the reification process of the fourth stage of knowledge consciousness in its previous cycle.

In this process, being is in fact the being grasped by the preexisting cognition. That is, it is the world^{n-1} that is tainted with colors – knowledge consciousness^{n-1} that has gone through the reification process. But 'n' means an infinitely many number of experiences (or relations). Then, 'n-1' also means that the process of countlessly many experiences has already been established. This is to say that we see, again with colored eyeglasses (karma consciousness^n), the features of something that is not the being itself because it has been tainted with colors not just a few times but innumerably many times. The features of 'the world tainted with colors (manifestation consciousness^n)' are different from the features of 'the world' without n (the accumulated amount of experiences). 'Manifestation consciousness^n' is a being that can be defined only in its relation to the process of 'karma consciousness^n' and 'rotation consciousness^n.'

In this regard, it would be an error if one should believe that pure and simple 'manifestation consciousness^n' exists independently as a real being separately from its relation to 'karma consciousness^n' and 'rotation consciousness^n.' We can substitute many concepts for 'manifestation consciousness.' All the words that can have noun forms, such as matter, languages, mental phenomena, the subjectivity 'I,' ideologies, systems, and gods, belong to the domain of this 'manifestation consciousness.' And not to reify this 'manifestation consciousness,' that is, to know that the process of 'knowledge consciousness' is an error is what 'ontological emptiness' is about.

Then, what is 'epistemological emptiness'?

This means to have a state of an open mind that is not obstructed by a certain preconception or a narrow-minded view when we face things, situations or phenomena. This is to be free from all preceding experiences, and it is a state free from any form of realist thoughts. This will set us completely free from all the senses of memberships to belong to a biological human species, an anthropological classification like people or race, other political standpoints such as nation or ideology, and the preconceptions coming from social statuses and class memberships. This is to be liberated from such idolatrous mechanisms as language, culture, custom, god, opinions limited by the category of space and time, etc. as well. And this also means to transcend an individual's unconsciousness, desire and psychological complex. All this surely sounds like an enormous job to accomplish, but it is not really such an insurmountable task once you look at it closely. The following is the reason.

"A fish is liberated from water" or "A fish is free in water" does not mean that a fish has nothing to do with water, it can live without water, or it can handle water at its will. However, a fish and water exist without any incompatibility or pretense as the fish follows its own way of life and water follows its nature of flowing. When a citizen of Korea says "I am liberated from Korea," this does not mean that she does not set a foot in the land of Korea. This does not mean that she does not follow the laws or customs of Korea, either. She is well aware that laws, customs, systems, etc. constitute the ethic of given situations, and she believes that they must be righteously and correctly implemented. And she thinks that although they may vary, they must be observed when it is the time they need to be observed; she also thinks that when people want revision and reformation, they need to be changed by the will of the majority of the people. Although she was born as a citizen of Korea, she understands that Korea is a member of the international community of the world; and she is well aware that she must play some historical role as a citizen of Korea for the universal prosperity of all of humanity. Also, she knows that although it is necessary and unavoidable for all nations to have mutual exchanges and to influence each other, none of these should make one subordinate to the other, or let exploitation or infringement take place.

And she believes that this world should be like a flower garden that has various flowers joining and blooming together – that is, the world should be such that, although each nation and each people develop their own unique cultures, they have political, economic and social exchanges based on the belief in mutual prosperity. This way, she believes, they do not lose their independence or uniqueness, but, at the same time, they form a harmonious community as a whole. All these are of course a kind of metaphor, but we can now say "She is free from Korea" or "She is liberated."

Let me add one more point. The following is how a Zen master of Buddhism who achieved enlightenment described the realm of his own enlightenment: "I eat when I am hungry, and I sleep when I am sleepy."

The desires for food and sleep are the two of five desires in Buddhism – the desires for wealth, sex, food, fame and sleep. Buddhists proclaim to overcome these five basic desires. However, the Zen master is not said to be constrained by the desires of food and sleep although he says "I eat when I am hungry, and I sleep when I am sleepy." Then, what state is this? Doesn't this state address 'epistemological emptiness' which is the stance of a liberated mind that is free of preconceptions or perversion? To transcend even the unconscious desires or psychological complex does not mean that the desires or complex disappeared or we have come to have nothing to do with them. There still are desires, and psychological complex continuously functions. We live a tough life if it has to be tough, a small-scale of life if it needs to be small, and a fastidious style of life if it has to be so. It is just like the way a craftsman uses tools well and dexterously whether they are of superb quality or have defects. Desires and complex still function, but we are free from them. We do not eliminate desires or complex; instead we can free ourselves from them by accurately comprehending their natures.

The Vimalakirti Sutra, one of the major Mahayana sutras, shows us the state of this 'epistemological emptiness' with an interesting fable.

At that time, there was a heavenly being, a goddess, in Vimalakirti's room who, seeing these great men and hearing them expound the Law, proceeded to make herself visible and, taking heavenly flowers, scattered them over the bodhisattvas and major disciples. Then the flowers touched the bodhisattvas, they all fell to the floor at once, but when they touched the major disciples, they stuck to them and did not fall off. The disciples tried to shake off the flowers with their supernatural powers, but they could not do so.

At that time the goddess said to Shariputra, "Why try to brush off the flowers?"

"Such flowers are not in accordance with the Law," he replied. "That's why I try to brush them off."

The goddess said, "Don't say these flowers are not in accordance with the Law. Why? Because the flowers make no such distinctions. You in your thinking have made up these distinctions, that's all. If one who has left the household life to follow the Buddha's Law makes such distinctions, *that* is not in accordance with the Law. One must be without distinctions to be in accordance with the Law. Look at the bodhisattvas – the flowers do not stick to them because they have already cut off all thought of distinctions. Just as evil spirits are able to take advantage of a person who is beset by fear, so because you disciples are fearful of the cycle of birth and death, the senses of form, sound, smell, taste and touch are able to take advantage of you. But once a person has done away with fear, then the five desires that arise from these senses will not be able to get at him. So long as one has not done away with all such entanglements, the flowers will stick to him. But they will not stick to someone who has eliminated them all."

– Chapter 7 Regarding Living Beings, *The Vimalakirti Sutra*[77]

'Nirvana,' which is the ideal realm of Buddhism, means the state in which the flame of suffering is extinguished. We can obtain this realm of nirvana only when we have the stance of fundamental 'epistemological emptiness' of Mahayana Buddhism that teaches "Do not eliminate suffering; but do not generate a mind that is attached to suffering."

Let us compare and contrast this 'epistemological emptiness' with my view that each of the nine stages of 'consciousness' is all 'empty.'

'Epistemological emptiness' is a concept that denies 'the reification of rotation consciousness' of the fourth knowledge consciousness. The rotation consciousness is the state in which we see (respond) with the newly formed cognition (karma consciousness^n) which is defined by being, and it is the autonomous activities of karma consciousness^n. But this karma consciousness (colored eyeglasses)^n is the state of a newly defined consciousness influenced by the mode of being that went through the reification process of its previous stage of knowledge consciousness^{n-1}. 'Karma consciousness' is formed by the accumulation and influence of mutual experiences repeated innumerably many times notated by 'n-1' or 'n'. The function of karma consciousness is 'rotation

---

77 *The Vimalakirti Sutra*, translated by Burton Watson, Columbia University Press, 1997, pp. 86-87.

consciousness.' Karma consciousness and rotation consciousness interact with each other and go through changes. To reify this process and see it as the realm of real being of the cognizing subject is the very 'reification of rotation consciousness' which is one of the reification functions of the fourth knowledge consciousness. The stance of 'epistemological emptiness' means to be liberated from countlessly many experiencesn of the mode of being and actions that come to develop due to the reification of knowledge consciousness.

The revolutionary nature of enlightenment

All history is consciousness. Consciousness is emptiness [Consciousness is empty]. However, people cannot grasp consciousness as empty, and they instead reify it. As we discussed above, this reification has roughly two kinds: one is the reification of the cognizing subject, and the other is the reification of extant phenomena as objects. Cognition and being are thoroughly overlapped with each other, and thus neither of them can be reified. Accordingly, the twofold structure of 'epistemological emptiness' and 'ontological emptiness,' which is to correct these two forms of errors, does not have each of them as an independent part; each of them includes the other, both of them together form a stance of 'one emptiness,' and neither of them can be separated from the other.

We need to cognize history as history itself and being as being in its true features without any preconceptions or restricted mind. Only when we accomplish this, we can establish our stance for life that follows this understanding. However, the open stance of 'epistemological emptiness' that embraces the view 'Do not generate a mind that is attached to suffering' must be preceded, after all, by the stance of 'ontological emptiness' that knows 'the emptiness of suffering.'

We must have truly open minds. We should face history candidly and objectively without being attached to desire, bigotry, complex and ideology, properties, machine, god, the laws that we believe as truths, etc. The achievement of this ($\rightarrow$ to have the stance of epistemological emptiness) is possible only when we cognize that all these are experiences[n], that is, consciousness, and they are 'emptiness' that are not real being ($\rightarrow$ when we have the stance of ontological emptiness).

On the other hand, however, we come to find out that this 'ontological emptiness' is on the level that can never be reached unless the state of the open mindset of 'epistemological emptiness' is presupposed. If we face a being with the cognition tainted, even a bit, by a certain experience or by a view of values, then the being never manifests itself as 'emptiness' and this is to taint the being with a certain cognition. Then, this comes down to the point that 'epistemological emptiness' and 'ontological emptiness' become each other's preconditions.

If I may summarize these two aspects of emptiness, one is 'the liberation from cognition ($\rightarrow$epistemological emptiness)' and the other is 'the liberation from being ($\rightarrow$ontological emptiness).'

However, since the cognition in 'the liberation from cognition' originates from being, 'the liberation from cognition' contains 'the liberation from being.' And, since the being in 'the liberation from being' comes from cognition, 'the liberation from being' comes to mean 'the liberation from cognition.' So, we come to obtain such a dynamic structure of a conclusion as "We cannot be liberated from being unless we are liberated from cognition, and we cannot be liberated from cognition unless we are liberated from being." For since these two form each other without one preceding the other, the liberation from one should be done by untangling both of them simultaneously. Therefore, 'the liberation from cognition' and 'the liberation from being' are each other's necessary and sufficient conditions. This is not a process that can be achieved by one after another following a temporal procedure. The situation that leads to these two cannot but come simultaneously, after all. Then this realm may well be said to be a revolutionary situation that is separate from the concept of causality.[78]

The view that the enlightenment of emptiness is of a revolutionary nature came from the Chinese Zen masters of old times. They described this revolutionary enlightenment as 'Sudden Enlightenment.' 'Sudden' means 'all at once,' 'all of a sudden,' and it is in sharp contrast with 'in an orderly fashion,' 'gradually' and 'through a certain process.' It was Huineng Sunim (AD 638-

---

78 The current perspective to see the concept of emptiness as a concept of liberation requires us to learn by experience that all phenomena that exist consist in the relations of dependent arising. And this realm is called the state of nirvana. *The Nirvana Sutra* summarizes the merits and characteristics of nirvana with the following three expressions: dharma body, prajna [wisdom] and liberation. So, the undistorted manifestation of the being itself, that is, of the relation of dependent arising among dharma body, prajna and liberation is named 'the unfathomable realm of liberation.'

712), the *de facto* founder of Zen traditions, who specifically grasped enlightenment with this aspect of revolutionary features. His famous poem that manifested his view of revolutionary enlightenment criticized the majority of monks of his time who understood enlightenment as a result of gradual practices.

Let us first see the poem of Shenxiu Sunim who viewed enlightenment to be achieved gradually.

The body is the Bodhi Tree,
The mind is like a clear mirror standing.
Take care to wipe it diligently,
Keep it free from all dust.

Huineng's poem of revolutionary enlightenment, which was composed to refute the view of Shenxiu's poem, went as follows:

Bodhi has no tree to begin with,
The clear mirror is nowhere standing.
Originally there is not a thing [there is no real being],
Where can there be any dust?

"When there is originally not a thing, where can there be any dust?" – that is, it is nonsense to say that there is dust on the non-existent real being. Zen Master Shenxiu understood enlightenment as a product of gradual efforts. However, Huineng Sunim thoroughly kept his stance of emptiness in such a way that he did not even postulate any fixed criterion of cognitive system symbolized by the 'clear mirror' or any criterion of truth indicated by 'bodhi.' And thereby he showed that the way to enter enlightenment was not a gradual process. In other words, one must realize not only that the dust itself was not real but also that there was not even any real basis to which dust could stick. Naturally, there was no problem of dust that was supposed to stick to the basis because there existed no such a basis to begin with.

In other words, what is the point of trying so hard to remove color or dust from eyeglasses? These are unnecessary efforts even if the glasses become colorless and transparent. Why do you think you should wear eyeglasses at all (why do you need to illuminate things with such and such a criterion or from a specific system of logic)? That is an error. Take off any eyeglasses. Smash them. This is what Huineng meant with his line "Originally there is not a thing." To choose and wear a specific color of eyeglasses, to remove dust on the glasses, or to color the glasses is a gradual procedure; but to get rid of them is a revolutionary event.

These different views of Huineng and Shenxiu definitely influenced their followers. Their views earned the title of 'the Southern School of Sudden Enlightenment and the Northern School of Gradual Enlightenment' named after the places where they resided. It is needless to say that 'the Southern School of Sudden Enlightenment' symbolizes the tradition of the revolutionary teaching of Huineng who lived in Southern China. Huineng opened his mind to awakening for the first time when he heard of, among all the Buddhist sutras, the following passage of *The Diamond Sutra*: "A bodhisattva should use his or her mind without dwelling on anything." Ever since this awakening, he took *The Diamond Sutra* as the basic frame of his teaching. It is quite significant to notice that his own fundamental perspective of enlightenment was based on *The Diamond Sutra*, which is the representative sutra that illuminates the teaching of emptiness, if we relate his choice of *The Diamond Sutra* to his revolutionary stance on enlightenment.

'Sudden' in 'Sudden Enlightenment' means the elimination of all erroneous views at once and "Enlightenment" is not to accept a real being of any logic or contents, as Zen Master Huihae clearly commented. This view evolved into the famous but paradoxical proposition "The Great Way is gateless (There is no special point of access to the Buddhist Way or enlightenment)." This proposition is what Zen Master Haegyeo in Song Dynasty of China used when he taught his students. "The Great Way is gateless" or "There is no gate that opens up to truth" means that there is no 'method [way]' to enter the truth. It professes that no efforts or practices may make a necessary cause to let us enter the realm of truth.

If we think of the realm of truth as the state of liberated mind that knows the emptiness of all beings and thus is not attached to anything, all the efforts and practices, made before we arrive at this state, are directed by the awareness tainted by something. For whether they are attached to the epistemic level, to the ontological level, or to something that combines both levels, they are all captured by the erroneous view that things really exist as substances. No matter how much we have controlled and purified our mental states and awareness, as long as they are founded on the view of real being, they have, from a logical point of view, nothing to do with the world of emptiness that transcends the level of the awareness of real being. No matter how much and how deeply we have continuously made our efforts to liberate ourselves from the bondage of cognition, we cannot achieve it unless we are liberated from the world of being. Conversely, we are not able to liberate ourselves from the constraint of being, however hard we try it, unless we are free from the bondage of cognition.

All this signifies that any thoughts and actions before the realization of the world of emptiness, no matter how much they get accumulated, ordered and systemized, do not in essence have any necessary connections to the world of enlightenment. The proposition "There is no gate that opens up to truth" reveals to us, in a paradoxical way, the point that no effort or practice can make a direct cause that connects to the world of enlightenment.

This stance reminds us of the view of modern philosophers who raised questions on the inductive method of epistemology and science. For instance, David Hume (1711-1776) denied the classical idea of causality and pointed out that no matter how many individual observational statements we may collect, they do not imply any general statement that logically includes an infinite number of observational statements. Especially, he thought that no causal relation can be found in the physical world and that only constant conjunctions or regularities between event types takes place. The regularity of successive events creates a psychological association in our minds, and this association makes us predict the occurrence of subsequent event to follow when we observe the preceding event. However, according to Hume, this necessity exists only in our minds and we cannot find it in the things themselves.

A large number of people who maintained the traditional view, that is, the inductive method, raised questions on Hume's skepticism as follows. "Even if we admit that a general theory cannot be derived from individual observation statements, individual observations can still *imply* a general theory. In other words, they can bring about certain insight or imagination to scientists. Therefore, in fact, theories are made in such a way that observation cases lead to a general theory. Of course there is a logical leap or gap involved when a general theory comes out of individual cases. However, this process is not random or irrational at all. It seems that there is a kind of logic involved in the process, and it is what we call the method of induction."

However, Karl Popper[79] presents a unique view on the logic of scientific research and the characteristics of knowledge. His claim is grounded on the denial of the way of thinking based on inductive method. (It would be interesting to compare Popper's view and the claim

---

79 I believe Popper's view is in many respects closer to the basic Buddhist stance than any other philosopher's. But I do not think that his view is grounded on the completely same cognitive basis as the Buddhist stance. However, as he makes clear, he could nevertheless present the views close to Buddhism because the same propositions can be derived from different views or different cognitive bases. He admits that scientific theories which are not true can in reality reach many very important and useful conclusions. So, we cannot falsify our opponents' conclusion in an argument by falsifying its premise. For Popper, any scientific theory is a system of hypotheses produced as conjectures and it needs to be provisionally accepted as theory so long as it is not falsified by the tests on the deductive results of those hypotheses. And new evidence can falsify the theory and a given theory may be continuously replaced by a new theory. Popper's stance on, and approach to science is very friendly and encouraging to Buddhism because his stance accords with the Buddhist stance that does not view the mode of any existence as the mode of real being or of a completed state.

of Sudden Enlightenment. Try the following: substitute 'observation' and 'experiments' for efforts or practices to achieve enlightenment, and 'scientific theory' or 'conclusion' for 'the state of enlightenment' or the state of 'quasi-enlightenment' in which one believes that he or she is enlightened in his or her way.) Popper thought that the procedure with which a given theory is derived has nothing to do with its scientific status. Experiments and observations do not really produce a theory; to the contrary, they are the partial results derived from the theory, and scientists perform experiments and observations in order to test the theory.

Popper also says that the method of induction is not needed to solve the problem of scientific method and that in fact the inductive method does not exist. And the way the inductive theory is formed is a matter of psychological process, not a matter of logical process. For the observation itself cannot precede the theory itself and observations presuppose theories. Popper says that people do not realize this truth because of the defects underlying the foundations of the empiricist tradition. He explains his view introducing his own episode.

The following is his episode. The claim that science is theorized from experiences has been widely and firmly accepted and no one will listen to us if we should deny it. However, it is in fact ridiculous to be convinced that we start from pure experiences without having anything of theoretical nature. The following story shows well how ridiculous this conviction is. ... One day, decades ago, Popper started his lecture for a group of physics students in Vienna and asked them to follow his instructions so that he could explain the same logical points. 'Take your pencil and paper. Make a careful observation and write down what you have observed.' Students naturally asked him what it was that he wanted them to observe. The instruction 'Observe!' surely is ridiculous. Observation is always selective. It requires a selected object, specific assignment, interests, problems, etc. To describe [the contents of] observation, we need descriptive language; we also need the concepts of similarity and classification; and for classification, we require interests, perspectives, problems, etc.

Also, according to Popper, observation, observational statements, statements on the results of experiments, etc. are always the interpretations of observed facts. And they are the interpretations made under the light of theories.[80]

The following is Popper's conclusion on the method of induction. A new scientific theory or law does not come to appear as a consequence of the inductive method of research. According to him, as in arts, there is in science no fixed logic of methodology that leads to a new scientific theory. Every scientific discovery involves 'irrational elements' or 'creative intuition' in Bergson's sense. Einstein also said that he had searched for the most fundamental and general law that could be derived with the methods of pure deduction and should be that which could draw the way the world exists as its conclusion. However, he admitted that there was no law of logic that led to such a law. He agreed with Popper on his view that such a law could be reached by certain intuition based on something like an

---

80 Popper's view of this is the same as Thomas Kuhn's view that there is no research without any paradigm.

intellectual projection on the objects of experience, and Einstein said that a theory cannot be produced from the results of observations and that it can only be originally created.

If we see from the perspective we must accept in our pursuit of enlightenment, we will understand that even our efforts to get out of some specific views or preconceptions, as long as they are made before our realization of the truth of emptiness, have nothing to do with the open world of emptiness because those efforts are made while we still are captured by the erroneous background view of awareness of real being – the light of theory in Popper.

The following remarks of Zen traditions represent this stance. "You must see the nature[81] in order to become a Buddha. If seeing of the nature is not preceded, you cannot accomplish the Buddhahood even if you chant for the Buddha, read sutras, and strictly abide by the rules and precepts. Chanting, good conducts and others may bring about corresponding temporary good karmic consequences as the rewards of these good conducts, but you can never obtain the realm of the Buddha with them."

This stance of Zen traditions has often been criticized as paralyzing moral norms or historical, social awareness. However, this stance of Zen is based on their conviction that above all, it

---

81 'The nature' here means the true form of existence. 'Seeing the nature' is an exclusive term of Zen traditions and it is related to the following phrases in *The Flower Garland Sutra*: "If you wish to know the Buddha of the past, present, and future, observe the nature of the ontological world." *The Flower Garland Sutra* explains the features of the ontological world as the features of emptiness such that all beings overlap with and connect to one another and endlessly unfold themselves.

is 'enlightenment (seeing the nature)' that should be preceded in life and that only the historical life unfolding on the basis of this enlightenment can be a correct historical life. So, Zen traditions do not say that the practice itself is meaningless or should be ruled out; instead, they say that although enlightenment is not achieved, from a logical point of view, by the results of causal efforts, those efforts help make occasions to trigger enlightenment. They actually emphasize the necessity of consistent and steady efforts.

This particular stance led Zen traditions to choose a unique method of practices. It is a way to advance to enlightenment while avoiding two forms of error. The first of these two forms is all kinds of actions and thoughts (distractions) generated by the intention to pursue enlightenment. The second is a kind of nihilistic attitude (torpidity slumber and lethargy) that attempts to deny and eliminate not just any actions and thoughts but also even efforts. In other words, the pursuit of enlightenment itself needs to be controlled because it is a product of the idea of real being constrained by such things like 'truth or enlightenment.' On the other hand, however, although this is true, if we lose the direction of our conscious efforts and thereby give up our goals and try to eliminate even the function of consciousness itself, we will fall into lethargy and endless darkness. So, this should also be avoided.[82]

---

82 To avoid these two types of serious problems in practices, 'torpidity and slumber' and 'distractions,' the meditation method using a key phrase (hwadu) – Phrase-Observing Meditation, Key Phrase Mediation – is generally adopted. A key phrase may well be understood as a kind of 'form without content.' A key phrase is different from the propositions used as examples in philosophy of which the linguistic expressions have

The approach to a creative theory in science without an inductive process and the revolutionary enlightenment in Buddhism – are they of a similar kind? No, they are not. For although they are similar in the respect that the inductive method is not used to reach a scientific theory or enlightenment, a completion of scientific theory and an establishment of the Buddhist perspective of enlightenment belong to different dimensions. A creation of a new theory steadily continues in science, but in Buddhism it happens just once at the beginning. Let us see this difference with Kuhn's view.

We come to have the laws and theories of science not by reformulating them with the bases of experiments and observation; we come by them with creative intuition. This view helped beget Thomas Kuhn's new theory on the history of science. He views the history of science not as the process of accumulated progresses but as a series of revolutionary processes. According to his *The Structure of Scientific Revolutions*, the development in science is the ongoing process of the replacement of a given paradigm[83] by a new paradigm.

---

both contents and forms. It excludes contents and thereby shakes off the theoretical traces given precedingly and apriorily, but it maintains a kind of formal frame and thereby drives one's mind and efforts with a focused concentration to a certain intense form that does not have any contents. With this Phrase-Observing Meditation, practitioners avoid 'distractions' caused by the contents (a preexisting worldview, a stance) and at the same time they stay with an anchor and concentration away from 'torpidity and slumber' that make them lose tension. The features of Phrase-Observing Meditation that removes 'torpidity and slumber' and 'distractions' are characterized as 'Alertness and Quiescence,' 'Equal Maintenance of Alertness and Quiescence.' (alertness vs. torpidity and slumber, quiescence vs. distractions)

83 'Paradigm' is a concept that Kuhn uses in his own specific way. He uses it to refer to various meanings, but its generic meaning is that a paradigm constitutes the fundamentals of a scientific community and it refers to the theory, laws, knowledge,

There is normal science in which the members of a scientific society share a paradigm and conduct their research based on the paradigm. That is, there is a stage of research activities based on one well-established paradigm that makes current scientific achievements possible. As time passes by, however, this stage of normal science comes to face various scientific problems that cannot be solved with the norms of the paradigm that makes the research activities of the given normal science possible. A new paradigm, which can explain these problems, will appear as a response to the crisis. The new paradigm, with the support of many scientists, makes the foundation of scientific society that replaces the preexisting paradigm. And another stage of normal science based on the new paradigm continues. This new paradigm is not a result that is accomplished based on the research activities in the stage of preexisting normal science. To the contrary, the new paradigm comes to be created by those who have newly accessed the areas of the preexisting paradigm or by those who doubt its usefulness. As in the case of political changes in societies, the new paradigm, with the support of the majority of scientists, overwhelms the preexisting paradigm in a revolutionary way and makes the foundation of a new scientific society. We may summarize Kuhn's view as follows:

a pre-paradigm period→ paradigm 1→ normal science 1→ anomalies→ crisis → paradigm 2→ normal science 2→ ⋯ scientific revolution

---

values, traditions, etc. that are commonly shared by all the members of its community.

In a nutshell, Kuhn's scientific revolution is about the episode of change made not by accumulated processes but by a complete or partial replacement of one paradigm with a new paradigm that is incompatible with it. However, when Kuhn explains scientific revolution, he says that we do not know exactly how the revolutionary theory comes to be achieved (Popper and Einstein also agree on this point). We do not have a solution of the problem on how the norms of a new paradigm are devised, but it seems that those who primarily create a new paradigm are the people who are not attached to or constrained by the traditional norms of preexisting normal science. We can only presume that they are often pretty young or have recently come to approach the areas of the paradigm that they are changing. Also, as a revolution in the political system of a society is achieved by the support of the majority of the people on a system or ideology, Kuhn uses the concept of 'revolution' in the sense that more people have accepted the usefulness of a new paradigm that can solve the accumulated crises of the preexisting paradigm.

On this line of view, we can see that there is a conceptual difference between the scientific revolution of a new paradigm in Kuhn and the revolutionary features of enlightenment in Buddhism. For the revolutionary character of enlightenment is such that it is quite different from the preexisting view of values (perspective), and furthermore, the process or method of attaining enlightenment is the state that essentially excludes any preexisting conditions or processes. Enlightenment untangles the twofold structure of the awareness of real being instantaneously and simultaneously. Also enlightenment does not continuously change like scientific theories; it is accomplished all at once as a completed form. So, the revolutionary features of enlightenment have differences from Kuhn's revolution of a new paradigm.

To achieve enlightenment means to establish a perspective, which is basic but necessary, not distorted or refracted, in order to live a good and righteous historical life. What this implies is that we must have such historical activities as science, politics, etc. based on enlightenment to prevent errors and avoid going wrong. Accordingly, Buddhism respects and encourages as 'upaya-paramita'[84] only the theories, norms, and activities of social science that are unfolded based upon enlightenment.

From the perspective of seeing history as the world of emptiness manifested with dependent arising, no fixed stance or ism can exist. Accordingly, 'upaya-paramita' appears being set up appropriately in each stage of history or situation of the time. All our social activities can also be incessantly modified, changed and developed case by case as we appropriately apply them to the time and situation. However, enlightenment, which is the perspective that works as the basis making upaya-paramita always function in a good and correct way while not going astray, is far from being changed or modified. I have previously made it clear that enlightenment is not about an epistemic system of methodology that implies that 'we should see beings in such and such a method'

---

84 This is one of the features of historical practices exercised by those who have achieved supreme enlightenment. 'Upaya' is a variable form of truth that is appropriately applied to situations without losing the basics, and 'paramita' means the acts of advancement to the ideal realm.

when we face them. Enlightenment is not 'contents'; rather, it is a state in which any 'framework' or 'contents' are removed, that is, a state liberated from everything. To understand enlightenment as norms or laws that have certain contents is criticized as attachment to dharma [truth]. *The Diamond Sutra* has a refreshing phrase that is intended to help eliminate this attachment to dharma.

"What is called the Buddha's dharma is not the Buddha's dharma. It was only named the Buddha's dharma." That is, since enlightenment is a state in which one is liberated from everything, enlightened ones can face any historical situations with an objective and correct stance. Also, we cannot say that a liberated state undergoes changes, modifications or developments because it does not mean any 'contents.' Enlightenment is about the liberation from everything in itself, and it is a completed form of the correct, supreme and basic perspective with which the enlightened one faces all things in the world. So, Zen traditions have also called revolutionary enlightenment 'perfect accomplishment' and 'perfect awakening.' In this sense, this 'revolutionary enlightenment' is not something enormous that is to be completed in the last minutes of the process of one's life. To the contrary, it is the basic perspective that we should primarily assume in our lives, as we can correctly discern things only if we have eyes.

The difference between 'revolutionary enlightenment' and the laws of all sorts of scientific theories about humanity, society and nature is surprisingly clear. Enlightenment can be compared to healthy eyes, and upaya-paramita is historical activities to be accomplished with the visions possible through healthy eyes. To lack the perspective of enlightenment is to face history with colorblindness (or wearing colored eyeglasses). We could of course engage in historical activities without the perspective of enlightenment, but, then, it would be the history of delusion and errors to which the concept of 'upaya-paramita' cannot be applied. Logical consistency and the nomological nature of things lead to all scientific theories which are upaya-paramitas; enlightenment is not a distorted or refracted but healthy and open perspective that makes all scientific theories and activities deserve the title of upaya-paramitas.

Accordingly, the enlightenment in Buddhism and the creation of theories in science, although the processes that reach these two have equally revolutionary features, each of them has a different meaning. Also, the features of the mode of being, which can be described only as 'emptiness' as Buddhist sutras say, may be called 'an unfathomable realm of liberation'[85] in which innumerably many material and social factors become mutual conditions for each other and continuously change while they are tangled. On the other hand, scientific investigation will perhaps continue with no end and undergo revolutions of innumerably many theories and laws. A scientific theory is a system of hypotheses made by conjectures, and it will remain provisionally accepted as it undergoes deductive tests until it is falsified, as Popper's modest view shows. Also, as Kuhn says, the stages of normal science will develop into normal science 1,

---

85 This is an expression describing the features of the world from the perspective of enlightenment in terms of three characteristics: dharma body, prajna [wisdom] and liberation. This is not about the world made of alienation or distortion; it is about the liberation (moksha) and open realistic world (dharma body) that we enjoy through the stance of non-real-ness [non-substantiality] (changes and relations, that is, prajna).

2, 3, … with the appearance of new paradigms. In the area of social science as well, problems may be solved by gradual improvements and modification, as 'critical rationalists' think. Or, all sorts of problems in history may be solved only by revolutionary measures as is claimed by 'critical theorists' who aim for revolutionary changes. In either way, societies will steadily improve or change. What is important to notice is that historical theories and activities in the areas of the studies of humanities, social and natural sciences, whether they are revolutionary or gradually improving, belong to the realm of 'upaya-paramita.' 'Enlightenment' is, on the other hand, an original insight on the nature of being of all these historical conditions. That is, it is about the difference between 'wisdom (enlightenment)' and 'upaya (historical activities).'

The world of enlightenment seen through Ten Ox-Herding Pictures[86]

Let me summarize my points on 'revolutionary enlightenment' with an introduction to an interesting fable.

Zen Master Kuoan of the Song Dynasty in China compared the process of reaching enlightenment to the task of searching for an ox, and explained it with ten stages. This fable has been known as the story of Ten Ox-Herding Pictures or of Pictures of Searching for an Ox,[87] and it is composed of ten pictures and poetic

---

86 This is the name of the paintings on the ten stages of Ox-Herding.

87 This is about the famous fable in Zen traditions on the Songs of Ten Ox-Herding Pictures or Pictures of Searching for an Ox. Ten Ox-Herding Pictures became a main

interpretations on each of the pictures. The titles of the ten pictures
are as follows:

1. A man searching for an ox
2. Discovering its tracks
3. Seeing the ox
4. Catching it
5. Taming it
6. Controlling it at his will (Riding it home)
7. Ox forgotten/disappeared, man remains
8. Both forgotten/disappeared
9. Returning to the original place
10. Entering the dust of the world (Entering the path to history)

Many people have unfolded their various explanations and
interpretations on the symbolic nature of these ten pictures and
Kuoan's poetic interpretations. However, Kuoan himself and most

---

theme of the wall paintings of Buddhist temples, and even these days it is virtually
impossible not to find these pictures on the walls of Korean Buddhist temples.
Kuoan's Ten Ox-Herding Pictures are based on the 12 Ox-Herding Pictures of Quingju
Haosheng. The way of comparing the process or method of practices to the way of
taming an ox can be traced back to as far as the Buddhist *Agama Sutras*. *Agama* 46
Chapter 47 on Upaya has parts that teach monks' learning of good karma as they tell
a story of 11 ways to tame an ox, including 'corporeal aspects of knowledge' and
'characteristics of knowledge.' Also, *The Mahaprajnaparamita Sastra* Chapter 2
cites *The Comparison to Ox-Herding Sutra* which seems to be the translation of *The
Increased by One Agama Sutras*. Also, Kumarajiva translated *The Ox-Herding Sutra*.
As these examples show us, we can see that Ox-Herding has appeared as a symbol of
the practice process of practitioners since the early sutras. Toyenbee compared the ox
of this Ten Ox-Herding Pictures of Zen traditions with the monster of the Mitra myth
and regarded it as a symbol of the unconscious desire of humans.

people seem to have used Ten Ox-Herding Pictures as a tool to explain 'the gradual achievement' of enlightenment. Now I am going to present my view here as I set aside all the preexisting interpretations and transform these pictures into nice tools that illustrate 'revolutionary enlightenment.'

First of all, let us change the title of 'Pictures of Searching for an Ox' to 'Pictures of Teaching That an Ox Is Not an Ox (an Ox Does Not Exist).' For the preexisting interpretations take searching for an ox as an important task, but my view is exactly its opposite.

The first stage, a man searching for an ox

This is the beginning of delusion.

People hear a rumor that there is a wonderful ox. They believe that if a man could catch it and tame it, he could enjoy the highest form of life.

The ox is a symbol of 'mind.' It is otherwise called 'nature' – this is what Zen traditions mention as 'nature' in their point of 'seeing through the nature.' This 'nature' is 'the nature of dharma (being)' or 'the nature of things' – and it is at times thought as 'Buddha-

Nature' or 'the Way (Dao).' It may also be regarded as a symbol of fundamental desires such as 'honor,' 'wealth,' 'sexual desire,' etc. that we generally believe that people commonly pursue. Anyhow, whether it is 'mind' or 'wealth,' one believes that there exists some 'thing' that is symbolized by the ox. He comes to value it in his own way and then gets determined to search for it and get it.

The series of the ten pictures starts with the picture, without any explication, in which a man starts to search for an ox. If we assume that the ox is 'mind,' why did he decide to search for the mind? What is mind? With no reflection on these issues, he reifies the value systems of events and objects, the true nature, substance, etc. all of which are symbolized by 'mind.' And he moves forward pursuing them.

On this picture, the man is a symbol of reification of the cognitive subject and the ox is a symbol of reification of the being as object. The pictures following up to the sixth picture, which includes the story of the man encountering the ox, depict the way that 'the reified cognitive subject' and 'the reified being as object' interact with each other. So, the pictures showing that one believes there is an ox and then comes to start his journey searching for it signify the tainted mind that thinks that finding the ox and taming it is the realm of completed enlightenment and the way of a true life.

According to the theory of nine stages of consciousness, this is about the reification stage of the fourth stage knowledge consciousness[n] (For this, refer to the Section of 'All phenomena are consciousness'). So, although the man believes that this is the start of the practices that lead to enlightenment, in reality it becomes the start of delusion.

The second stage, discovering the ox's tracks

The third stage, seeing it

The fourth stage, catching it

The fifth stage, taming it

The sixth stage, controlling it at his will (riding it home)

From now on, it is about the features of delusion that unfolds unilaterally and necessarily because the man was affected and influenced by the reification process in the first stage 'search for an ox.'

The man first finds the ox's footprints, then finds the ox, and eventually captures it and tames it. The ox becomes more and more trained, the man can control it as he wishes, and both the man and the ox come to be completely united. And at last the series of the pictures reaches the stage in which the man returns home as he plays the flute while riding on the back of the ox.

What does the metaphor of these five stages signify?

To find the tracks of footprints or the ox means that the concept of ox (mind, the Way) one postulates is gradually and concretely reified. The black ox that used to be untamed gradually turns white and tamed. It becomes perfectly unified with the man. This signifies that the concept of ox gets forged, mature and purified. This level of stage may well be said to be the realm where supernatural powers – which are religious, mysterious phenomena – have been reported to appear. To name a few, they are "walking on water," "controlling freely sleep or dreams," "reading others' minds," "seeing objects through a veil or a wall," etc.

However, this realm is too great for most people to reach with their ordinary measures. Of course, one needs talents to accomplish this goal, but it would be impossible without the highest level of painful training that is as important as talents. We have observed this in the film *Jonathan Livingston Seagull*. Jonathan could reach the realm, after an enormous amount of training and meditation, where he learned how to fly transcending space and time. However, …, however, this realm, no matter how wonderful it might be, was not the realm of truth. It has nothing to do with the features of the Way (Dao). Even if you fly, or stand on your hands and walk dozens of miles, it is all irrelevant because "truth is not something that you can see even in your dreams." Truth is not such a thing.

There was a Zen master called Jinmook in the middle period of the Chosun dynasty of Korea. One day, an arhat wanted to play a prank on him. The arhat[88] transformed his shape to the figure of

---

88 "Arhat" is translated as 'No Birth,' 'Non-Birth.' Its original meaning is 'a sage who

a young boy, walked and crossed a deep river as if it were quite shallow, and he said to Jinmook to cross the river quickly. Jinmook had no suspicion and simply tried to cross the river walking, but he sank in the river. The arhat laughed at him, clapping his hands as he enjoyed the fun, and said, "You are a Zen master cultivating your Way. Do you not even have a supernatural power to cross the river?"

Jinmook finally realized that he had been tricked. But he said in a resolute manner, struggling to stay afloat, "My magic and supernatural powers are not as good as yours, but you will need to ask this old monk if you have questions about the Great Way."

This is a story included in *The Traces of Jinmook* compiled and edited by Zen Master Choeui.

The features of the Way or how to use it has nothing to do with supernatural powers or demonstrations of miracles. People of religious faiths these days expect to witness supernatural powers or miracles because they mistake the features of the Way for something that should be achieved by training, completion through purification, grace, etc. At least in Buddhism, however, enlightenment lies in the realization of the emptiness of being, and it means the liberation from all the structures of cognition and being.

The Way represents the features of liberation. Liberation

---

realized the emptiness of the phenomenal world that manifests itself in terms of dependent arising.' It was used mostly to refer to the disciples of Shakyamuni Buddha, and later, it came to mean later eccentric sages who obtained supernatural powers. Arhats have been said to be not engaged in historical or social issues and keep aloof attitudes towards them.

consists in being freed from 'the awareness of real being' which is commonly called suffering. We need the liberation from cognition and the liberation from being in order to be liberated from the awareness of real being and realize the truth of emptiness. As previously discussed, each of these two liberations is expressed as 'epistemological emptiness' and 'ontological emptiness,' respectively, and they are the necessary and sufficient conditions that must be simultaneously satisfied in the process of achieving enlightenment. The first six stages in Ten Ox-Herding Pictures show the man's struggle to understand and handle the emptiness of this twofold structure by starting from one or the other of the two or gradually following the temporal order of the process – when it has to be solved simultaneously in a revolutionary way.

We can never reach enlightenment if we practice, however hard we may try, with an intention to obtain some 'thing.' The harder we try to get it, the more distance we will have from enlightenment. For we got it wrong from the start. That is, since we postulate a real being to begin with and then try to find the Way based on this postulation, we come to be enslaved by the awareness of real being presupposed at the beginning, no matter how hard we train and how thoroughly we purify ourselves. So, if we think in our own way that such and such must be 'the Way' or the features of 'enlightenment,' everything we begin to do leads us, in fact, to a trap of another real being symbolized by the ox.

I do not positively evaluate training the ox and controlling it at one's will, but this does not mean that the initial motivation of all this is bad or meaningless. It is just that although the man tried to reach his own enlightenment, he eventually missed the Way.

In fact, no matter how hard one tries not to get caught in a trap of the ox, trying not to fall in the trap usually makes itself leads to, unbeknownst to him or her, another ox that stands tall.

If we substitute for the ox such things that we pursue as 'mind,' 'wealth,' 'honor,' 'sexual desire,' etc., this has nothing to do with the Way even if we can dexterously control the ox. For we cannot enjoy freedom (liberation) because we are constrained by real being. Also, it is because we cannot see things as things themselves due to the colored eyeglasses called 'the ox.' Therefore, as we saw in Ten Ox-Herding Pictures, even if the man and the ox come to be completely united and reach the realm where both are free and at ease, that is, even if our eyes get used to the colored eyeglasses and we come to feel that they are a part of our sensory organs, colored eyeglasses are unnecessary and they make us unable to see the original features of things. With this metaphor, we should now stop thinking, regarding 'Pictures of Searching for an Ox,' that to find the ox and tame it well is an important process in practices. And we should define the process that reaches up to the sixth stage as a process of delusion.

The seventh stage, ox forgotten/disappeared, man remains

I believe that we may well call this seventh stage the stage of 'quasi-enlightenment.' The disappearance of the ox signifies the disappearance of the concept of real being. It is to grasp that the ox, which the man has pursued and trained so far, is not real. However, what does it mean to say that the man still remains? This means that the preexisting traces of the cognitive subject still exist and that [mistaken] judgments before [correct] judgments also remain.

This means, whether the man is aware of it or not, that his awareness of self still exists. This may be compared to Descartes' view: although he can doubt everything else in the world, one thing still sustains its own existence, it is a thinking subject, and this cognizing act cannot be doubted, and all this primordial fact (ego cogito, I think) remains.

This seventh picture symbolizes the fixed state of the inner experience of the self. If the man stays in this state, he still remains, even if the ox has disappeared, on the level of the world, on the level of psychological cognition, and on the level of the natural knowledge of events and facts. And as long as the traces of the cognitive subject remain, it will be the psychological interpretation that the ox does not exist, whatever interpretation it may be, which will inevitably destroy the absolute nature and dissolve the objectivity in the relative subjectivism.

Remember that cognition and objects are formed simultaneously and that the liberation from them is also obtained at the same time. Accordingly, it is in fact impossible for the man to exist when the ox disappears. So, the real being of the ox has not really disappeared as long as the preconception of cognition remains. Perhaps the ox might continuously exist in an invisible, hollow shape, and it will be fixed as self-righteousness that begets chronic diseases and evil. The preceding process reaching up to the sixth picture was about how the man is constrained by the visible ox, but the seventh picture depicts how the man is bound by the invisible ox. However, the man himself does not think that he is constrained by the ox. This is because the traces of cognition still remain. In this regard, the seventh stage is nothing more than an extension of the sixth stage. Liberation achieved only half-way is not liberation at all. The true liberation, that is, enlightenment, is complete and thoroughly-achieved liberation that accomplishes the liberation from cognition and being simultaneously. Thoroughly-achieved liberation comes from thoroughgoing negation.

Masters in Zen traditions teach wholeheartedly. "Empty your mind," "Throw away your attachment," "Let go of all your thoughts," "Remove even the mind that seeks after the Way," etc. The following is a dialogue between Zhaozhou Sunim and Yanyang Sunim.

"I did not bring a thing. How is this state?"
(This means that Yanyang does not even have the mind that pursues the Way.)
"Unload it."
"Well, what should I unload when I do not even have a thing?"
"If you would not like to do it, load it up on you again and go back."

Teacher Zhaozhou baffles his student Yanyang. Yanyang

proudly declares that he is liberated from everything, but Zhaozhou sees how Yanyang still stands on a real being. So, Zhaozhou hits the nail on the head in a paradoxical way. "If you would not like to unload it, load it up on you again and go back."[89]

We need to overcome our conscious awareness that we have liberated ourselves from the awareness of real being. However, we must overcome even the awareness that we have overcome it. The following passage of *The Sutra of Perfect Enlightenment* aptly describes this spirit of thoroughgoing negation and the revolutionary nature of its process.

> "All bodhisattvas and sentient beings in the age of the decline of dharma[90] must shake off all illusions and illusory realms (the awareness of real being). And if you are captured by the awareness that you have eliminated them all, it is also an illusion and you must remove it too. Even the thought that you have removed it is also an illusion, so you must discard it. Get rid of it, eliminate it, remove it, shake it off, … you will have let go of all the realms of illusions until you will have nothing to let go of. …
> And you seekers of the Way! What is important is 'that to know

---

89 *The Compilation of Examinations of Verses on Ancient Precedents* also has the paragraph of the same significance in its Section 1018: A monk asked Monk Yunmen. "Do I have any fault when I do not even have a thought rise?" Yunmen answered, "As much as Mount. Sumeru."

90 The third and last period of a Buddha-kalpa; the first is the first 500 years of correct doctrine, the second is the 1,000 years of semblance law, or approximation to the doctrine, and the third is a myriad number of years of its decline and end. [from A. Charles Muller, *A Korean-English Dictionary of Buddhism*, Unju Publishing Company, 2014]

that it is an illusion is itself to get out of the illusion. There is no special methodology about it. Also, breaking free from illusion is called the realm of enlightenment, and this realm is not to be achieved through some gradual procedures."
The Sutra of Perfect Enlightenment, Chapter on Bodhisattva Samatabhadra

A Chinese Zen master described this spirit of thoroughgoing negations with poetic symbolism[91] :

The poverty of past days was not true poverty,
Today's poverty is genuine poverty.
In the past days I tried not to leave even a spot of land to stick in an awl,
Today I have finally thrown away the awl itself.

The eighth stage, both the man and the ox disappear

---

91 This is the verse that Xiangyan gave to Yangshan Sunim. *The Record of the Transmission of the Lamp*, Vol. 11, Chapter on Yangshan Huiji.

We have at last entered the stage that deserves the name 'revolutionary enlightenment, Sudden Enlightenment' or 'perfect enlightenment, Complete Enlightenment' which is our basic stance.

The disappearance of the ox symbolizes the disappearance of the concept of being as the object that has become a real being, and the disappearance of the man means the closing down of the cognitive subject that has become a real being. So, 'both the man and the ox disappearing' is the mode of 'revolutionary enlightenment' that has simultaneously achieved both the liberation from cognition and the liberation from being. In other words, it is to jump into the world of emptiness which has the twofold structure of epistemic emptiness and ontic emptiness.

The state of 'both the man and the ox disappearing' is the very stage where one has finally moved from the history of delusions to the place of enlightenment. This situation is about the realm of enlightenment that is to be achieved not by gradual and temporal procedures but through a revolutionary procedure. In this regard, it is a new level (dimension) that is differentiated from its previous stage.

There is no logical connection between (1) the training of the ox, gaining its free and easy control, and the man and the ox becoming completely unified, and (2) the realization that neither the man nor the ox is real. There is actually an unbridgeable logical gap between the two. This means that those efforts and actions before the state of both the man and the ox disappearing all at once, that is, before the state of enlightenment, are not the direct cause of enlightenment. However, we cannot look down on our efforts to achieve enlightenment only because the accumulation of actions and efforts made under the state of delusions does not [logically] lead to enlightenment.

Although these efforts are, from a logical point of view, not necessary preconditions that lead to enlightenment, they provide important occasions that trigger enlightenment.[92] So, any act or thought, even in the case that it needs to be rejected in our general stereotypical view of morality, may be regarded as a precious experience on the way to enlightenment as long as its intended goal is enlightenment. Nevertheless, however, it is an important fact to notice that there is a logical gap between the efforts prior to enlightenment and enlightenment. The acknowledgement of this fact suggests that what is fundamentally important in obtaining enlightenment is not the amount of accumulated time and efforts but the one-time change of perspective.

I believe that the following story of Huangbo Sunim, a great Master of Zen traditions, addresses the very same point.

"If those who learn the Way cannot reach at one instant the realm of no-mind (the state of epistemic liberation which has no preconception, which is, after all, the realm where one is liberated

---

92 Radical Zen masters have often ignored this point. For instance, they have the slogan of 'no establishment through words or letters' and ignore and deny scholarly efforts, and they reject social engagement and activities if these take place before enlightenment. This radical stance has been criticized as Silent Illumination Meditation because it makes all conscious efforts lose the regulative goal and leads and drowns practitioners into the problem of endless lethargy, torpidity and slumber.
Mahayana Buddhism provides its features of practices, in order to overcome this problem, with the bodhisattvas' acts of 'illusory compassion' and the Phrase-Observing Meditation of Alertness and Quiescence that connect 'meditation and practices before enlightenment' to 'enlightenment.'

from both cognition and being), they are not able to achieve the Way no matter how long they continue their practices. For they cannot obtain liberation because they are constrained by their determination and efforts to achieve the Way. However, depending on individuals, it takes a longer or shorter time to arrive at the realm of no-mind. Some directly reach this realm of no-mind at the spot right away – where and when they listen to the teaching of the Way. Others reach the state of no-mind in the process of their believing, following, and practicing (the ten stages of faith, the ten abodes and the ten dedications). Yet another group of people achieve the state of no-mind only after they go through the ten grounds of sages, the completion of which enables them to become liberated from the domains of matter and mind.

Accordingly, the process of practices may be long or short depending on individuals. However, we can achieve the Way only when we reach the realm of no-mind, and the efforts themselves made during the process of practices are not essentially related to the Way. Reaching the realm of no-mind does not imply that we understand or obtain some contents in this realm. What it means is only that although we do not even assume any fixed stance or perspective, we come to have a genuine perspective that functions soundly when we see things. In this realm of no-mind, regardless of whether it has been reached at one instant or through the efforts made for an indefinitely long period of time, there is no difference in its capacity if viewed from the standpoint of enlightenment."

– From *The Dharma Essentials for Mental Transmission*
(Huangbo Sunim, *The Record of the Transmission of the Lamp, Book 9*)

The world of enlightenment, where it is said that 'both the man and the ox disappear,' does not imply that this world should fall in the state of non-existence. To the contrary, it is the world that makes manifest itself the relation of dependent arising between consciousness and the world, which is hidden (or distorted) in our natural attitudes.

The disappearance of the ox means the liberation from objectivism (naturalism) or metaphysical realism. The disappearance of the man signifies the freedom from psychologism or subjectivism. All this says that Buddhism has nothing to do with realism or idealism. That is, it is to stay away from the temptation of psychological subjectivism and overcome its chronic accidentality and relativism (the man disappears), and to be protected from realism and naturalism (the ox disappears). Nevertheless, however, Buddhism can remain as a thoroughgoing empiricism, which is the greatness of enlightenment and also the twofold duty of 'both the man and the ox disappearing.'

Therefore, the true meaning of 'both the man and the ox disappearing' is not that the man and the ox are eliminated but that they do not turn real. The man and the ox still persist and continuously act. This is the genuine world of enlightenment. Enlightenment does not eliminate or reduce all things – whether it is an ox or a man; it just sees through them in terms of their changes and relations and it does not make them fixed or real (substantialized). This way, all beings come back alive with their new (or original) features. In other words, all beings, up to this point, have been distorted beings, not genuine beings.

The world of 'to the thing itself'[93] unfolds simultaneously with the revolutionary enlightenment of the eighth stage 'both the man and the ox disappears.' So, the eighth and ninth stages are simultaneous situations as well. "Mountain is mountain, water is water." No other expression describes the contents of 'to the thing itself' more easily than this phrase. It originated from Monk Yunmen's phrases,[94] but it has been circulated in Zen traditions from the ancient times. It surely sounds plausible as we appreciate it more. Does it mean that, before one's enlightenment, mountain was not mountain and water was not water? We might have seen mountain and water with various colored eyeglasses of real being. However, we have gotten rid of all varieties of colored eyeglasses and accepted

---

93 'To the thing itself' may remind us of Husserl's slogan 'Zu den Sachen Selbst.' Epoche and intentionality in phenomenology may well be compared to the stance of epistemic emptiness and dependent arising in Buddhism, and 'to the thing itself' to 'to the unfathomable realm of liberation.' However, the thing itself in 'to the thing itself' is, unlike Heidegger's Sein, not real or substantialized. Also, the tenth stage of 'entering the path to history' is not Sartre's venture for the future full of Angst.

94 *The Compilation of Examinations of Verses on Ancient Precedents*, Section 1055.

the nature and all things as themselves through the revolutionary enlightenment of 'both the man and the ox disappears.'

To be in the world of enlightenment is to return to the thing itself. This is to deny the superficial, utopian concept of enlightenment that one can easily postulate. The world of enlightenment does not refer to a transcendental or special world, and it is about the perspective with which one correctly sees the life of reality distorted and refracted. Accordingly, the ground as the base of enlightenment is nothing other than this reality and history. That the content of the world of enlightenment is returning to the thing itself is an important point that differentiates Buddhism from other religions. However, even devout Buddhists with deep faith are sometimes confused and believe erroneously that the world the Buddha's dharma teaches us is a transcendental world which is separate from this secular (saha) world. That is, they believe, at times, that the world of liberation, the world of nirvana, is a certain world that is transcendental, divine, and full of truth.

"Let us board the ship of prajna (wisdom, the world of enlightenment) and cross over to the other shore of nirvana" – this kind of phrase of the Buddhist sutras occasionally makes Buddhists feel as if the world of enlightenment kept spatial distance from this saha world.[95] However, it is clear that what we obtain through enlightenment is not the shortening of spatial distance or crossing over but the turnover of the content of each individual's life. The

---

95 'The saha world' is our world – the world where we humans and other sentient beings reside, not the world of demons or the world of gods.

truth is that Buddhism has never departed from our lives and the reality (history) of this land from its starting point to the destination it reaches – from its interest and problems to practices and solutions.

The Buddha's motive to renounce the secular life, which is the content of what the Buddha found as problems, is the very problems of our lives that are symbolized with the four kinds of suffering, the eight kinds of suffering,[96] and the Buddha's determination to solve them. And his final conclusion of the solution was to correctly see through the problems of life (the true form of things as they are) and manage life in a correct and appropriate way. The Noble Eightfold Path and six-paramitas are the methodology to reach enlightenment and at the same time the maxim of the enlightened one's ordinary life.

This is in sharp contrast with the view of Western religions that think of the problems and conclusions of life and history with the dichotomous religious perspectives of the holy and the secular, God (the transcendental realm) and humans (the history in space and time). Buddhism does not introduce God or the holy as a transcendental value system. It does not presuppose the absolute spirit as the framework of ideas that penetrate history, or the realism of force (Chi) or matter – whether it is the real being to return to and rely on, or

---

96 The four kinds of suffering are birth aging illness and death. The eight kinds include these four and the suffering of not-getting when we want, the suffering experienced when we are separated from the persons and things that we love, the suffering experienced when we are forced to associate with people and things that we dislike, and the suffering due to the five aggregates. These generally imply all the physical, mental, social and institutional, and existential sufferings of life.

the real being that transforms itself. Still, Buddhism has reached a teaching that explains the problems of all sentient beings and saves them in a great way. It was to accept life as something dependently arising, that is, as something that is of non-realist features.

The world reached through revolutionary enlightenment is not an enormously mysterious world, and it is not a peculiar world of transcendental truth. This fact may incidentally embarrass and disappoint those who have fantastic expectations and imaginations. The delusions of sentient beings make extravagant even their expectations of the Buddha's dharma. However, enlightenment says, in a resolute manner, "The world we reached is 'the thing itself.'" After all, Buddhism has never departed from the history of this life from the beginning till the end.

'To the thing itself' is about the features of a liberated life as well. 'The metaphor of ice' that discussants of Buddhism often cite is quite appropriate to explain this case. This metaphor compares to ice the features of an unliberated life inculcated with various kinds of realism, and to water the features of a liberated (enlightened) and open life.

It may be understandable to compare to the fixed state of ice the stance of life doctrinally constrained by the worldview based on various forms of realism, or the stance of life captured by the ideology or methodology which is postulated on the level of upaya (convenient tools). This kind of stance of life cannot read or recognize the changes and dynamism of life. However, what does it mean to say that the features of enlightenment are like water in a state of flux? What else could it be if it does not mean that the world of enlightenment does not discard any part of life? It is not to throw away ice and water and go out of the water. It is not to make water evaporate, either. It just means to melt the fixed (or frozen) state and accommodate all of it as water in totality.

Subjective realism (the man), objective realism (the ox), monistic, dualistic, and pluralistic versions of various realism fix and freeze our lives like ice and make it unable to accommodate things as things themselves. As 'the metaphor of ice' suggests, it is clear that although the enlightenment of Buddhism stands by the non-realist worldview based on dependent arising, it does not go as far as to anti-being or non-being.

The (non-realist) worldview based on dependent arising accepts all beings soundly and wholly. It does not impair any being even a bit, and it is an ontology that does not reduce or abandon any being. It does not make us static like ice; it does not make us individualized, fixed and real, either; to the contrary, it guides us to 'the thing itself' that manifests and unfolds itself in the midst of changes and dynamism. Therefore, to live in the world of enlightenment is to return to history, as one corrects the misguided postulation of the realm that we believe we should pursue separately outside the field of history. This is the right way to meet history, and it is an honorable way to face it. And it is to live, yet again, in the real world of agony, suffering and desires. However, it is not to be enslaved by anything called good or evil because we will see through them once again, and it is to understand the identity of all human factors and social factors whether they are called good or evil.

To have the stance of not making anything real and substantial (to have the stance that changes ice to water), but at the same time to closely observe everything and accept them, and thus to make all things manifest themselves as things themselves – this is the teaching that 'returning to the thing itself' gives us. On the other hand, although one has by now grasped the non-realness of beings (true emptiness) through enlightenment, this is the stage that makes him or her comprehend at the same time the phenomenal existence (mysterious existence) of beings. In other words, this stage emphasizes especially that there is also a positive interpretation of beings, and moreover, it makes this interpretation stand out as its original point.

It is very important to understand the difference between the non-realness [non-substantiality] and realness [substantiality] of being although in both cases its existence is equally emphasized. And we need to know that, if we understand that to deny the realness and to emphasize the non-realness is to deny the being/existence itself or to regard it negatively, it is nonsensical and preposterous.

The tenth stage, the path to history

The stage of 'Enter the market place and engage,' the stage of the path to history, means the historical activities of those who have obtained enlightenment by experiences. From now on, therefore, the story unfolds from the realm of enlightenment to the realm of history. And the division of Mahayana and Hinayana finally begins to appear at this stage. How are enlightenment and historical practices correlated to each other? Enlightenment is naturally the enlightenment on history. However, even if it is the enlightenment on history, it is not a methodological enlightenment on how to engage in history or how to construct it.

Then, what is enlightenment?

It is to be enlightened on the ontological nature of history. It is a correct insight on the ontological nature of all forms of being subsumed under the categories of mind, matter and concept. The contents and the gist of this insight are such that there should be no certain mode of being individualized, fixed, and made real and substantial, that it is to accept the mode of being in terms of changes and relations, in terms of dependent arising, and that it is to remove all veils of real being and accept things as things themselves.

It has been pointed out, though, that this way of Buddhist enlightenment has made many Buddhists face the problems of history only passively. This is on one hand the error of Buddhists who misunderstood enlightenment; on the other, it was because they let enlightenment remain only at the level of enlightenment. We have noticed above, with regard to 'the metaphor of ice,' that some people have from time to time misunderstood it as teaching the negation or elimination of water, not as teaching a way to melt the frozen state. Likewise, when we say that some people have misunderstood enlightenment, it means that they made a mistake in accepting the non-being or anti-being of things when enlightenment is a matter of shaking off the awareness of real being and accepting things as things themselves. This really is a case in which enlightenment was misunderstood in an absurd way.

Enlightenment is a positive perspective of history that embraces comprehensively all beings and history without distortion. However, many Buddhists have often degraded the historical perspective of enlightenment to a relativistic perspective of history. This case of relativistic features is grounded on a destructive and skeptical perspective on beings, and it has the ahistorical and anti-historical stance that does not attribute meaning or value to any historical facts or phenomena. This is another twisted form of enlightenment, and we can correct its mistake with the lesson of the ninth stage 'returning to the thing itself.'

However, even if we have clearly overcome this trap and correctly learned enlightenment by experience, it is obvious that enlightenment as enlightenment has its own limit in its historical applicability. For enlightenment is enlightenment about the nature of beings, not about the contents and method on the change and reform of beings. In other words, it is because enlightenment is not about how to transform or accumulate 'a certain thing' but it is to see through, beforehand, the nature of being of that 'thing' in 'a certain thing' (or, it is to read the changes and relations of innumerably many things).

Enlightenment is in this regard not about mentioning the 'how' part, for it is not an essential character of enlightenment. Accordingly, although enlightenment enables us to overcome the original fetters (the form of real being) of history and secure the liberation from history, what is important to notice is that we cannot get, with just enlightenment, any explanations or answers to a specific prospect, choice or action in life. So, we cannot have any historical prospect or vision as long as we remain on the level of enlightenment.

Then, how should we continuously solve all the problems of history and establish a new history?

It is clear that the solution to the problem of progress and changes in history does not deductively derive, or is analogically inferred from the basis of enlightenment, if we view this issue in light of the nature of enlightenment. After all, we solve the problems of history with our historical efforts. We must have the perspective of history that does not make anything real [substantial] or absolute, which is the greatest lesson for life obtained through enlightenment. As we proceed fearlessly and passionately with this open perspective of history, we will continuously solve the problems of history.

Enlightenment, which is to see through the emptiness of the ontological nature of history, and the problem of how to manage history are not applied to the same category of logical realm. However, as the whiteness and hardness of a white Go stone are different from each other but are still unified as one stone, enlightenment and historical practices are the twofold structure that sustains our lives.

Why would an enlightened one go out on the path to history rather than remain content and satisfied in the realm of enlightenment? It is because of the loving-kindness and compassion for beings. Compassion is the driving force of historical actions and is also a link that connects enlightenment to history. The specific forms in which this compassion is manifested are the Buddhist modes of actions called upaya [skillful means], vow and power. Vow is about the setting of a goal for history, power means the indomitable faith that makes vow ultimately accomplished, and upaya is the specific methodology and practices to achieve the goal of the vow. Therefore, vow, power and upaya are nothing other than the historical manifestations of compassion.

Those who have achieved just enlightenment are called arhats. Those who have compassion, vow and power as well as enlightenment are called bodhisattvas. "Arhat" is made of a single word meaning 'enlightenment,' and "bodhisattva" has the complex concepts of 'enlightenment (bodhi)' and 'history (sattva).' The life of an arhat is the life of Hinayana, and bodhisattvas live the life of Mahayana.

'The path to history' in Ten Ox-Herding Pictures is nothing other than the path of bodhisattvas. Arhats of course enjoy in their own way the highest degree of tranquility and contentment. No historical action can fundamentally hurt them. An arhat said quietly, when he was about to be hanged due to political persecution, "To hurt my body is just like cutting the spring breeze."

Enlightenment is complete and perfect as enlightenment itself.

Staying alone on the top of a high mountain peak does not increase (or diminish) enlightenment, and making oneself busy in market places does not decrease (or increase) enlightenment, either. The precious value of enlightenment remains independently of whether there are historical activities or not, whether there are more or less activities, or whether they are successful or not – although the criterion of their success is also a product of history. An arhat's life of contentment is compared to the life that has obtained freedom from all eyeglasses.

On the contrary, the life of bodhisattva is the life free to any eyeglasses. A bodhisattva's freedom to history is possible only when an arhat's freedom from history is presupposed. Bodhisattvas are protected from absolutism through their enlightenment. Their historical activities chosen without attachment or fixation transcend relativism. Bodhisattvas' historical practices, which go beyond absolutism and relativism, will transform this world to the Pure Land. However, bodhisattvas do not make the Pure Land a real being. For, as mentioned in sutras, bodhisattvas are aware from the beginning that even the Pure Land they try to establish is also empty. So, bodhisattvas' historical will and determination are called 'compassion like an illusion [illusory compassion].' Perhaps it means that a being like an illusion establishes the Pure Land like an illusion with historical activities like illusions?

Now we can see that how and what bodhisattvas choose and implement depends on how to unfold upaya, vow and power on the level of history (sattva) which is a further step made from the level of enlightenment (bodhi). Upaya, vow and power will come to life only when they are based on realistic and specific grounds. Then, which upaya should the bodhisattvas of our time unfold and with what historical vow and power?

First of all, bodhisattvas need to observe the forms and situations of all our lives, what problems we have, and what tasks we have to solve them. And they should be seriously and passionately concerned about all these. Based on such historical examinations, bodhisattvas will be able to finally choose, decide on, and establish history. For they exert their irresistible loving-kindness and compassion to history.

4

Critique of
Sudden Enlightenment and Gradual Cultivation
and
Sudden Enlightenment and Sudden Cultivation

This article "Critique of Sudden Enlightenment and Gradual Cultivation
and Sudden Enlightenment and Sudden Cultivation" has evolved from my
lecture notes used at Haeinsa Buddhist Seminary in 1985.

Critique of Sudden Enlightenment and Gradual Cultivation and Sudden Enlightenment and Sudden Cultivation

The rise of debate

Korean Buddhism raised an important issue in the 1970's on the history of Buddhism, especially on the history of Zen traditions. It started when Seongcheol Sunim, who was the Spiritual Mentor of Haein Comprehensive Training Monastery, proposed 'Sudden Enlightenment and Sudden Cultivation.'

'Sudden Enlightenment and Sudden Cultivation' is a theory of practice that has, as its basic structure, 'Sudden Enlightenment' which grasps the process and contents of enlightenment as revolutionary. 'Sudden Enlightenment and Sudden Cultivation' assumes a fiercely critical stance against 'Sudden Enlightenment and Gradual Cultivation.' 'Sudden Enlightenment and Gradual Cultivation' was at times mentioned and supported in the literature related to Zen traditions of ancient China and Korea. In contrast, although 'Sudden Enlightenment and Sudden Cultivation' originated from Zongmi Sunim's (AD 780-841) classification of the seven forms of Sudden and Gradual, I believe it was Seongcheol Sunim who named and argued for it as a serious theory of practices.

Shenhui Sunim (AD 685-760) of China first raised the view of 'Sudden Enlightenment and Gradual Cultivation' and Zongmi Sunim established it as a theory of practices. The core of this claim is that one must go through some significant process of practices in order to arrive at perfect enlightenment even after he or she obtains enlightenment. This view, as it was combined with many sutras and treatises of the Doctrinal School and made plausible, was more readily accepted by practitioners. Such writings as *The Secrets on Cultivating the Mind* and *The Excerpts from the Dharma Collection and Special Practice Record with Personal Notes* of Bojo Sunim in Korea, along with Zongmi Sunim's *Duxu*, include the theory of practices on Sudden Enlightenment and Gradual Cultivation. These books have become representative required texts of the curriculum in Buddhist seminaries.

'Sudden Enlightenment and Sudden Cultivation' and 'Sudden Enlightenment and Gradual Cultivation,' as obvious from their expressions, both have the procedure of 'Sudden Enlightenment.' However, although I will discuss more later in this article, there was clearly a difference about the way of grasping enlightenment – 'Sudden Enlightenment' – and this difference resulted in contrastive cultures of practices. But, then, which of these two is correct? If only one is correct, the other must be incorrect. However, I am going to suggest in this article a new and fundamental interpretation of enlightenment and argue that both of the claims may have problems. That is, this article aims to point out the problems that not just one of the two but both claims have.

'Sudden Enlightenment' emphasizes the revolutionary character of enlightenment. The word itself is a combination of 'enlightenment' and 'sudden,' the latter of which implies the meaning of 'all at once, altogether.' There was a debate between Huineng Sunim (AD 638-713) and Shenxiu Sunim (AD ?-706) on whether enlightenment is a gradual process or a revolutionary one. This idea of Sudden Enlightenment came to form the mainstream method of practices after Huineng's view of Sudden Enlightenment, according to which enlightenment is of a revolutionary character, was received through this debate as the orthodox view of Zen traditions. All this happened in Tang Dynasty of China. The idea of Sudden Enlightenment of Huineng, who is called the Sixth Patriarch of Zen traditions, was fully established as the orthodox method of practices. After Huineng, his disciples, especially Shenhui Sunim, theorized the revolutionary characteristic of enlightenment, and this view of Sudden Enlightenment has been received as the orthodoxy of Zen traditions ever since.

On the other hand, however, those who disagreed with the method of practice conducted on the line of Sudden Enlightenment raised the following question: "If enlightenment is to be achieved all of a sudden through such a revolutionary process, why is it the case that those Zen practitioners who have obtained Sudden Enlightenment cannot exhibit the mysterious supernatural powers and various wonderful features of the Buddha?" Also, they asked, "How would you explain the passages of the sutras that report that practicing bodhisattvas arrive at the Buddha's realm only after transmigrating across innumerably many lifetimes for a staggeringly long time and cultivating all wholesome practices of bodhisattvas?"

The exponents of 'Sudden Enlightenment' did not give clear answers to these questions, and distorted the idea of Sudden Enlightenment. We can see this chaotic state as early as in such writings as *The Exposition on Determining Right and Wrong [with respect to] Bodhidharma's Southern school* and *The Record of the Zen Discourses by Monk Shenhui* of Shenhui, who could be said to have started the idea of Sudden Enlightenment. By the time the traditions reached Zongmi, the concept of 'Sudden Enlightenment' had completely undergone uninvited changes. It was Bojo Sunim of Korea who fully accepted this changed view of Sudden Enlightenment.

The criticisms waged on the idea of Sudden Enlightenment were neither clarified nor responded to. And 'Sudden Enlightenment and Gradual Cultivation' was the distorted product of the rough-and-ready compromise of the idea of 'Sudden Enlightenment' and 'Gradual Cultivation' as its complementary function. Zongmi's attempt in his *Duxu* to combine Zen and Doctrinal Studies was a great scholarly achievement which was conducted with excellent sense and acuity. However, we should not overlook the problem that his view underlies a biased interpretation of the sutras that purported to justify 'Sudden Enlightenment and Gradual Cultivation' which may be said to be a distorted idea of Sudden Enlightenment. In particular, Zongmi's view of 'the ten stages to eliminate suffering and achieve enlightenment' and 'the ten stages to result in the samsaric life [the life of transmigration] of an ignorant person' in the second book of his *Duxu* is a good example of a problematic interpretation that may very well mislead readers.

Seongcheol Sunim's 'Sudden Enlightenment and Sudden Cultivation' raises fundamental criticism against this 'Sudden Enlightenment and Gradual Cultivation,' and claims that Sudden Enlightenment needs to be understood as including in itself Sudden Cultivation. He argues that Sudden Enlightenment is the state of completed practice and the place of final and ultimate realm, and that it cannot be an incomplete enlightenment or the starting point of practices, as shown in Sudden Enlightenment and Gradual Cultivation. There is no room for any further practices to perfect enlightenment which has eliminated even the most subtle form of suffering, that is, even the habituated tendencies of the eighth consciousness (alayavijnana). So, this is called the realm of Sudden Cultivation where not only enlightenment but also practices are completed and finished. In this regard, an enlightened one has no need for post-enlightenment practices to complement his or her own life. It is claimed to be the realm of awakening in which one is unfettered and liberated, neither arising nor conditioned. According to Seongcheol Sunim, enlightenment is a state in which there is no agitation in our ordinary life of coming and going, it remains the same even in dreams, it is thoroughly clear from both the inside and the outside, and all these can be represented with the dictum, 'Sudden Enlightenment and Sudden Cultivation.' But this view also seems to have an issue in comprehending the concept of enlightenment, and accordingly it ends up with such a problem as implying mysticism or a non-historical tendency.

There has been lots of debates in the history of Zen, but I believe that the gist of them may well be summarized as the disputes between Sudden and Gradual. For instance, the competitions between Southern Sudden and Northern Gradual represented by Huineng and Shensui, the differentiation of Tathagata Zen from Patriarchal Zen, and those arguments presented by Baekpa and Choeui of Korea have proceeded as they have been roughly based on the theoretical frame of Sudden and Gradual. In a nutshell, all these debates are about what enlightenment is and how to achieve it.

This debate on the method of practice has continued to date, and it has reached 'Sudden Enlightenment and Gradual Cultivation' and also finally 'Sudden Enlightenment and Sudden Cultivation' that refutes its predecessor. This way, Korean Buddhism has come to have not only different theories on the level of practices but also different practice cultures of actual Zen meditation centers that have resulted from the different views on Sudden Enlightenment and Sudden Cultivation and Sudden Enlightenment and Gradual Cultivation. Naturally, all the confusion caused by this situation has been getting worse. We may recognize the doctrinal stances that these two claims are rooted in and also admit a significant portion of the various usefulness and merits produced by these views; however, we must guard ourselves against the basic fallacy committed by these two claims. It is what these two views equally imply – that is, they are confused about and between 'the aspect of enlightenment' and 'the aspect of history.' And we must also examine the problem they themselves caused about the refraction and distortion on the concept of Sudden Enlightenment – the revolutionary characteristic of enlightenment – which may very well be regarded as Zen traditions' most important contribution to the history of Buddhism.

Enlightenment (bodhi) and history (sattva)

First of all, let us examine the enlightenment that these two views share with their claims of Sudden Enlightenment before we criticize 'Sudden Enlightenment and Gradual Cultivation' and 'Sudden Enlightenment and Sudden Cultivation.'

What is enlightenment? It is etymologically a noun form of the verb 'enlighten,' and it seems to imply a meaning of 'enlightenment on some thing.' But, then, of what is the enlightenment in Buddhism? As we can see in the case of the Buddha, it is nothing other than about the problems of life which is represented by the problems of birth, aging, illness and death; in other words, it is about all our sentient beings. Many people with religious backgrounds or philosophical ideas presented omniscient and omnipotent God or postulated a transcendental realm and values in order to solve the problems of life. They also argued for some absolute value system immanent in history – for instance, the absolute reason (the world spirit) or scientific laws (the laws of social sciences or the studies of humanities). In contrast, the enlightenment in Buddhism generally has the following three features.

Firstly, it is the enlightenment about the truth that there cannot be any other form of existence outside the realm of all our sentient beings. The well-known phrase "There is not a thing outside the mind" in fact refers to this point. The mind is, in Buddhism, not the subjective frame of cognition as a psychological phenomenon. This is as good as to say that any form or mode of being, be it psychological or conceptual, needs to be understood as formed with a harmonious combination of the subject and object. All modes of being with these complex meaning and forms were expressed as 'mind.' This mind is called 'all sentient beings' and is also named 'the Buddha.' There cannot exist any separate realm of being or system of values outside the world of all sentient beings called 'mind.' And this is because of the second feature of enlightenment, which is as follows.

Secondly, enlightenment is about the realization that the true forms of all sentient beings are neither substances nor real being. All elements that constitute our lives change and develop in terms of mutual relations and conditions. One must realize, with an examination on this feature, that all forms of beings are not some fixed and unchanging subjective beings or self-caused beings that spontaneously exist without any cause or conditions, but that all forms of beings are the modes of beings that change and unfold with no substance or realness. This realization is also the goal of Buddhist practices. It is to be liberated from all forms of the awareness of real being, so it means the realization of the truth of non-self or non-birth.

Thirdly, one comes to achieve this enlightenment not through a gradual process but by a revolutionary conversion. Zen traditions describe this revolutionary achievement as Sudden Enlightenment. Philosophers and natural scientists have these days agreed that the discovery of knowledge and laws are obtained not through an extension or improvement of the existing knowledge and laws but by a revolutionary conversion or creative intuition. So, the denial of inductive method and research programs has become a characteristic of the contemporary method of scientific investigation.

It may not be an accurate comparison, but the enlightenment in Buddhism may also not be achieved through the accumulation or forging of the existing knowledge or perspective. And this becomes so obvious if we pay attention to the fact that the preexisting view, the view before enlightenment, is in a state tainted with delusions. To be enlightened is to strip off the veil of the awareness of real being. That is, it is to take off the veil of real being from the reified cognition and objects as reified beings, and it is to accept all modes and forms of life that these two jointly create without the awareness of real being. Due to the mutual relations of the modes of beings and changes, breaking the awareness of real being may not come true through temporally ordered procedures. Any view or stance has to presuppose preceding conditions and perspectives, and it cannot be independent or liberated from them. So, enlightenment requires us to shake off localized, partial and individualistic perspectives, and it also demands a comprehensive and holistic perspective on organic relations. This process of enlightenment can only come to us through creative intuition, not through inductive cognition.

I have so far discussed the characteristics of enlightenment. But they could serve only as a partial exposition on enlightenment and all sentient beings which are the targets and contents of enlightenment. Accordingly, it is important to elevate this issue to the problem of life which is the problem of the more comprehensive and dynamic reality.

If we first take a look at the word "all lives (all sentient beings)," although it has an implication of objectivity, vitality and comprehensiveness, it cannot but give us an impression that it lacks a realistically concrete and tangible characteristic. So, let me replace this word "all lives" by "history" as long as I can avoid undermining too much of its meaning. We can of course give many different definitions to the word "history," but let us consider that a little more concrete and realistic character of history be added to the Buddhist concept of 'all lives.' So, history becomes a domain where such subjective value judgments as 'I like it' or 'I do not like it' are added to the factual features like 'black, white, hard, soft, high and low.' Also, history is about the general features of dynamic lives which are in the process of changes of 'wishing to do things this or that way and things are eventually proceeding in such a way.'

We can see, in light of this perspective, that getting enlightened is seeing through this nature of history not as fixed and unchanging substance but as non-real modes of being, and getting enlightened is also being awakened to the domain of history. This means that Buddhism is neither history-transcending nor antihistorical or ahistorical. It is properly historical and all about sentient beings. However, we need to note carefully that getting liberated from the realist idea of beings and history, that is, getting enlightened, does not mean actually controlling, changing and supervising beings and them at will. Actual changes in history happen with the beings' actual empirical properties, routines and selective efforts. But enlightenment means the liberation from the realist fetters in such historical features and situations. In other words, the historical aspect in which we try to change and improve some thing in a certain way, and the aspect of enlightenment in which we take off the realness from the 'thing' in some thing – both of these address the same domain but at the same time emphasize different aspects. So, it is important to recognize the logical limit or the limited domain of the application of enlightenment in history.

Getting enlightened is obtaining fundamental liberation by seeing through the non-realness of all historical beings. Actual history has the mode of being that changes and pans out without assuming the existence of real being. If described in Buddhist terminology, history comes to have the features of dependent arising (changes and relations). So, it is more important than anything else to carefully identify the relations and contents of the beings' dependent arising when we face the problem of managing actual history. In fact, there is no logical basis in believing that we can measure and infer qualitative changes only in real beings. As is actually manifested, the modes and forms of all sentient beings in history, although they are not real beings, go through changes consistently in countlessly many conditions and relations with their own features of non-realness. And the modes and forms of all sentient beings let us measure some level of temporal variability and spatial relations.

Realistically, however, it is often convenient to view the problems of history while recognizing the provisional and hypothetical realness. For, although we cannot admit the existence of any real being from a logical point of view, it is often quite useful for the management of life to intentionally postulate the existence of the provisional and hypothetical real beings. So, although it is true that such features of reality do not always unfold following only the rational and causal – inductive – laws, we do not have to refrain ourselves from provisionally relying on such lawfulness, if needed.

Anyhow, enlightenment is enlightenment about history, and it is to see throught and realize that historical beings change and unfold with non-real properties. On the other hand, nevertheless, the progress and change of history follow their own various factors and conditions. So, it is very important to understand these two aspects. What this means is that even if we obtain enlightenment we cannot come to freely handle all beings in life of this history.

For instance, how can we understand the following? "I have achieved enlightenment and gotten out of the bondage of transmigration. I have gotten out of the cycle of birth and death." This means, at least, that one has liberated oneself from the awareness of real being on the phenomena of arising and ceasing with the enlightenment on the phenomena of transmigration of arising and ceasing. This does not mean that the phenomena of arising and ceasing themselves get reduced or eliminated but that we change our stance to accept them. After all, to be detached from the awareness of real beings [oneself, people, all sentient beings, life span] and accept life is called the permanent termination of transmigration. This enlightened one will still be situated among the various constraints and alienation in beings (history). However, enlightenment will enable him or her to keep the fundamental bliss of nirvana even among the actual joy and anger together with sorrow and pleasure.

If we follow this line of view, we will come to see that the Buddhist goal of the elimination of all suffering is not the termination of all psychological phenomena in order to become a tree or stone. The sutras say, "To eliminate suffering is the opinion of ordinary people, but Mahayana bodhisattvas realize the emptiness of suffering and become free from suffering." No matter how subtly habituated tendencies there might be, if one would try to eliminate and terminate them, it would be evidence that he or she is still captured by the realness of the suffering itself.

Huineng Sunim's teaching that criticizes the ignorance of the efforts to wipe off the dust on a mirror has not yet had its roots thoroughly planted. The clear and definite stance of enlightenment that does not even recognize the existence of any real being, not to mention 'mirror' or 'dust,' is a basis in managing one's historical life.

The expression of 'bodhisattva' is the masterpiece phrase of Mahayana Buddhism that describes the features of this historical life quite appropriately. 'Bodhi' means enlightenment, and 'sattva' is all sentient beings, that is, history. When we normally describe enlightenment (bodhi) and history (sattva) in a row, these two words might at first glance be understood as belonging to different domains, but they can never be separated from each other. For the concept of 'bodhisattva' is a fundamental insight (bodhi) about the mode of being in life and also about the features of actual progress of life (sattva). So, we need a name that always keeps both the two combined, and we call the life that deserves this name 'bodhisatttva.'

Bodhisattavas are liberated from the awareness of real being. From this basis of their fundamental enlightenment, they meet all the challenges of actual life with realistic upaya-paramitas and pursue their historical achievements (the adornments of the Buddha Land) through the historical design based on upaya-paramitas. They know that the genuine happiness of all lives lies, regardless of the degree of historical achievements, in the liberation from the realiness of beings. They take this achievement of liberation (enlightenment) as their basic goal that supports all historical practices and adornments from behind.

The lives of bodhisattvas proceed in such a way that they live in reality, without fundamentally being constrained by itself, and they exert their affections and passion to it while being not restricted by it. A transparent and pertinacious perspective of history – this may well be the bodhisattvas' very perspective of history. It is transparent because bodhisattvas see through that history is not a real being and they are thus fundamentally not constrained by it. However, although it is not a real being, this does not mean that it does not exist. To the contrary, it unfolds endlessly in terms of changes and relations. It is said to be pertinacious because we 'cultivate' it with various historical imaginations and practices in addition to such features of changes and relations. 'Enlightenment' is about the realization that history (being) is not real. And 'historical acts' are about how we should manage with what stance. 'Enlightenment' and 'historical acts' are to be combined through the excellent dialectical lives of 'bodhisattvas.' And these lives of 'bodhisattvas' come to emerge as the most desirable forms of lives that are free from evils and sufferings.

The problems of the two views

Let us examine 'Sudden Enlightenment and Gradual Cultivation' and 'Sudden Enlightenment and Sudden Cultivation' in light of our understanding of what we call 'bodhisattva.' I believe it is a triumph of Chinese Buddhism that Zen traditions describe 'bodhi (enlightenment)' in 'bodhisattva' as 'Sudden Enlightenment.' For the phrase 'Sudden Enlightenment' manifests at first sight the important characteristics of enlightenment. However, as previously discussed, some significant distortion happened in the process of putting in theoretical order the view of 'Sudden Enlightenment.' Its representative example is the view of 'Sudden Enlightenment and Gradual Cultivation' established by Guifeng Zongmi. The problems of this Sudden Enlightenment and Gradual Cultivation are as follows.

Firstly, this view went overboard trying to explain the aspect of enlightenment and the aspect of history as issues that belong to the same domain. The enlightenment side is in the domain in which one realizes the non-realness of the nature of beings. The history side is about the domain where beings change and unfold in terms of their own conditions and factors on the basis of such (non-real) nature. So, from a logical point of view, it is clear that these two sides do not belong to the same system of meaning. The problem of 'Sudden Enlightenment and Gradual Cultivation' is that it tries to include the domain of changes and progress in history – this domain includes an individual's habits, physiology, improvement of psychological states, and normalization of all actual problems – within the area controlled by enlightenment when enlightenment is a matter of breaking down the awareness of real being on beings (history).

Enlightenment in Buddhism is not to make beings reduced, separated or change in order to improve them; it is to see through their nature of being (that is, their non-realness). And the issue of beings' changes and unfolding is a problem of history and it belongs to the area of upaya. In other words, it is in the domain of 'sattva.' The logical confusion on bodhi and sattva begets unreasonable attempts to add the problems of the domain of historical progress in the matters to be controlled by enlightenment. So, this issue leads to the loss of the original significance and function of enlightenment and makes all the problems of history connected to the value system of enlightenment. Accordingly, it commits the fallacy of making history unilaterally consistent, schematized, and mystified on the level of 'the attachment to dharmas.'[97]

Secondly, the confusion on enlightenment and history makes

---

97 'Dharma' has a variety of different meanings. In this context, it means 'the Buddha teaching' or 'truth.'

vague even the basic characteristic of enlightenment as 'Sudden Enlightenment.' 'Sudden Enlightenment and Gradual Cultivation' claims that one should complete enlightenment through a long time of bodhisattvas' wholesome practices after Sudden Enlightenment. This view might easily be misunderstood as a claim that enlightenment can be obtained through gradual processes, and it will result in the loss of the genuine meaning of enlightenment. We must notice that the contents of 'Sudden Enlightenment' and 'Gradual Cultivation' are neither that their concepts are on different parts of the same area nor that the concept of one area is an expanded concept of the other.

'Sudden Enlightenment and Gradual Cultivation' may be compared to mean with a metaphor that one finds a real being, the ox (Sudden Enlightenment), and then tames and trains it (Gradual Cultivation) and freely plays around. However, the path to enlightenment is not the way of ox-herding. It is to know that the ox is not an ox, that is, it is to know that it is not an objective real being, and then become liberated from the ox. At the same time, it means to be freed from the state of subjective awareness of real being that takes the ox as its object. That is, the way of enlightenment is to break down all forms of real beings, but it seems that Sudden Enlightenment and Gradual Cultivation is still fixed on and bound by the idea of real being. Everything proceeding under the view of real beings cannot but go through gradual processes, but getting out of all that awareness of real being is accomplished simultaneously (at once), on the temporal point of view, and altogether, on the spatial point of view. Zen traditions have described all these features as 'Sudden.'

Thirdly, although the exponents of the view of Sudden Enlightenment and Gradual Cultivation attempt to secure from the sutras theoretical supports for their claim, their interpretations of the sutras have a lot of problems. Zongmi was also known as a scholar monastic in the Flower Garland School, and in particular he used extensively the theories of the Flower Garland School to establish Sudden Enlightenment and Gradual Cultivation. In his theory on the ten stages to achieve enlightenment, he explains specific practices for these processes in comparison to the order of the five stages – faith, abode, practice, intention and ground – of *The Flower Garland Sutra*. And he tries to implicitly emphasize that the sutras like *The Flower Garland* teach that one enters the ultimate status of the Buddha through gradual bodhisattva practices (gradual cultivation). However, as the Flower Garland's doctrine is expressed as the Sudden Teaching or Complete Teaching, it is not such a simple matter.

Such Flower Garland thoughts as 'One is all,' 'One moment of thought is equal to eternity' and 'Enter the status of the Buddha with one leap' constitute the theoretical foundation of the idea of Sudden Enlightenment. The types of bodhisattvas' practices that unfold quite extensively in the Flower Garland may look like showing gradual achievements and progress due to the order of narrative developments in the sutra. However, the doctrine of the Flower Garland is replete with basic teachings that would not allow for such interpretations. A variety of dharma talks were collected, edited and published under the same name of the system 'Flower

Garland.' We need to examine these factors from the perspective of the history of the sutra's establishment. However, more important than anything else is that we must pay attention to the fact that each and every phrase and item of practices in the Flower Garland has a self-completing structure of the Flower Garland doctrine. For instance, as we can see in the sutra with the metaphor of "Every piece of sandalwood has its scent to the fullest, and every drop of the sea tastes [fully] salty," such features of practices in *The Flower Garland Sutra* as the ten abodes, the ten practices, the ten dedications and the ten grounds do not have their hierarchies of importance determined by the order of their enumerations; each practice includes in its own features the realm of the Buddha.

The Flower Garland Sutra has the following passage in its Mystic Talk (Book 5, 7~10).

> … Various features of bodhisattvas' practices need to be understood in two aspects: Gate of Difference in Level and Gate of Perfect Interpenetration. The Gate of Difference in Level enumerates each bodhisattva's forms of practices in order (the ten abodes, the ten practices, etc.), and the Gate of Perfect Interpenetration shows that one form of practice includes other forms of practices in their entirety. For instance, the ten abodes contain the ten practices, the ten grounds, etc.; further, the first abode of awakening operation among the ten abodes includes the other nine abodes and at the same time the ten practices, the ten dedications and the ten grounds.

The 'Mystic Talk' says that although innumerably many features of bodhisattvas' practices are enumerated in a row in *the Flower Garland* world, they do not obstruct one another, they are harmonized, and they include one another in terms of the features of Difference in Level and Perfect Interpenetration. In this regard, we come to arrive at a conclusion that bodhisattvas' various forms of status mentioned in the *Flower Garland* may not be understood in terms of gradual processes. So, many problems emerge when we interpret the theory of bodhisattvas' ranks in the sutras with the frame of Sudden Enlightenment and Gradual Cultivation.

Fourthly, there has recently been an attempt to interpret 'Sudden Enlightenment and Gradual Cultivation' in such a way that this view has both the aspect of wisdom and the aspect of compassion. Wisdom is about the enlightenment on beings, and compassion is a matter of saving all sentient beings based on such enlightenment. However, although I can sympathize with the intention of this attempt, I believe that it is basically rather far away from the original view of 'Sudden Enlightenment and Gradual Cultivation.' For, although I admit there is a sense in which we can see the original 'Sudden Enlightenment and Gradual Cultivation' as having both the aspects of 'wisdom and compassion' like this case, the basic structure of this recent claim is a theory that unfolds on the domain of enlightenment. The essence of 'Sudden Enlightenment and Gradual Cultivation' is based on this theory, and it makes the problem of the historical domain belong to the problem of enlightenment, that is, it extends the issue of enlightenment to the domain of history. I believe that it is appropriate to have the theory of 'wisdom and compassion' approached under the light of 'bodhi and sattva' rather than of 'Sudden Enlightenment and Gradual Cultivation.'

'Sudden Enlightenment and Gradual Cultivation' had a plethora of problems as mentioned above. Let us now examine 'Sudden Enlightenment and Sudden Cultivation' that was presented criticizing 'Sudden Enlightenment and Gradual Cultivation'.

I believe there was the same basic problem in 'Sudden Enlightenment and Sudden Cultivation' in that it attempted to handle the aspect of enlightenment and the aspect of history within one frame, as 'Sudden Enlightenment and Gradual Cultivation' did. 'Sudden Enlightenment and Sudden Cultivation' recognizes Sudden Enlightenment (or, Complete Actualization, Perfect Awakening) only when one eliminates even the subtlest habitual traces of suffering and comes to have majestic power and merits as an awakened one while clearly penetrating one's inside and outside. 'Sudden Enlightenment and Sudden Cultivation' has a rigid and perfect standard, and thus creates a noble culture in which practitioners should not fall in laziness or take pride in one's superiority. However, as I have already discussed above, enlightenment is not about the elimination of suffering, the possession of supernatural marvelous power, or the complete freedom in managing historical matters. 'Sudden Enlightenment and Sudden Cultivation' demands a satisfaction of all these requirements as a basic qualification of enlightenment, and thus it faces the same problems of 'Sudden Enlightenment and Gradual Cultivation' that it criticizes. So, 'Sudden Enlightenment and Sudden Cultivation' as well as 'Sudden

Enlightenment and Gradual Cultivation' verges on realism when it handles various features of history.

All this comes to cloud even the basic characteristic of enlightenment called 'Sudden Enlightenment.' Sudden Enlightenment is nothing other than getting out of the realness of all beings, and as I said earlier, it comes as a revolutionary conversion. However, 'Sudden Enlightenment and Sudden Cultivation' reifies the habitual traces of suffering and all those various merits that enlightened ones must have, and thereby it makes the features of 'practice accomplishments' pick up tendencies of gradual 'meditation cultivationism.' In other words, to the contrary of the grandiose title of 'Sudden Enlightenment and Sudden Cultivation,' its contents come to have the characteristic of 'Gradual Cultivation and Sudden Enlightenment (Sudden Cultivation).' The problematic situation is actually even worse than this. Neither 'Sudden Enlightenment and Gradual Cultivation' nor 'Sudden Enlightenment and Sudden Cultivation' can properly reflect the characteristics of enlightenment which is Sudden Enlightenment. So, depending on expressions, although 'Sudden Enlightenment and Gradual Cultivation' emphasizes the characteristic of Sudden Enlightenment with its 'Sudden Enlightenment' and 'Sudden Enlightenment and Sudden Cultivation' focuses on Sudden Enlightenment with its 'Sudden Cultivation,' we need to see and examine if both of them are, in fact, approaching the features of 'Gradual Cultivation and Gradual Enlightenment.'

Another worry is the mystification of enlightenment that the meditation-cultivationist tendency, which 'Sudden Enlightenment and Sudden Cultivation' exhibits, comes to produce. 'Sudden Enlightenment and Sudden Cultivation' requires the elimination of the subtle habitual traces of the eighth consciousness alayavijnana, and also utter clarity under any situations, both of which tend to make an enlightened one regarded as possessing supernatural powers like a superman. Enlightenment does not mean controlling or governing freely all phenomena – including psychological states of suffering – and events of history. Enlightenment is to see through their natures and realize their non-realness. The fundamental freedom (liberation) brought about by enlightenment makes one always maintain the nirvana-bliss in spite of all the constraints and changes of history. So, we will enjoy the three virtues of liberation, dharma body and prajna even with the constraints of the world. Sitting quietly at the top of a high mountain peak does not increase or decrease one's enlightenment, and neither does working hard at the center of busy streets.

Jinmook Sunim has already taught that supernatural powers and marvelous functions have nothing to do with the Way, and sutras and sastras also tried to illuminate this point seriously. Weishan Sunim's dictum, "A fish does not change its scales when it becomes a dragon, and a layman does not alter his face when he becomes a sage," tells us straightforwardly that it is not the case, *pace* our social stereotypes, that the general appearance of an enlightened one shows a loftiness of character or that this enlightened one's abilities can be absolutely mystified. We just need to note that an enlightened one is liberated from the bondage of the realness of all historical beings by dint of his or her enlightenment.

Another problem of 'Sudden Enlightenment and Sudden Cultivation' is that it declares a clear and rigid distinction between doctrinal [scholastic] studies and Zen, although 'Sudden Enlightenment and Gradual Cultivation' tries hard to harmonize with sutras. I do not really think that this stance of 'Sudden Enlightenment and Sudden Cultivation' was designed to protect the weakness of its own position that cannot adapt to, and harmonize with the doctrines of sutras. However, it will be a serious problem if the doctrines and the bases of the ideas of Zen traditions are different from the bases of the ideas of doctrinal/scholastic schools. So, even if 'Sudden Enlightenment and Sudden Cultivation' bases its own status on the actual situations of practices, it cannot but be pointed out as a problem that 'Sudden Enlightenment and Sudden Cultivation' degrades various teachings of sutras to [what they call the inferior teachings of] the level of 'intellectual understanding' or 'understanding-awakening,' gives a hierarchy to Zen and doctrinal studies such that Zen is superior to doctrinal studies, and begets the alienation and unbalance of ideas. For if Zen is in its way thoroughly an actual method of practices, the experiences of doctrinal studies are also actual manuals of practices described in light of different cultural approaches.

Therefore, as it is not fair for 'Sudden Enlightenment and Gradual Cultivation' to unilaterally interpret sutras and sastras and use them to support its claim, I believe that it is not desirable for 'Sudden Enlightenment and Sudden Cultivation' to interpret the teachings of sutras and sastras as heresies and disparage them. In fact, as all those orthodox Zen masters emphasize, the Buddha's instructions in sutras and patriarchs' dharma talks on Zen are of the same teaching if we just set aside the difference in their expressions and descriptions. Even 'Sudden Enlightenment,' the most precious expression of Zen traditions, gained its theoretical inspiration from such Mahayana sutras as *The Lankavatara Sutra, The Vimalakirti Sutra, The Diamond Sutra* and *The Flower Garland Sutra.*

Conclusion

The debate on 'Sudden Enlightenment and Gradual Cultivation' and 'Sudden Enlightenment and Sudden Cultivation' has transformed the problem of 'Sudden' and 'Gradual,' which is the primary point of discussion in the history of Zen traditions, to actual problems in actual practices. It has unfolded the issue of enlightenment and practices in much more depth and width, and thereby opened a new horizon in the theory of Buddhist practices. On the other hand, however, these claims have more than a few problems. The most basic and important one among all these problems is that these claims use the concepts of enlightenment and history outside the categories of their logical applications. They accept, deep down in their claims, each of the domain of enlightenment (bodhi) and the domain of history (sattva) as the other's extended and expanded concept, and thus they actually regard both as belonging to the same domain. Further, they try to explain historical matters mainly with the domain of enlightenment. So, due to this confusion of the basic perspective, 'Sudden Enlightenment' in the orthodox Zen traditions, and 'Sudden Enlightenment' in 'Sudden Enlightenment and Gradual Cultivation' and 'Sudden Enlightenment and Sudden Cultivation' have become different concepts that do not have an intersection.

Korea's Buddhist culture of practices is currently divided by the two mountain chains of 'Sudden Enlightenment and Gradual Cultivation' and 'Sudden Enlightenment and Sudden Cultivation.' However, if these two views do in fact have as many problems as I pointed out earlier, Korean Buddhism will inevitably beget a lot of obstacles in achieving enlightenment in the midst of practices, and it is obvious that the bodhisattva practices in history will also face many constraints and limits.

Then, which meditations and practices should we conduct? It is the Sudden Enlightenment culture of Zen traditions that we must maintain because, in this way, we can have the way of enlightenment (bodhi) most correctly conform to enlightenment, and we will also be able to achieve the original goal of enlightenment which is to remove the veil of realness from beings. And, based on enlightenment which is the open stance of life to accept historical matters with the awareness of real being taken off, historical practices will be to read historical experiences and their correlations and boldly open oneself to the applications of enriched historical imagination and hypotheses.

In this case as well, we should not evaluate historical matters with the value system of enlightenment as if we were trying to see whether the matters of historical domain conform to the Buddhist truth (or enlightenment). In the matters of history, such value judgments as the meaning of merits and demerits, good and evil, beauty and ugliness will need to be transferred to the area of historical experiences.

The most desirable life will be to understand, this way, the characteristic that enlightenment and history belong to the same area but they are systems of different domains (dimensions), and then dialectically combine and synthetically harmonize these two domains in a life. By doing this, we transcend the level of a one-sided Zen practitioner (bodhi) or the level of simple history (sattva), and become 'bodhisattvas.'

5

Buddhism Approaching History

Buddhism and Society

This story is not to propose a specific sociological theory of Buddhism but only to address the essential relation between Buddhism and society. This essay is in this regard a small story about Buddhism's stance on history, that is, a small story that may well be included in the category of Buddhist philosophy of history.

These days, many Buddhists have faced a problem regarding their relation to society. However, it is not just a problem of methodology on how to participate in society. More important is the problem that precedes this methodological stage. I believe the problem is that we are wandering about in front of the following question: "How should we view what is called 'society'?" Buddhists are captured by the dichotomous view that sees Buddhism and society as belonging to essentially different areas, and they struggle with such questions as follows: "Isn't the history of society something useless that does not have any substantial value deserving our efforts and passion?" and "Isn't what the Buddha suggested as his teachings not about this society or history but about a different, transcendental world?" Those who wish to discuss today's Buddhism and society should examine this issue first.

Buddhism and society are one

We usually define Buddhism as 'teachings of the Buddha,' 'teachings about the Buddha,' 'teachings to become a Buddha,' etc. Then, how are 'Buddhism' and 'society' related to each other when Buddhism is defined this way?

It is not just these days but also from a very long past that many people have thought that Buddhism has nothing to do with society, it goes beyond this society, and it intends to reach a certain realm that transcends this society. Those who have held this view will probably be surprised when told that Buddhism and society are essentially related, and furthermore, they are a perfectly unified area, although they are expressed differently in our language with the language of religion and the language of secular society. However, it can be said that they are, in reality, one area, and they aim and strive for the same area.

If what I have said above is true, then why do most people misunderstand it and why are even devoted Buddhists sometimes misled? Perhaps we have misunderstood the Buddha's life and his teachings? Or, have we misunderstood the language of Buddhism? Only if we examine and reflect on this problem will we be justified in believing that Buddhists should discuss history and society and that they should take part in this history with affection and concerns.

Buddhism, the way to solve the problem of suffering of all sentient beings

When we say that Buddhism is 'the Buddha's teaching,' 'the Buddha' is of course 'Siddhartha Gautama' who lived 2,500 years ago.[98] As widely known, he was the one who renounced the secular life, searched for the Way, and taught dharmas and practiced them after his enlightenment. It is clearly known to us what was his motive to come to live an excellent life, what was the problem that he tried to solve in the process of his renunciation of the secular life and also of his search for the Way, and what he taught about.

He responded to the unhappiness and suffering of all sentient beings as if they had been his own. So, he chose a special type of life and tried to concentrate on comprehending this problem to find its solution. He explained the solution of all sentient beings' unhappiness and suffering during the 45 years of his dharma teaching. Since there would be no move for a solution if there exists no problem, the problem of all sentient beings was truly the first starting point and also the final destination of Buddhism. The suffering of all sentient beings that the Buddha took seriously as a problem is usually represented as the eight kinds of suffering:

---

98 Of course, in this case as well, orthodox Buddhists [of Mahayana traditions] do not limit the reference of "the Buddha" to just Siddhartha Gautama. So, this issue comes to beget the fundamental question 'What is the Buddha?'

birth, aging, sickness, death, separation from that which we love, association with that which we hate, inability to fulfill our desires, and the suffering from the instability of the five skandhas.[99] These eight kinds of suffering include all the physical, mental, socio-institutional, and existential sufferings that exist in our lives. The Buddha made his start with this problem and then saw through that the problem of suffering and unhappiness was brought about by the various erroneous judgments, misunderstandings, and preconceptions on the being and life. So, he emphasized, above all, that these unfortunate situations could be overcome when we are established on the 'correct understanding (bodhi).' According to his teaching, whether it be an individual or a whole, materialistic or idealistic, whether it be a situation derived from the being or it itself be a movement, no being exists really or substantially and all beings mutually relate to and constitute one another. 'The correct understanding (bodhi)' is to know this truth, and this 'correct understanding' is the most basic and primary key to solve the problems of all sentient beings.[100]

This perspective of 'correct understanding' is called 'the law

---

99 Five skandhas are five aggregates that constitute a human existence: its material basis and four kinds of psychological states.

100 What we need to heed here is that it is not the case that 'such and such things' exist and they interact among one another but that even 'such a thing' should not be thought of as independent being, that is, substance. And all things determine and constitute one another, and they are also determined and constituted by one another. Above all, we must note that all these things are in the process of changes. This point is the important difference between dialectical logic and the law of dependent arising (interdependence).

of dependent arising (interdependence)' and is otherwise described as 'emptiness (the mode of being formed in terms of dependent arising).' If one examines the first starting problem with 'correct understanding,' she will realize that the problem of life that she used to have gets untangled from a new perspective. That is, it will be illuminated through this new horizon of understanding that the problem of life is not a problem of an individual, of an independent situation, or of a substantial, fixed and unchanging nature.

So, the problem of one life comes to be elevated to a problem of social nature, which amounts to say that Buddhism started with the problem of life, that it came to grasp the connectedness of lives as it went through the process of the Buddha's enlightenment, and that it reached the level to see through the social nature of all lives. We can notice, through the Buddha's life, that he gave his dharma talks to teach this very point for all his life and he also drove his efforts to reconstructing the society of his time and the stance of life. The place he aimed for was, after all, not heaven or a transcendental realm of life. It was the very ground and problem of our lives, and it is clear that these were the problems of mutual relations among the beings that are exposed to the process of changes.

The Buddha is society

When we define Buddhism as 'the teaching about the Buddha,' the most important question is what 'the Buddha' truly is. And it is the Buddhist view of the world and history that gives an answer to this question.

"What is it like to be a Buddha?" is the best of all the serious questions that a seeker of the Way should have. And the answer to this question may be said to be the issue of Buddhism in its entirety. But, then, how is it if we say, in the Zen masters' lightening manner of speech, 'The Buddha is society' to answer the question "What is it like to be a Buddha?" or "What is the Buddha?"

The understanding of the Buddha was the issue that started as early as the Buddha's own time, but the responses to this question reached the very climax about the time the Mahayana sutras were completed. According to *The Flower Garland Sutra*, which is the quiescence among Mahayana sutras, the Buddha is not just 'Siddhartha Gautama.' "The Buddha" has also come to refer to all 'beings in general in their entirety.' And these 'beings in general in their entirety' is the field where each and every situation or domain changes by interacting with one another, and 'beings in general in their entirety' are both a part the field and the field as a whole simultaneously. Also, this sutra uses different descriptions such as 'all sentient beings' or 'mind' to describe this 'field of beings,' and it also says that 'the Buddha,' 'all sentient beings' and 'mind' are only varied expressions that refer to the exactly same 'field of beings.'

"Mind" in this context does not designate the mind that people in the contemporary time understand as a psychological phenomenon. It means 'the field of beings' where the subject and object determine each other and get put together harmoniously. It can be neither divided as material or mental nor described with a noun because it does not have its own proper domain. 'Mind' is only the term agreed on in this context that describes this 'field of beings.' So, when Buddhism is usually called the religion that searches for 'mind,' awakens 'mind,' and explains everything with 'mind,' 'mind' in these cases also has the same meaning as 'the Buddha' or 'all sentient beings,' and is completely identical in its meaning with 'beings in general in their entirety.'

The following passage in *The Flower Garland Sutra* may also be understood in this way: "If you wish to know 'the Buddha' manifested on the line of time that is connected with the past, present and future, observe the nature of 'beings in general in their entirety.' You will then come to realize that all these are the manifestation of 'mind.'" Also, such words as "the Buddha," "mind" and "all sentient beings" do not refer to the concepts of real beings, as "A" is assumed to do in a sentence like "A is such and such." In contrast, they need to be understood as symbols or terms agreed on like "A" in "Such and such are agreed to be called A." All this becomes clear and obvious if we apply to language the Buddhist ontology that views all beings not as a collection of real beings but as phenomena of interrelations.

In this regard, it is actually appropriate to read from right to left, not from left to right, all sentences that have a subject part and a predicate part, and this tip may well be circulated as useful, though paradoxical. All the phenomena of reification, absolutization, and even mystification of many Buddhist terminologies should now be eliminated in light of the original ontology of Buddhism.

This point needs to be applied not just to 'Buddhism' but also to 'society.' 'Society' means an organic entity made up of multiple persons, but the issue of these many lives is not only about a quantitative collection of persons or individuals. The life of a part is interconnected to the lives of the other parts or of the whole. And if we consider the interrelations in which the life of the whole is entangled under the influence of one part's inter-determination, constraint, connection, etc., we can see that 'society' is not just a one-directional 'total society' bound by blood ties, customs, laws, and so on. Society may have to be understood, if described with Buddhist terminology, as 'something made up of organic relations which is neither one nor many, neither identical nor different.'

'Society' is in this regard so much alike with 'the Buddha,' 'all sentient beings,' 'all beings in general in its entirety,' and 'mind' in 'Buddhism.' If Buddhism is 'a teaching about the Buddha,' couldn't we also say that it is 'a teaching on society'?

To become a Buddha is ...

We have by now derived a comprehensive and dynamic concept of 'the Buddha.' It was to signify 'the Buddha' not just as a person, 'Siddhartha Gautama,' but also as all 'beings in general,' that is, 'history' and 'social phenomena.' When we examine the final definition of Buddhism, i.e., 'a teaching to become a Buddha – to achieve a Buddha' from this perspective, we can see right away that this proposition implies a very significant historical meaning.

To become 'a Buddha' is to become 'beings in general,' and it is none other than to become 'history' and 'society.' In other words, it is not an issue of one individual or a part; rather, it is for the whole and its parts to remain harmonized. Only in this way can we leave behind individualized and narrow-minded phenomena brought about by an erroneous understanding and shake off unhappiness and suffering caused by it. 'To become a Buddha' is to lead all beings and lives to comfort and peace. This point helps us realize that 'to become a Buddha,' 'the realization of straightened-out history,' and 'the accomplishment of a healthy society' are only different expressions of the same content.

However, we see that we are caught in an unexpected trap although we have in our hands a clear 'teaching to become a Buddha.' This trap is nothing other than the confusion between 'the language of religion' and 'the language of the mundane world.' All Buddhist terms such as 'achievement of Buddhahood' and 'salvation of all sentient beings' are symbolic jargons of religion. And Buddhism is a form of ideas made of this kind of system of language, but its basis and mission (destination) are the history of actual reality.

We should not think of Buddhism as an independent domain of real being. To the contrary, we need to understand Buddhism as a collected system of religious meaning and language that is derived from concrete history and reality. And it comes to fit in the Buddhist perspective only if we can see even Buddhism (dharma) in the structure of laws of dependent arising (interconnections).

These days, people are trapped in a dualism that regards Buddhism and society as different worlds. Buddhism is a system of teaching that came into existence to explain the problem of history and reality. Buddhism explains reality as full of various changes, and although it borrows the expressions of the symbolic language of religion to obtain objectivity and universality, it actually addresses exactly the same problem and situations. Buddhists should be able to interpret and read this language of religion in terms of our ordinary, mundane language. When we read sentences of a foreign language, we do not translate them after we read them, but we translate and understand them simultaneously. Likewise, we should think and practice the language of Buddhism with our everyday language in the same way. Buddhist language will then be connected to our specific problems that are constantly developing, and thereby the views of Buddhism, which have obtained the historical and social nature, will be realized on the basis of specific social science.

Buddhists say, often rather excessively, that we should save and lead all sentient beings, never commit evil deeds, put into practice what is good, realize the mind, become a Buddha, establish the Pure Land of the Buddha, and so on. If we lack a clear and specific understanding of these sentences, we will not only fall in a trap of the circular logic of tautology but also we will not know in reality from which problems we have started and which lives and practices we are aiming for. We must understand seriously that this is as good as not even knowing who died after you have cried for him or her all day.

Buddhism must return to assume its original historical stance

The most important agenda in Buddhism is to return to its original historical features from its [currently] non-historical attitude, and to come back to the concrete language of reality from the system of religious symbolic language. Also, it is to read the logic of social science from the logic of tautology, and engage in the reality with the theory of practice and the high-level of morality (great compassion) linked to the problems of our real lives. We call the people standing on this realm 'bodhisattvas.' This word means that 'the worldview illuminated under the correct understanding (bodhi)' is tied with 'the actual, historical reality (sattva),' or that 'concrete history' is built on 'the correct perspective.'

On the other hand, there is another trap, in this concept of 'bodhisattva,' that even the theory of universal social science itself is not properly a problem of the real world. In contrast with the case of natural science, we cannot but doubt if there truly exists in social science a 'paradigm' which is rooted in the shared support of an entire society. No theory of social science can be universally applied everywhere all the time. Accordingly, if a 'paradigm' of social science becomes fixed and absolutized, the social evils that follow it will inevitably be devastating. For this reason, although socio-scientific ideologies have recently contributed to explaining history and society, their absolutization has on the other hand obstructed the true growth and the realization of the lives of most social classes and their members.

So, when we say that Buddhism needs "to become a social science," "to acquire historical and concrete nature," it does not simply mean to wrap it up with today's socio-scientific language and theory or to make it fixed as a universal and objective theory of society. It means that Buddhism needs to constantly face, recognize, and meet the challenge of the reality of lives which is our problem. It is not easy to become a bodhisattva, yet this is possible only by incessantly leaving behind any given frame and confronting the changing reality.

(bodhi + sattva)	+	sattva	+	sattva	=	bodhisattva
⋮		⋮		⋮		
symbolic		social science		concrete		
⋮		⋮		⋮		
the language of religion		theory		reality		

The lives of bodhisattvas constantly aim for bodhi and sattva, and they live their practical lives with historical awareness. But, then, how should today's bodhisattvas in Korea live their lives?

To have the perspective of bodhi is the essential duty that any Buddhist should basically perform, so it is not necessary to raise questions about it. However, how good is our understanding of the real situations in which the perspective of bodhi should return, get rooted and realized? How do we understand today's social ideologies, systems or social norms that define contemporary people or Koreans? Or, to say again from the start, what is the perspective of bodhi originally? – It is nothing other than the correct perspective on the present world in general. However, those who are ignorant about our contemporary world, history and society may not be said to have bodhi. The concepts of bodhi and sattva are mutually connected (dependent arising), and they can never be separated from each other. However, those who do not understand Buddhism in the right way fix their perspective in blank space and claim that we can participate in history and society only after we establish such a perspective. They suggest that we should not have concerns about, or even pay attention to society or history before such a successful establishment of the correct perspective.

"If you wish to know all 'the Buddha' in the past, present and future, in other words, if you want to obtain the perspective of bodhi, you should first see through the nature of all beings in general."

This is a passage in *The Flower Garland Sutra*. We should now come back to reassume the original stance of Buddhism as follows:

"The Buddhist way of life is to be concerned about history and society, to cognize their issues correctly, and to live a life of practices in the right way, and Buddhism has only described this story with the symbolic language of religion."

This essay "Buddhism and Society" was Hyun-Eung Sunim's manuscript prepared for the lecture he gave for Summer Camp held at Haeinsa Buddhist Monastery in 1985.

The Social Practice of Buddhism

Waiting for the Buddhist methodology of practice

The question "How should Buddhists engage in social practices?" requires responses to the issues of 'the logical ground' of Buddhist social practices, 'the methodology of practices' and 'the stance of practices.'

These days, Buddhism is undergoing a sincere and reflective self-examination with the suspicion that it might be getting behind, voluntarily or involuntarily, in its efforts to find the solutions for the problems of history and society. So, we have come to raise serious questions in order for Buddhists to regain their more active and leading stance in today's historical situations. Also, on the social level as well, researchers in social science are listening carefully, through these questions, to the teachings of Buddhism to further elevate their theory and practices.

It is fundamentally the eternal problem of humanity to realize a good and righteous society and construct a healthy and sound history. Concerns and practical efforts for all these are no longer limited or defined as the exclusive area of a number of leaders or special classes, and they now seem to be extended to the area of the people's level. Following this movement of history, Buddhists should also play a role – hopefully, a leading role – in social engagement and the construction of good and just history. Buddhists share in their wishes that the specific method for this participation may well come from the methodology and forms of practice based on the Buddhist teaching (thoughts) rather than the preexisting sociological theories or modes of practices. Can these wishes come true? If so, how does it happen and what is it like?

The Buddhist ontology – dependent arising (emptiness) and the Middle Way

There were many philosophical schools and religions in the Indian society that begot Buddhism. As commonly expressed with the 62 views or 96 views, it was the time when all the ideologies and thoughts were flourishing and competing with one another. In this ideological and religious climate, the Buddhist teaching had an enormous difference that brought a great qualitative change to the perspective of the preexisting ideological system and worldview. As is manifested in such sentences like "It is red (or it is blue)" or "We should make it this (or that) way," the preexistent teaching of thoughts accepted, in its explanation on the problem of beings (the world) or life, all parts of beings as established facts – with the presupposition that they exist as real beings – and then focused on discussing the issues that appear only after this acceptance and presupposition. However, Buddhism started to solve all the various problems of unreasonableness, suffering, and other issues in life. And Buddhism suddenly raised doubts, while it was examining the problems derived from life, on the realness of all forms of life themselves that precede inessential derivative phenomena. That is, Buddhism came to make a judgment, before discussing whether this is 'a red thing' or 'a blue thing,' that this 'thing' itself is in fact not 'a real phenomenon (real being)' of our generally accepted view.

Whether it is physical, mental, or whether it belongs to the third areas such as language, laws, customs and culture, all beings in this world are not substantial real beings – to describe this point, Buddhism uses an expression 'dependently arising being (or, emptiness).' If we view all beings from a spatial perspective, what this means is that we cannot separate the cognitive subject from the object of cognition due to the phenomena of mutual determination, inter-formation, and inter-penetration of the subject and object. All beings in this world are so closely connected to, and mutually affecting one another, as we can see how a whole building would collapse if a part of it were removed. On the other hand, if we view all beings from a temporal perspective, every being changes every moment corresponding to every instant of which the duration is the infinitely divided time period, which means that there can exist no area of any independent real beings that last even for the shortest time.

The Buddhist perspective that sees through the mode of existence of all beings in this world as dependently arising (emptiness) has nothing to do with the view that all beings do not actually exist at all (nothingness). The Buddhist view is that it recognizes all the areas of beings in this world but that none of them substantially exist as real beings. That is, it may be said to be of the mode of existence in the Middle Way that is neither 'real being' nor 'complete nothingness,' and the sutras also describe this rather differently as 'This world (of all sentient beings) exists like an illusion." This 'illusion' here is not only distinguished from something faint and unreal that is associated with 'violet,' but it is also not real being with substantiality. It means that the feature of being is revealed in the process of changes as overlapped fields, not as an independent substance.

Even though we know that life is only a scene of a dream or a play

This worldview that sees all beings as illusory came to bring Buddhism its own unique mode of practice for life. Let us have a look at a passage in a Chinese classic that clearly implies the Buddhist view of practices.

> Who has awakened from a great dream.
> I have known its meaning for a long time.
> I had a good nap in this thatched cottage on this spring day,
> But the sun outside the window still has a long way to go.

This is Zhuge Liang's poem in Luo Guanzhong's *The Three Kingdoms*. It appears in the famous part related to Liu Bei making three calls at the thatched cottage to ask Zhuge Liang to take up a government post. This scholar, who was cultivating his farm land in Nanyang with no government position, regarded history as a great dream. So, he chose not to take part in any activities that might constrain or make himself suffer, and only read books, cultivated his field to grow crops and vegetables, and relaxed. One day, however, he found himself in a situation where he had to be trapped in a gigantic whirlpool of history. In the end, he decided to proactively engage in history. According to *The Three Kingdoms* and historical records, he remained very prudent and diligent until the magnificent moment of his death, and, through this kind of dedicated life, he struggled with all his efforts for the political group that he supported. Still he continuously held the view of history he had had in Nanyang, and further, he had already predicted that the group he was going to support would never succeed.

How, then, should we accept Zhuge Liang's stance on history? If we closely examine his case as is described in the novel from a Buddhist point of view, although he knew that history was only a bout of a dream, he threw himself in there rather than withdrew from there. On the other hand, according to the author's view of history manifested in the introductory poem, any historical task that people wish to accomplish is only transient regardless of its success or failure.

I believe that the basic stance on how to participate (practice) in history must be founded on the Buddhist perspective that the world in which we live is only a scene of a great dream and this realm of all sentient beings is also an illusion.

The following is a part of Chapter 7 Regarding All Sentient

Beings in *The Vimalakirti Sutra.*

Manjushri: How should Bodhisattvas regard all sentient beings?

Vimalakirti: The being of all sentient entities is illusory. As the wise view the moon reflected on the water, or a face seen in a mirror, as shimmers of fire, as echoes, as clouds, … Bodhisattvas should see the world this way.

Manjushri: How, then, can they have compassion or practices, and in what forms can they be implemented?

Vimalakirti: The compassion and its practice in Buddhism are to let all sentient beings know and realize that this world is illusory. And this is the very practice of true compassion.

Manjushri: Then, what are the concerns we have for them, and what are the practices of giving help because we feel pity?

Vimalakirti: That is to share all our practices with all sentient beings.

Manjushri: How do you explain the joy and dignity of practices?

Vimalakirti: It is the attitude to be joyous at historical achievements with no regret.

Manjushri: What about the dedicated spirit of sacrifice to give alms with unsparing hands?

Vimalakirti: It is not to expect any recompense or any return for one's acts to help others.

According to this sutra, there is something out of focus in the goal-oriented intentionality behind the given title 'What Is the Social Practice of Buddhism?' In Buddhism, we call the conscious efforts to turn to and achieve a goal 'turning to set a direction to go in' (setting a direction, hereafter).[101] In this regard, we believe, in Buddhism, that we should direct and converge 'all our actions and will' eventually in the solution of three problems. These three are bodhi (correct perspective), actuality (the features of beings revealed by the correct perspective), and all sentient beings. These three issues cannot be separated from one another, and they may well be understood to belong to the same dimension. The first reason of this is that all practices and concerns are ultimately for the issues of all our lives (setting a direction to all sentient beings). The second is that we must, first of all, correctly understand this world including our lives in order to resolve those issues (setting a direction to actuality). Its third reason is that we must, for the same purpose, have the correct perspective (setting a direction to bodhi). So, we call these three 'setting directions to three places,'[102] and they are understood as extended issues of the same problem.

Accordingly, when such a Mahayana scripture as *The Flower Garland Sutra* [*The Avatamsaka Sutra*] mentions 'setting a direction to all sentient beings,' and when Zen traditions encourage the pursuit of enlightenment (setting a direction to bodhi), we must understand that these

---

101 In Buddhism we usually use this concept to signify 'transferring to neighbors and society the merits and value of the Buddhist ceremonies and events after we carry them out.' However, I believe it will be correct to see that the true meaning of this concept is not about what should be done after actions are completed but that it is rather about the goal-oriented intentionality that precedes actions. So, to have the awareness of 'setting a direction' is to have a consistent awareness of the goal from the beginning stage of actions till the end.

102 *Dasheng yizhang (Essay on the System of Mahayana)*, Vol. 9, by Huiyuan in the Sui Dynasty.

two traditions are, in essence, implying 'setting directions to three places,' although each of them is emphasizing a different aspect of the same issue.

On this view, all those representative practical endeavors that Buddhism advocates – for instance, the six paramitas: generosity without hesitation (dana-paramita), putting into practice moral virtues (sila-paramita), patience (kshanti-paramita), exertion (virya-paramita), having the clear mind of concentration (dhyana-paramita), and bright wisdom (prajna-paramita) – should ultimately be directed at the aforementioned three places: bodhi, actuality and sentient beings. Furthermore, each and every move of our life and all the efforts we make in our social activities regarding jobs, environments and patterns of behaviors must also be directed in the end toward these three issues.

However, if we examine the contents of these three places, we will come to see that they are not different from the perspective of viewing things as illusions (bodhi), the world realized as illusions (actualities), or the feature of all sentient beings that live illusions and are formed by illusions (sentient beings).

Understanding the twofold structure of life

Then, what does 'the social practice of Buddhism' mean from a sociological point of view?

The issues of the increase of productivity and distribution, of politics and economic structure, of the unification of the two Koreas and of realizing various equal conditions for the social lives of people, of war or of the preservation of environments, etc. – what utilities does the Buddhist stance of practices have to solve all these accumulated social problems?

The goal that Buddhism aims for and its mode of practice, and the socio-historical task that is aimed for on the social level – strictly speaking, these two are problems that belong to different levels, but they seem to be thought and practiced together. As religion, philosophy and all sciences – natural science, social science, etc. – have been separated in modern society, it seems that the Buddhist way of practices should also have its characteristics rigidly distinguished, although it has some partial similarities with socio-scientific practice and its area.

Let us return to the perspective with which we first discussed the difference that Buddhism had from the preexisting systems of thoughts. Social sciences are concerned about the problems of seeing beings as blue, red, or how to construct them. In contrast, the basic concern of Buddhism is to investigate the genuine feature of beings themselves and respond to it. These two are, from a philosophical point of view, clearly problems of different levels. In other words, there are two different levels of perspectives to see the same domain of all sentient beings.

For instance, consider a theory that handles the issue of whether the hardness and whiteness of a stone in Go game are the same or different. Let us compare the softness and hardness of a stone to the issue of a social task, and the whiteness and blackness to the issue of whether the stone is a real being or an illusion.

The whiteness and hardness of the stone is an issue that cannot be separated from each other and they are descriptions made on different levels about the same event (or fact). Likewise, the

Buddhist practices directed to the three places and the practice parts on social tasks are the issues of different levels in the same life. However, as the whiteness and hardness are unified in a stone that cannot be separated, the Buddhist practices and social practices are also overlapped with the problem of the same sentient beings.

Understanding this twofold structure of life is directly connected to the problem of Buddhism's social practices. As the issue of the whiteness and blackness of a stone cannot be used to solve the problem of its hardness or softness, the Buddhist practices that aim for the three places – whether they are individual practices or social practices – cannot have a logical correlation with the solution of social tasks. Also, as making a soft thing hard cannot solve the problem of whiteness and blackness, even if we solve all the social problems, we cannot arrive at Buddhism's conclusion that beings themselves are illusory (non-real).

We can see from this understanding that the purpose we had behind the topic of 'the social practice of Buddhism' must be, in fact, an incorrect requirement that resulted from a conceptual confusion. That is, we should handle all social tasks through a scientific stance of approach based on sociological laws, and we need to learn in Buddhism a problem of beings on a different level.

Also, Buddhists should also revise, with regards to social issues, their stance to search for theoretical or practical bases to solve social problems from the Buddhist doctrines. Such Buddhist practices as the six paramitas, the Noble Eightfold Path, and the 37-aids to enlightenment can of course prove their partial usefulness for social practices. However, since the goal-directedness of such

Buddhist practices are intended for different places to begin with, the features of these practices cannot always be said to be useful for the specific social problems of reality.

Construct the Pure Land among all sentient beings

Let us now conclude our discussion on the topic of 'How to engage in Buddhist social practices' with the following passage in the chapter of 'Buddha Lands' in *The Vimalakirti Sutra*.

The rich man's son, Jeweled Accumulation: All of us have set our minds on attaining bodhi (correct perspective). We now wish to hear how one can purify the Buddha Lands, and what should the practices to be carried out by bodhisattvas be like?

The Buddha: 'The Buddha Land' is the world of all various sentient beings, but one should not think of this Buddha Land as something to be built in a transcendental place like an empty space. So, bodhisattvas must come to construct the Pure Land in all our sentient beings. And the Pure Land should be built with an upright mind, a deeply searching mind, the six-paramitas, various upaya (expedient means), compassion and almsgiving, the 37-aids to enlightenment including the Noble Eightfold Path and others, the ten good actions,[103] and so on.

---

103 (1) not killing, (2) not stealing, (3) not committing adultery, (4) not lying, (5) not speaking harshly, (6) not speaking divisively, (7) not speaking idly, (8) not being greedy, (9) not being angry and (10) not having wrong views.

Buddhists understand social practices on the level of the construction of the Buddha Land. Therefore, under the proposition of the construction of the Buddha Land, we must be looking for the harmony between Buddhist practices and social practices.

If we adopt the Buddhist point of view, we must understand that unless we realize that all of society, history and life are illusory (dependently arising = empty) beings, we would have to face a necessarily tragic consequence regardless of what achievements we make out of social tasks. So, Buddhists have, even amid all the same historical efforts, an additional historical task to realize that all these sentient beings are illusions.

And although the Buddhist practices set in the direction of the three places might be an issue of a different level than the level of social problems, this Buddhist stance does not imply an indifference or contradiction to social problems. To the contrary, they complement each other and can be sustained as and in a harmonious life. Therefore, 'the Buddhist social practices' may well come to deserve its title only when the Buddhist practices, set in the direction of the three places, and the socio-scientific practices to solve all the problems of society are to be combined and overlapped. It is these social practices of Buddhists that accomplish the world of sentient beings as illusions, and it is called 'the purification of the Buddha Land.' And, finally, these historical efforts of Buddhists are called 'illusory compassion (compassion like an illusion).'

This essay "The Social Practice of Buddhism" was Hyun-Eung Sunim's manuscript prepared for the lecture he gave for Summer Camp held at Haeinsa Buddhist Monastery in 1985.

For the Mahayanist Progress of People's Buddhism Movement

The rise and background of People's Buddhism

It has been some time since the Buddhist movement that pays sincere attention to social problems and history has been called the 'People's Buddhism movement.' People's Buddhism movement is concerned about the lives of sentient beings – to be more specific, the lives of people in our time - and their problems, and this movement is to participate in their lives and solve their problems together. The origin of its spirit and traditions traces back as far as to the teaching of Shakyiamuni's time and the history of Buddhist orders. In Korea, this People's Buddhism has continued since Wonhyo, Shindon, Seoshan, Samyung, through the Maitreya Buddhists of each era who professed their will of change, to the nationalist Buddhist spirit of Baek Yongseong and Han Yongwoon, and after the liberation of Korea in 1945, the socialist Buddhists on the line of reform alliance.

Korean Buddhism used to participate directly in social issues and the problems of sentient beings, and was called the 'Buddhism protective of the nation.' However, it must be the recent 'People's Buddhism movement' that finally started to make Buddhists actively engage in our society consciously, systematically, and in an organized way with more self-confidence in the Buddhist doctrines and with the people's perspective with regard to the issues of history.

The new interpretation of Buddhism and practices, which is these days called 'People's Buddhism,' began to develop in the mid and late 1970's while the Revitalized Reform system[104] was heading for its collapse, and it used the hope and frustration of democratization in the early 1980's as a stepping stone and started to emerge in full scale in the history of South Korea. Although People's Buddhism movement has been active for only about ten years, it has already established its experiences and theories within the Buddhist society, its own significant status from the perspective of its doctrines, and its position within the Buddhist order. It has also exercised its own influence that corresponds to its status. And, since it has invited many expectations that it will take the initiative in the future Buddhist movement, Korean Buddhism may now well be said to have started a new era of People's Buddhism. On the other hand, although People's Buddhism movement is somewhat radical compared with the preexisting features of Buddhism, it has settled relatively easily in the Buddhist order and society

---

104 This is a political system devised primarily to prolong the dictatorial and authoritarian government of Korea in the 1970's.

despite many trials and vicissitudes because there was a necessary factor that required People's Buddhism to be established in the order and society. However, still being in its early stages, People's Buddhism movement has many problems and I believe it needs to be continuously revised and complemented.

First of all, although the rise of People's Buddhism is on one hand a consequence of the continuous and devoted efforts of Buddhism's theorists and activists, it has on the other resulted from the historical situation in which Buddhism was placed. This historical situation means none other than the nationalistic situation where a political and social engagement of the religious society takes place in full scale, which is one of the features of third-world societies. The nation's situation after the liberation in 1945 was quite abnormal. Comprador capital prevailed in this political structure, and foreign culture came to eliminate and interrupt traditional and national culture. Accordingly, the self-contradiction of politics, economy, society and culture was naturally deepening amid discords and disagreements, and the system of military dictatorship become prolonged on this distorted foundation.

The political participation of religious societies started in this crippled structure from the 1970's. It is because the only group of people or classes who could lead others to correct and reform the faulty society under the social reality in which silence and obedience were coerced was only religious societies and students. This political and social engagement of religions was of course the invocation of the era that was placed in front of the self-contradictory social structure, but this change that the conservative and sycophant religious societies showed was based on an epoch-making awakening on history and moral decision. In other words, Buddhism was impressed with this movement of society, and the 'People's Buddhism movement' emerged as Buddhism's self-awakening movement necessary to take part in this current of history.

The time that People's Buddhism movement started coincides roughly with the period when the Korean Buddhist order's traditional culture of practices and the primitive and self-sufficient mountain communities [monasteries] were rapidly transferred to, and included in the capitalist structure of South Korean Society. The stagnation and isolation of the Korean Buddhist order lasted for five hundred years of the Chosun Dynasty, through the period of Japanese occupation, and until the 1970's. It was clearly symbolized with the one fact that the candles and private electric generators were used until the 1970's by not only major monasteries in the mountains but also most other temples. The lay society was only an outside world that required at least several days for a round trip. The foods from vegetable gardens and croft land, some economic income, chanting, reading, meditation, and the dharma talks of Bodhidharma, Huineng and Linji Sunim were the entire world that Buddhism had. As Buddhism had little and rare access to society, the society and general public also found the way to approach Buddhism as too far and remote. In short, Korean Buddhism was isolated and closed like an island in society.

From the 1970's, though, the policy to turn prominent Buddhist monasteries into national parks and tourist attractions was implemented in full throttle. For this reason, Buddhism came to be open, with no control, to Korean society, people, and the world. So, Buddhism had to face a lot of confusion in its doctrines, and damages and destructions in the structure of its order. However, on the other hand, the dialectics of history mysteriously gave Buddhism opportunities to be awakened to the lives of history and sentient beings and participate in them.

Korean Buddhism has finally been modernized (?) as roads stretching to the temples have been built, so many people came to visit temples in mountains, and electricity and the methods of mass communication were introduced to temples. Korean Buddhism has become a member of the social structure this way, but the truth is that Buddhism could not have normal or desirable meetings with society and that the meetings were made on the negative and distorted frame. Various evil laws related to Buddhism, with 'the law of property management for the Buddhist order' as its representative, were prepared to make Buddhism subject to the government and refracted by the ruling ideology. The government controlled the property management right and even the personnel management right of the Buddhist order, and the order was forced to become conservative and patronized by the government.

Also, the expansion of monastery economy due to the income from tourism severed the relation with the fourfold community – male/female monastics and male/female lay people – that should have been made through normal missionary works, and caused disputes over the high-ranked positions of the order involved in interests and privileges. The tradition of pure white to be respected has been plundered by decadent Western culture and ugly and evil capitalist culture, and the secular values have become replete in Buddhist temples as well. However, although Buddhism has, on the surface, collapsed, become subordinate, and been undermined in front of the indiscreet opening to society, the Buddhist spirit and tradition, which is what is truly important, has actively coped with this challenge of history and civilization quite straightforwardly.

Such efforts were manifested roughly in two directions. The first is the efforts to revitalize Buddhism, and the second is the endeavor to fully participate in society. The former has, as its gist, the contents of the plan to revive the Buddhist spirit with the culture and tradition of the Buddha and patriarchs, renovate the education and administrative systems, and actively drive forward missionary work while dealing with the situations in which the Buddhist order has been pillaged and collapsed absurdly under the capitalist political and economic structure. The latter has its contents that, since Buddhism is also a member of the society and people, it should not remain comfortably only within the issues of the order, and that it should proactively have more concerns about reality and the issues of society and take initiatives in solving these problems. Society needs to be normalized and developed, and Buddhists should actively participate in and contribute to this task – these two are directly connected to the issues of the Buddhist society's autonomy and revival. This stance of bodhisattvas is the very original meaning and spirit of Buddhism.

All these efforts showed dualistic features at the early stage. From the 1980's, however, the Buddhism movement that started from the level of the order's own efforts to help itself and the level of the revival of Buddhism, and the social reform movement that focused on the reality of people, came to form a confluence with one frame in harmony and balance through the change of doctrinal understanding and historical awakening. 'The autonomy of Buddhism' and 'anti-dictatorship democratization,' which People's Buddhism professed to make efforts to achieve since 1980, are the outcome of this understanding on Buddhism and history. Based on this result, People's Buddhism movement came to set up the issues of 'the liberation of people' and 'the unification of people' as the primary tasks of the current stage.

As we saw above, People's Buddhism movement is the justified feature of self-manifestation of Buddhism begotten by the consequence of historical impact and awakening that resulted from the traditional Buddhist order becoming a part of capitalist society. This is to defy the conservative and compliant attitude to conform to the ruling system and distorted cultural order. It is also different from the helpless and selfish stance of Hinayana that gives up the essence of Buddhism. It is a progressive Buddhism movement that purports to establish the correct ideology of Buddhism and its status of practices in front of the open society. And, on the other hand, it is a new Mahayana Buddhism movement in that it tries to lead history and the lives of all sentient beings to the Buddhist world and realize the ideal of the Pure Land afresh.

People's Buddhism movement tries to succeed by itself the outcome of the correct self-development of the history of Buddhism. Accordingly, it must converge all the achievements and mistakes of the past Buddhism as its own issues and deal with them, and thereby it should go accomplish the tasks that Buddhism nowadays has. At the same time, People's Buddhism movement must also assume the responsibility to dauntlessly accept the demands of the whole – of Buddhism, of society, of people, of humanity, etc.

The characteristics and several problems of People's Buddhism

People's Buddhism started from the nationalistic situation where Buddhism was placed and, with its acute concerns about social problems, it tried to identify the problems of society and people with the problems of Buddhism. Strictly speaking, the present People's Buddhism involves the following two cases: One is when a Buddhist approach is applied to social issues, and the other is when the efforts to resolve social conflicts and problems are applied to Buddhism. But this is only a natural socio-cultural phenomenon and it seems to serve as a complementary factor that enriches and vitalizes People's Buddhism even more. And, above all, both cases have a basic and common stance to see the problems of Buddhism and society from a unified perspective. Although it still is in the early stage, People's Buddhism has already produced many outcomes pertaining to both Buddhism and society. All this results from the major characteristics of People's Buddhism and the efforts that followed them.

The characteristics of People's Buddhism may be summarized as follows.

Firstly, it has a people-centered perspective. Many new theories and discussion are still being presented on the 'people' in People's Buddhism, but there is a general consensus that 'people' signifies not only the concept of 'sentient beings' with the meaning of universal lives, deluded lives, and suffering lives, but it also refers to the class of lives who are, in their current social stage, suffering, alienated, suppressed, and exploited politically, economically, socially and culturally. People's Buddhism claims that we should take 'people' most seriously in Buddhism and that we need to proactively engage in solving their problems. Since the 'people' are the sentient beings that are suffering more among all sentient beings, the society where the suffering of 'people' is eliminated, that is, the society where the suffering of all sentient beings is eliminated is an ideal society, and it is what Buddhism calls 'the Pure Land.' This is the background of the establishment of People's Buddhism's worldview 'People are the Buddha' which was transformed from the Buddhist doctrine 'All sentient beings are the Buddha.' In People's Buddhism, the 'people' ordinarily include 'all sentient beings,' and People's Buddhism chooses the 'people' as the subject of social reform in order to implement sociological upaya-paramita that fits better in the realization of the Pure Land.

Secondly, People's Buddhism has a strong will to reform society. The preexistent Buddhism was different from People's Buddhism in that the former saw society and history, that is, the world of sentient beings as something static, and thereby understood beings as things that essentially do not change, increase or decrease. This is due to the influence of Laozi and Zhuangzi's Daoism, and it is also because the preexistent Buddhism accepted the Buddhist doctrines in a mistaken way. So, Buddhists used to live passive lives accepting the given modes of being as fate or they relied on the choice and control of their subjective consciousness. Or, they prayed to the Buddha and bodhisattvas and formed a faith-centered religion that depended on higher powers. However, People's Buddhism claims that only social reforms can solve the problems of sentient beings and people, and to make this happen, the people should become the leaders of reforms and conduct social practices with a strong will to build an ideal society.

Thirdly, it claims that the world of the Buddha or the Pure Land is what we establish here on this land, not the world after death or a transcendental world. It also says that the Pure Land means none other than the social community full of happiness where all people rejoice equality, peace and freedom.

Fourthly, the center for Buddhist practices has changed from the monastic community or the order to bodhisattvas who implement People's Buddhism. These bodhisattvas are not just women lay Buddhists in Korea or just lay Buddhists. They are, as the sutras note, monastic bodhisattvas and lay bodhisattvas. That is, whether they are monastics or lay Buddhists, all Buddhists who agree on the ideals of People's Buddhism and jointly implement them come to have the central role in the practices of People's Buddhism as comrades of equal status – but of course this is what should ideally be the case in principle, and in reality there are hierarchies and the relations of instructions between juniors and seniors, more experienced and less experienced people, and monastics and lay people. This perspective is an enormous change compared with the image of Buddhism usually associated with the scenes of Buddhist monastics, as the main subject of Buddhism, chanting and meditating at traditional Buddhist temples in the mountains.

Fifthly, the field of People's Buddhism's practices is not limited to mountain monasteries and mission centers; it includes the field of reality in society as well. For instance, they hold chanting ceremonies and training camps, and offer seminars on Buddhism and society in schools, office buildings, factories and mission centers, and if necessary, in preexisting temples, on streets, etc. They also engage in various fights and strikes to reform the conditions of reality. This way, People's Buddhism, leaving mountain monasteries and the limited space of faith, tries to approach the lives of people closely, share their lives in depth, and solve their problems together. In contrast with the traditional Buddhist meditation and practices that were limited practices in a fixed and closed space, the practice area of People's Buddhism is directed to the field of all sentient beings where its characteristics of ideology-, field-, mobility- and multiplicity-orientedness can be brought to life.

On the other hand, this is also proof that People's Buddhism still lacks such material bases as temples, offices and auditoriums. This is partly because People's Buddhism movement has been led mostly by young monastics and young lay Buddhists. However, there are many positive aspects in this because the effects of practices can propagate through a vast range of areas rather than remain static.

Sixthly, the Pure Land that People's Buddhism depicts and the features of the ideal society it wishes to achieve have significantly socialist – even communist – characters. This point tells us that People's Buddhism is in a politically tricky position in the current South Korean society. That People's Buddhism aims to achieve a socialist or communist world may be said to have resulted from the political and economic situation of South Korean society. The structure of the South Korean economy is such that it introduced foreign capital and maintained a high economic growth policy with exports, which begot a class of so many people in relative poverty. And any attempt to solve this problem cannot but fail due to the desire of self-reproduction of monopoly and comprador capital and the exploitation structure resulting from craving. In the end, they began to recognize that this structure was the capitalist structure of distorted form. Also, they came to know that the political and social system which perpetuated this structure was supported by strong military forces and foreign powers. They started to think that the way to solve this problem lies in changing this political and economic system from the foundation. They found the model of this solution in the socialist (communist) system that proclaimed to be overcoming the evils of capitalism, and they came to pay much attention to it.

These thoughts and perspective were seriously accepted by the people of many classes who believed that social reforms could solve their and their neighbors' problems, and also by the intellectuals who did not comply with the dishonest and immoral forms of social order in South Korean society. So, the people with this perspective built up a wide range of people's movement power. People's Buddhism movement was affected by this influence, and People's Buddhism came to align with the group of people's movement because it also thought of the liberation of people as a primary issue. The only difference between these two movements is that People's Buddhism movement added the Buddhist meaning of the Pure Land to the world that people's movement in society was directed to. For this reason, People's Buddhism movement could have, on one hand, an occasion in which it could socio-scientifically strengthen the characteristics of the Pure Land; and, on the other, the world that society's people's movement aimed for received the grandeur and contents of the Buddhist ideal and religious Pure Land and could come to depict the vision of society that has more enriched contents.

China and many Buddhist countries in Southeast Asia had socialism or communism as their political and economic ideologies, which was closely related to the background that People's Buddhism came to be interested in socialism. The Japanese and English translations of the texts of Southeast Asian Buddhism were introduced to South Korean Buddhist society. These texts described how Buddhism encountered Marxism, how it reacted to Marxism, and how it changed, which clearly taught many points to young Korean Buddhists who were struggling with the reality that the people in South Korea were facing.

Seventhly, People's Buddhism's basic worldview and ontology are grounded on materialist or objective realism. This is closely related to the socialist characteristics of the society for which People's Buddhism aims. With this worldview, People's Buddhism explains the current society and comes to have the future prospect of the world. Accordingly, it makes steady efforts to understand and interpret Buddhist doctrines from this perspective. The writings of Yeo Ikgoo, who tries to create the philosophy of People's Buddhism through the critiques of Mahayana Buddhist thoughts, are especially well-known.

Eighthly, People's Buddhism implies the characteristics of class strife. We can detect the presence of the theory of class struggle beneath the people-centered practices and fight that People's Buddhism puts up. This point also aligns with People's Buddhism's consensus with the assumption of objective reality, the materialist view of history, and the establishment of socialist society. The nonnegotiable line of class strife is received as the basic principle among the leading activists of People's Buddhism movement. Hence, People's Buddhism may be said to be based on the perspective that all intellectuals, the people of religion and students should go ahead for the movement of social reform with the workers' class at its center and that they should help make the workers' class stand tall as the subject.

Ninthly, People's Buddhism is friendly with Early Buddhism but keeps its distance from Mahayana Buddhism. The spirit of People's Buddhism seems to be close to the spirit of Mahayana Buddhism in that both of them emphasize the salvation of sentient beings and participation in history, but the truth is that some activists of People's Buddhism movement criticize firmly Mahayana Buddhist thoughts as idealistic – or, as objective idealism – and are trying to find the theoretical ground and force of materialist thoughts and objective realism from early sutras like *Agamas*. In the theory of People's Buddhism, Mahayana sutras are cited effectively only relative to passages, and People's Buddhism tries to secure its ideological basis from early sutras. This has a lot to do with the following: most of the communized countries in Southeast Asia belong to the regions of Hinayana Buddhism, the foundational texts of these countries are the sutras of *Agamas*, and, above all, early sutras in *Agamas* are relatively realistic and have many parts that can be connected to socialist thoughts.

People's Buddhism has the features roughly summarized above and it has a good purpose and spirit of its own. However, it has many points that need to be revised and complemented. Among these, there are issues that are related to the features of People's Buddhism and thus require serious examinations in depth.

Let us now examine the problems of People's Buddhism, the points that are thought to need revision and supplementation.

Firstly, People's Buddhism suffers from the poverty of historical philosophy based on the Buddhist worldview. People's Buddhism movement trapped Buddhists in puzzlement that was brought about by the theoretical discrepancy that resulted from the movement's intense claim of social engagement. This is because the historical understanding of many Buddhists still remains on the level where they think that the Buddhist world and the problem of history are separate issues. This tendency is generalized to both monastics and lay Buddhists, and it is deeply rooted in history. That is, they believe that Buddhists' getting involved in the problem of history in the name of Buddhism is a corruption of Buddhism or its secularization in a pejorative sense. Therefore, if the social engagement movement of People's Buddhism is to be positively recognized, the historical perspective of Buddhism, that is, its historical philosophy must be established as soon as possible so that Buddhists' social engagement and their concerns about history can be justified. And this historical philosophy needs to be suggested and recognized along with socio-scientific practices.

The philosophy of People's Buddhism would claim, even now of course, that they have their own historical philosophy and they conduct their practices based on that philosophy. But most Buddhists suspect that such historical philosophy of People's Buddhism is similar to the historical philosophy of Marxism, and they do not see how it is connected to preexisting Buddhist thoughts. It is important to have a theory that connects historical philosophy based on materialist realism to Buddhism. However, since the status and role of People's Buddhism need to be considered, it is more important and desperately needed than anything else to derive historical philosophy from the original doctrines and thoughts of Buddhism. For this purpose, I believe that People's Buddhism should pay more attention to Mahayana Buddhist thoughts that may well be said to be a treasure chest of Buddhism's historical philosophy.

Secondly, there is a problem of incomplete understanding of doctrines due to People's Buddhism's preference of Hinayana Buddhism, that is, Early Buddhism and their exclusion of Mahayana Buddhism. This problem is also related to 'the realist worldview' that People's Buddhism accepts. As was mentioned above regarding the features of People's Buddhism, there are ample reasons that People's Buddhism is interested in Early Buddhism.

However, it seems that such a preferential thought might be functioning in terms of the criteria on which of the two has more socialist elements, Mahayana or Hinayana, which is materialistic, and which recognizes the existence of objective real beings more easily. However, this is not a fair stance to understand Buddhism. Even if we accept these criteria to play a devil's advocate, we must notice clearly that Early Hinayana Buddhism never recognized materialistic or objective real beings, and, likewise, that Mahayana Buddhism is neither idealistic nor an objective idealism.

This perspective of People's Buddhism resulted from their confusion and preconception in understanding Buddhist doctrines. Early Buddhism is not materialistic and Mahayana Buddhism is not idealistic. To the contrary, it seems that Early Buddhism exerted all its efforts to deny objective real beings – whether they are physical, mental or conceptual – and that Mahayana Buddhism started from the denial of subjective real beings.

The theory of five aggregates, 12 sense fields, and 18 compositional elements of cognition[105] in early sutras does not explain the real being of objective elements; to the contrary, it denies the realness of beings. For instance, the five kinds of elements of beings called five aggregates (form [matter], sensation, conception, volition and consciousness) are not real (substantial) elements of various kinds of realism in Greek Philosophy. As the word 'aggregate' signifies, it means 'accumulated and piled up' and 'arising dependently on conditions' and expresses non-

---

105 The six sense faculties, their six objects and the six consciousness.

independency and non-realness.

> Form [matter] is like a collection of foam.
> Sensation is like bubbles.
> Conception is like shimmers in the air.
> Volition is like a banana plant.
> Consciousness is like magic.
> This is what the World-Honored One [the Buddha] taught.

This passage of an *Agama* explains well the characteristics of five aggregates with metaphors. The theory of 12 sense fields and 18 compositional elements of cognition does not mean that there are various kinds of real beings which relate to one another and change, but that all forms of being – whether they are form [matter], sensation, conception, volition, consciousness, subjective domain, or objective domain – are formed in their mutual interrelations through the process of changes. Hence, the theories of five aggregates, 12 sense fields, 18 compositional elements of cognition, impermanence, non-self and dependent arising, which are discussed in the first half of early *Agamas,* have as their goal the denial of the realness of whatever forms of being they are.

Therefore, all this is to say that all forms of being are formed and go through changes based only on non-realness. This view is actually radical and hard to understand from the general perspective of people who are familiar with the way of viewing the world grounded only on realism. Be it materialism or idealism, or monism, dualism, or pluralism, the Indian subcontinent at the

Buddha's time had cultural and religious climates in which the realist worldview could not be doubted as an obvious truth. So, the explanation of beings, like the worldview that the Buddha suggested in early *Agamas*, which does not presuppose – which denies – realism must have been quite shocking and leaving a lot of room for confusion.

On this understanding, it will be a serious mistake that People's Buddhism interprets, when it accepts the teaching of *Agamas*, the theory of five aggregates, 12 sense fields and 18 compositional elements of cognition as belonging to the category of realism or as a theory on materialistic factors.

On the other hand, I believe that the view of some activists of People's Buddhism that Mahayana Buddhist thoughts are idealism or objective idealism is, in fact, also a misunderstanding. First of all, People's Buddhism has been raising criticisms that Mahayana Buddhism is an alienated system of ideas that excludes reality and practices because of the Mahayana sutras' splendid, vast and profound style of description, that Mahayana sutras use more conceptual terminology compared with early sutras, and that Mahayana Buddhism shows the pinnacle of idealism where various passages of its sutras seem to turn everything to the subjective domain – for example, mind, True Suchness, Consciousness-Only, etc. However, I believe all this resulted from the rash judgements of some activists who did not really have time to calm down and examine the vast volumes of Mahayana texts that assumed historical forms and became historical philosophy in various ways such as Prajnaparamita, Vaitulya, Flower Garland, Lotus, Consciousness-

Only, Zen, Pure Land, etc. – these Mahayana thoughts, of course, have cluded the ontology and worldview of early sutras.

Mahayana Buddhism is not an idealism. To the contrary, we should pay attention, especially in the sutras of Prajnaparamita traditions, to the efforts that these texts make to break down idealistic real beings – or, subjective real beings. Early Buddhism objectivized not only material factors but also psychological factors and emphasized that they are the forms of beings arising dependently on conditions. But it could not point out many defects of subjective preconceptions and the criteria of judgment. That is, Early Buddhism analyzed all forms of being by objectivizing them and performing on them anatomists' rigid surgical operations, but the tenacious delusions and stubbornness of sentient beings made many subjective problems deepened inside. This is why Mahayana Buddhism began to point out the problems that those various, deep-rooted subjective attachment and preconceptions are reified and fixed.

What Mahayana sutras including *The Prajnaparamita* added to Early Buddhism's teaching of dependent arising is the denial of the fixation of this deep-rooted subjective real being. As Mahayana Buddhism handled the issues of subjective errors and bias, its teaching, including *The Prajnaparamita*, came to face a misunderstanding that it was supporting a subjective domain. *The Diamond Sutra* points out and rejects the four marks (the mark of self, of personality, of sentient being, and of life) and it has the famous phrase "A bodhisattva should produce a mind which dwells upon nothing whatsoever," and, in *The Heart Sutra*, there is the following phrase "There is neither wisdom nor the attainment of wisdom" –

all these are related to this issue. Also, the phrase "If a mind arises, all dharmas arise; if a mind ceases, all dharmas cease" in *The Awakening of Faith* and the teaching in *The Flower Garland Sutra* "All things are created by the mind alone" should not be accepted with ontological interpretations; to the contrary, they must be understood as propositions regarding practices. In other words, they should not be interpreted as subjectivism in such a way that beings arise and cease depending on the way a mind works, but these propositions need to be accepted as remarks that encourage and elevate a bodhisattva's will to engage in practices. They must be accepted with the interpretation that, even in such a culture like India's caste system where everything is accepted as fate, a bodhisattva can change his or her own form of being and the form of being of the society with his or her own ontological decision and practices.

This initiating-subject view of Buddhism – which denies reliant, static and fatalist worldviews – was already quite a revolutionary idea on practices at the time Mahayana Buddhism started. And, of course, the term 'mind' frequently used in Mahayana sutras has a completely different meaning from the mind in the area of contemporary psychology. The mind in Buddhism meant a special name or a general term for the organic relations and changes of all sentient beings, as repeatedly emphasized in *The Awakening of Faith*, *The Flower Garland Sutra*, the studies of the Consciousness-Only School, etc. The 'consciousness' in 'Consciousness-Only' means the same.

As shown above, interpreting Mahayana Buddhist thoughts as idealistic is completely mistaken. The basic stance of both

Mahayana sutras and early sutras is non-realism. The only point that distinguishes Buddhism from other religions or thoughts will be whether the given system is a realism or a non-realism. To overcome real beings and to explain, live and practice in the world with no presupposition of real beings are the features and pride of Buddhism. Hinayana Buddhism focused on the denial of objective real beings, and Mahayana Buddhism added subjective real beings among its targets and pointed out their problems. (Of course *Agamas* also emphasize, with the theory of five aggregates and 12 sense fields, the truth of dependent arising in the various domains of cognition, but I believe that Early Buddhism kept its composure to correctly cognize even these domains by objectivizing them.)

On the other hand, People's Buddhism has often criticized Mahayana Buddhist thoughts as 'objective idealism,' but most of these criticisms have also been brought about by the lack of understanding of the terminology and concepts of sutras, and by the misunderstanding of dependent arising and emptiness. And if we wanted to address this issue further, there would be too many other cases of misunderstanding of this sort to enumerate one by one. The world of dependent arising and the world of emptiness are the basic thoughts of Buddhism that have continued from early sutras to Mahayana sutras, and to interpret even these thoughts as subjective or objective idealism is to seriously distort Buddhism. 'The world of dependent arising' means that, if we view beings from the mode of their formation and also from the point of present time, these beings are not the forms of real (substantial) being due to spatial interrelations and temporal variations. This is a completely different story from the denial of the existence of real being behind ideas [Vorstellungen], that is, the denial of the external world as in the case of idealists' claims.

Let us look at 'idealism' for a while. Fichte's early philosophy sees the self as the only real being which is the origin of action and thinking, and it takes this world as established by the self so that the self can act in there. This philosophy is called subjective idealism. Schilling's early and middle period philosophy supplemented objectivity to this philosophy of self and established natural philosophy. Through the system of transcendental idealism, he arrived as far as at his identity philosophy that, although the subject and object, or the mind and matter confront each other independently, both of these are in fact none other than the two phenomena, forms, attributes, or modes of the absolute identity which is their common essence. This philosophy is called objective idealism.

However, what is obvious is that, whether it is subjective idealism, objective idealism, or Hegel's absolute, logical idealism, all these views are based on realism. And this is the point that differentiates them from Buddhist ontology. Neither Hegel nor Marx, Marx who is claimed to have overcome Hegel, could get out of the idea of Western dualistic realism, which started from Descartes, that saw as separate entities the cognitive subject and the being as object. In contrast, Buddhism belongs to a different level than any kind of realism regardless of its being monism, dualism or pluralism; and Buddhism has the worldview of non-self, impermanence, dependent arising and emptiness.

In addition, let me briefly address the difference between

Western dialectics and the Buddhist teaching of dependent arising. Western dialectics is such that there exist A (for instance, matter), B (cognition), C, D, … and they relate to one another and undergo changes – this is the dialectics based on dualistic or pluralistic realism. Or, it is about the way A progresses to B, C, etc. through A's self-alienation, change and development – this is the dialectics grounded on monistic realism. In contrast, Buddhism does not even recognize the realness of A, B or C. This is due to the features of dependent arising, and, according to Buddhism, the world is those dependently arising factors (aggregates, sense fields, compositional elements of cognition) changing and developing. So, although both Western dialectics and the Buddhist teaching of dependent arising address the relations of changes, since the former is based on realism but the latter is not, the difference in their perspectives can never be bridged. From this discussion, it is clear that the way People's Buddhism understood Mahayana Buddhism as idealistic and Hinayana Buddhism as materialistic or as an objective realism was completely absurd.

Let us examine one more problem. People's Buddhism praises highly the norms of practices and virtues encouraged in early sutras including *Agamas* but criticizes Mahayana Buddhism as abstract and [un]realistic.

First of all, compared with Mahayana sutras, early sutras like *Agamas* have many dharma teachings that are based on more ordinary, everyday lives of the people at that time and are also close to the historical Buddha's teaching. So, it is understandable that people feel more familiar with, and more easily accept early sutras. However, if People's Buddhism wishes to address the issues of history and social practices, it must know that what early sutras teach with the Four Noble Truth, the Noble Eightfold Path, the four bases of mindfulness, and the 37-aids to enlightenment, and so on, do not belong to the level of constructing a new history or of setting a direction to sentient beings, but that all these are the virtues of practices directed only towards enlightenment (bodhi).

The enlightenment and liberation in Early Buddhism means the realm of arhats (non-birth, no arising) who have realized by experience impermanence, non-self and dependent arising. So, what early sutras teach as the virtues and practices of practitioners may be said to have the characteristics as the methods of realizing the dependent arising of beings (five aggregates) rather than to discuss social practices. Compared with this, Mahayana Buddhism clearly made one more step forward. This is why Mahayana Buddhism may well be called 'Sentient Beings' Buddhism' and 'Historical Buddhism,' and this point is manifested even from the title of 'bodhisattva,' who is the initiating-subject of practices in Mahayana Buddhism. "Bodhisattva" is a combination of the two words "bodhi" and "sattva" where 'bodhi' is enlightenment and 'sattva' has the meaning of 'history,' 'all sentient beings' and 'reality.'

To explain this again, it is bodhisattvas or Mahayana Buddhism that added, to the arhats' transparent and static worldview, the historical features that incorporate vow, upaya and wisdom within the will [to] change. The features of bodhisattvas' practices and the world that Mahayana sutras depict in lengthy and extensive ways are about the historical practice (sattva), which is full of a variety of will to experiment, that is based on the worldview of dependent arising (bodhi).

This way, bodhisattvas make Buddhism proceed from the domain of Hinayana arhats, who settle comfortably in the level of enlightenment, to the world of history, to the world of space and time, to our very reality of the present day. Therefore, I believe that it is not just Early Buddhism but also Mahayana Buddhism that People's Buddhism must necessarily examine once again and learn from as the origin of teaching.

Thirdly, People's Buddhism is inclined to socialism. This is also a feature of People's Buddhism, but I believe there are many points that need to be revised and supplemented. People's Buddhism is paying attention to socialism probably because its attention is based on its socio-scientific judgements, or because it might be grounded on the way People's Buddhism understands the Buddhist doctrines. However, from the perspective of Buddhist doctrines, we can see that Buddhism has a lot of capitalist characteristics as well as socialist tendencies. These days, most of progressive Buddhists in particular, frequently admit implicitly that the doctrines Buddhism presents and the world it aims for are socialistic, but we need to examine this point one more time.

People's Buddhism understands Buddhism in terms of socialist characteristics, and this is because it follows the various doctrines and virtues of practices in Early Buddhism. For instance, the teachings of 'no desire,' 'no possession,' 'diligence,' 'frugality,' 'equality' and 'no killing (no extortion),' or the sangha community [in this context, the monastic community] which is morality- and ideology-oriented but with a smack of communist character – all these are close to the virtues that socialism has tried to instill and realize from the outset. Also, the teaching of dependent arising looks like materialist dialectics to People's Buddhism. Due to these reasons, there is much possibility to interpret Buddhism as having a socialistic character (actually, the communist blocks in Southeast Asia are these days attempting to combine Buddhism with Marxism in such a way).

I find this rather positive, of course, because it shows us that we can apply and realize the doctrines and thoughts of Buddhism appropriately in accordance with the situations of the time and also with the perspective needed. However, the problem is that there are many particular and universal conditions involved in the issues of the future of humanity and Korean people. And, above all, these conditions change and undergo revisions amid their dynamic relations. For this very reason, we should not nail Buddhist thoughts as having a socialist character at the start. Furthermore, Korean people are facing a situation in which they should complete a world-historical task to nationally harmonize and unify the capitalist system and the socialist system in their future. This task requires wise and creative thoughts and practices based on justice and morality in all aspects of culture, thoughts, ideology, politics and economics.

Therefore, considering the historical task that People's Buddhism should assume in the future, I believe that understanding Buddhism only in terms of socialist colors is, in fact, voluntarily reducing and standardizing the various and rich assets of Buddhism. To make my points somewhat schematic and simple, let me say that we need to affirm that the thoughts of Early Buddhism have strong socialist colors, but, along with this, we must notice that Mahayana Buddhist thoughts are intensely adding the capitalist spirit to such a socialist character.

We do not even have to mention that both Early Buddhism and Mahayana Buddhism start with the basic virtues based on equality, harmony, no-killing, fraternity, temperance and diligence. However, we must pay attention to the point that Mahayana Buddhism is making an extraordinary, historical interpretation of these virtues compared with the interpretation of Early Buddhism. Early Buddhism takes desire as something negative, but Mahayana Buddhism gives it a positive interpretation. But of course this presupposes the insight into the essence [?] of desire, its non-realness. Further, Mahayana Buddhism takes desire as a basis and uses it actively to obtain enlightenment and achieve the Pure Land. This may be called 'a conversion of ideas.'

The compassion and love of bodhisattvas are affections directed toward history and all sentient beings, and they are enormous historical desires that aid and liberate sentient beings and build the Pure Land. However, this is taboo in Hinayana Buddhism. Arhats see through the non-realness (dependently arising features) of life and history and aim to be liberated from the bondage of realness, that is, from the suppression of history. However, Mahayana bodhisattvas, having active affections and desires as their bases, take one more step forward from there and try to transform impermanent and illusory beings and history to a magnificent suffering-free world of the Pure Land. Of course the Pure Land that bodhisattvas want to achieve is also empty and arises dependently. So, they know that the

Pure Land is an illusion [an illusory phenomenon], but it is the world of history, and also it is bodhisattvas' practices that they are making while knowing their illusoriness. This is called 'compassion with no conditions,' and it means 'compassion not grounded in realism.' Also, it is the 'compassion like an illusion [illusory compassion],' and it means 'historical practices like illusions [illusory historical practices]' that 'beings like illusions [illusory beings]' make in order to achieve 'the Pure Land like an illusion [the illusory Pure Land].'

Mahayana Buddhism also notes that ordinary people's selfish and deluded desires are of course vices that should be rejected. However, it claims that bodhisattvas, who have seen through the truth of dependent arising, can sustain open attitudes to change and develop history and that they can also demonstrate relaxed and rich historical imagination. This Mahayana Buddhist perspective is different from the capitalist ideas that guarantee and stimulate a person's desires and his or her will to increase desires. What I am saying is, though, that Buddhism should not be generally accepted, in such a simple way, only from the Hinayanist stance that discards desires, will, and even the active stance of engagement. Mahayana Buddhism accommodates the basic thoughts and norms of practices taught in Hinayana Buddhism, but it still implies an active view of ontology and the awareness of history that make us take a step farther and accept positively, expand, and enrich everything.

Hinayana Buddhism teaches that we should not be attached to or acquire any forms of being – be it mental or physical – due to their impermanence. Nothing deserves any special affection or attention. We should discard everything one by one so that we can be thoroughly 'poor.' It goes the same with history. In Mahayana Buddhism, however, although everything is a being of impermanence, non-self, and dependent arising, our accepting and actively manifesting everything cannot obstruct us even a bit as long as we know their impermanence, non-self and dependent arising. History becomes a ground for the practices of bodhisattvas' infinite self-realization (this point may be closely related to the issue of 'freedom' in humanity's historical manifestation).

The sangha, which was the community of no possession, was the center of Early Buddhism, but, in Mahayana sutras, it expanded to the various lives of bodhisattvas, businessmen, lay men and lay women. The people of various jobs such as merchants, boatmen, soldiers, slaughterers and farmers appear as bodhisattvas. These various features might not have to be compared with the modern economic system called socialistic or capitalistic. However, some hasty activists of People's Buddhism movement might have understood that Buddhism is the kind of religion that denies desires and possession, and thereby they might be thinking that Buddhism cannot meet with capitalism and that it is socialism that is friendly with Buddhism. If this is the case, they must examine and reflect on their mistakes.

Anyhow, People's Buddhism can now choose the line of socialist orientation, of capitalism, of compromise and supplementation of both, or of a third kind of social system and character based on both the two. However, what is obvious here is that everything belongs to the domain of historical upayas that must be chosen according to the situations of the time. Therefore,

I do not believe that there can exist any fixed or confirmed special characteristics of society that People's Buddhism should aim for.

If People's Buddhism has another realistic and practical problem, it is that it neglects the internal issues of Buddhism, for instance, such issues as the effective and rational reform of the order's administration, missionary works, education, translation of sutras, etc. These are in fact important issues where People's Buddhism secures the support and affection of their own followers, but it has a significant tendency to overlook them due to practically imminent conditions and insufficient capacities. If People's Buddhism has a will to truly inherit the traditions of Buddhism and explore future Buddhism, it must deal with Buddhism's proper problems. I also believe this is a very important problem in that it is directly connected to People's Buddhism's capacities and the expansion of its conditions.

The theory of practice in Mahayana Buddhism

What would be the most Mahayanistic in Mahayana Buddhism? It would probably be its unifying character. Would there be anything more enormous and ambitious than the task of tying enlightenment (bodhi) and history (sattva) together?

The two mainstreams of contemporary philosophy, that is, (1) the efforts to research the process with which knowledge is obtained and the criteria of knowledge, and (2) the persistent investigation of personal and social situations we are in, are both contributing to the issues of humanity with significant appeal and merits. The truly unifying factor underlying modern philosophy is the efforts to comprehensively understand the epistemic and social restrictions that limit the scope of our choices but at the same time help us make choices. Due to these efforts, the work to organically connect the understanding of these two kinds of restrictions has become the present task of practical sciences.

This discussion coincides with the necessity to make our philosophy proceed, on one hand, in the direction of abstract discourse and establishments of criteria, and at the same time, on the other hand, provide more concrete and specific modes for social issues. I believe that demanding these two requirements simultaneously cannot be said to be a contradiction. And it seems to me that the primary reason that contemporary humans are experiencing the confusion in the studies of liberal arts and the conflict in sociology is that we have not yet succeeded in combining the thoughts and practices of these two kinds of characteristics. So, analytic philosophy and phenomenology have been helpless in front of historical imagination and special social problems, and Marxism and utilitarian social sciences have showed a lot of unreasonableness and loopholes in their application of epistemic issues and logic and thereby have had to face skepticism about their historical achievements. Would it be an excessive dogmatism if I should say that the solution to these current problems was already conceived in the thoughts of Mahayana Buddhism?

The distinguishing mark of Mahayana Buddhist thoughts was the task of combining nicely the aspect of 'bodhi' and the aspect of 'sattva': the former grasps the structure of beings and the characteristics and principle of arising and change, and the latter involves the ideological stance and norms on social practices. This was to unify, in one life and this life as the ground of history, the epistemic aspect and the domain of practices both of which belong to different levels from a logical point of view. This might be about the same principle that whiteness and hardness are unified in one Go stone. That is, 'bodhi' is to anatomize the realness of being and to be liberated from its fetter, and 'sattva' is various practices of lives that unfold based on temporary and provisional realism. 'Sattva' is to see this as red or blue, go left or right, or build a one-story or two-story house; 'bodhi' focuses its ontological contemplation on the 'thing' in 'this thing' in such a sentence as '…. does this thing,' and secures the original source of the domain of practices.

It is clear that 'bodhi' and 'sattva' belong to different levels of logical application, and I believe that each has constructed its own domain of self-contentment. Perhaps this is why practitioners in Hinayana Buddhism could settle comfortably in the aspect of 'bodhi' but still remain in the realm of nirvana. However, the various actual problems of history, that is, the issues on the level of 'sattva' were too severe and intense to have our faces turned away from them. Masters in Zen traditions could not contribute to the achievement issues of society or history, even after they attained enlightenment, because the logical levels were different. In a nutshell, their lives had only 'bodhi,' and they were biased and limping historical lives.

On the other hand, however, People's Buddhism currently seems to be engrossed in the social and practical problems of 'sattva' and neglects or misunderstands the 'bodhi' aspect. I believe that the stance that People's Buddhism has at this present stage may well be regarded as 'Marxismsattva,' not as 'bodhisattva.' When we nowadays say 'Let us negate the weaknesses of both Mountain Buddhism [106] and People's Buddhism, combine their strengths, and make both of them better," it purports to mean that we should combine in a unifying way the stance inclined to 'bodhi' and the features of Buddhism biased in favor of 'sattva.'

Mahayana Buddhism does not simply or easily accept the concept of 'bodhisattva' as a universal or abstract concept. 'Bodhi' is a logical understanding about the truth of being, and 'sattva' means some modes of practice and stance that correspond to specific and concrete realities at a given time. Especially, 'sattva' is a task to connect a domain of specificity and concreteness to the domain of universal 'bodhi,' and the most important and expansive contents of 'sattva' are upaya-paramitas. "Upaya-paramita" is a word combining "upaya" and "paramita." This word means that a specific historical upaya is neither fixed at the upaya itself nor changes simply following the flow of history; the word means that it is the upaya that has obtained the original freedom from the feature of history itself (this is because upaya is united with the basic stance of 'bodhi').

In Mahayana Buddhism, 'sattva' is 'bodhisattva' and 'upaya-paramita.' It is concrete, realistic and specific. And the principle that makes all this possible is bodhisattvas' transparent but ardent vows and compassion. Sattva is about the positive, warm and caring mind concerned about history. It is about the active nature of being that

---

106 By 'Mountain Buddhism' is meant 'traditional Buddhism found in mountain temples.'

makes sitting or lying impossible. Mahayana Buddhism made 'sattva' strongly connected to Hinayana Buddhism in which only 'bodhi' existed, and this is why Mahayana Buddhism is called Historical Buddhism, Sentient Beings' Buddhism and Practical Buddhism.

I am convinced that the historical spirit and practice of this Mahayana 'bodhisattva' will give an important ideological inspiration for the problems of thoughts and practices that contemporary humanity are facing. It will make the combination of liberal arts and sociology possible, and it will have philosophy and society meet. In social sciences as well, it will unify critical rationalism and critical theory, combine the issue of freedom and the issue of equality, and have capitalism and socialism reconcile and learn from each other's strengths. And it will eventually let all people in the world make peace and love one another.

This essay "For the Mahayanist Progress of People's Buddhism movement" was Hyun-Eung Sunim's manuscript prepared for the class of the members of 'The Monastic Community Association of Mahayana Buddhism.'

6

Basic Buddhism and Mahayana Buddhism

"Basic Buddhism and Mahayana Buddhism"
appeared in *The Buddhist Review* 44 (Fall 2010).

Basic Buddhism and Mahayana Buddhism

What is 'Basic Buddhism'?

I have always thought that most people do not really understand the characteristics and meaning of Mahayana Buddhism. In other words, I believe that they do not accurately understand the difference between Basic Buddhism (all branches of Buddhism that take as central teachings impermanence, non-self, dependent arising, emptiness, prajna, etc.) and Mahayana Buddhism. This might be excessive arrogance or misjudgment on my part, but I have thought about it for a long time. It was presumptuous of me but I had this suspicion when I listened to the dharma talks and lectures of senior monks, and some feeling of complaint found its place on one side of my mind when I reviewed Korean and foreign Buddhologists' views and claims through books and other publications. The reason is that there was something mostly unsatisfactory about the contents of those dharma talks and publications because they did not clearly know the difference between Basic Buddhism and Mahayana Buddhism.

First of all, I propose to classify all the various teachings that appear in the 2,600-year old stream of Buddhism mainly with the terminology of 'Basic Buddhism' and 'Mahayana Buddhism.'

This is the first time that I try the new name of 'Basic Buddhism.' This Buddhism is a separate kind from the series of Buddhism called Early Buddhism, Fundamental Buddhism, Hinayana Buddhism, etc. With this terminology of Basic Buddhism, and by having it compared with the teachings of Mahayana Buddhism, I am going to talk about the Buddhist prospect needed in our time.

Then, what are the contents of Basic Buddhism and Mahayana Buddhism?

Although 'Early Buddhism' is value-neutral in its expression, terminologically it does not show the features or status of the contents of Early Buddhism. It only has a meaning of 'the Buddhism that was chronologically at the beginning stage,' and it seems to be used to refer to the Buddhism that lasted for some period from the time of the Buddha.

'Fundamental Buddhism' is another term that refers to Early Buddhism. Since 'Fundamental' is understood in relation to 'root, source, origin, etc.,' this word is preferred by those who emphasize the original prototype's rightfulness and absoluteness, and thus it is a rather argumentative expression.

'Hinayana Buddhism' refers to all of Early Buddhism, Fundamental Buddhism, Theravada Buddhism, Nikaya Buddhism, etc., but the truth is that it is a term that Mahayanist Buddhists used to refer to Nikaya Buddhism with a pejorative nuance. These days, we use this term rather cautiously, or we use it in special occasions when we compare Nikaya Buddhism with Mahayana Buddhism.

In contrast, 'Basic Buddhism' uses the term 'basic' that has the meaning of 'foundation, ground, basis and standard.' Accordingly, the expression 'Basic Buddhism' signifies that it is the Buddhism that keeps both the contents of 'impermanence, non-self, dependent arising, emptiness and prajna,' which are the most basic teachings of Buddhism, and the contents of all the upayas and efforts to know those teachings (not only the four bases of mindfulness and the Noble Eightfold Path, but also the 37-aids to enlightenment, the practice of cessation and observation, meditations in Zen Buddhism, and so on).

Since the contents of this Basic Buddhism constitute the basis of Early Buddhism and abhidharmas, the teachings of Early Buddhism and abhidharmas can be called Basic Buddhism.

Also, although the mode of expressions is different, Zen Buddhism also has prajna and emptiness as its basic contents and thus may well be regarded as Basic Buddhism. Mahayana sutras and treatises have as their basic contents impermanence, non-self, dependent arising, and prajna and emptiness. For this reason, we may also say that Mahayana Buddhism basically has the teachings of Basic Buddhism. However, since Mahayana Buddhism addresses a separate domain of different character in addition to such basic aspects, we call it Mahayana Buddhism and distinguish it from Basic Buddhism.

Accordingly, the concept of 'Mahayana Buddhism' is actually in contrast with the concept of 'Basic Buddhism' rather than with the concept of 'Early Buddhism' or 'Fundamental Buddhism.' Then, what is it that was included in Mahayana Buddhism as a separate domain in addition to the domain of Basic Buddhism, and why did it have to be added?

The emergence of Buddhism and its background

The basic teachings of Buddhism are the teachings of impermanence, non-self, dependent arising, emptiness and prajna. These teachings brought about the effects that helped people realize the transience and groundlessness of being and thereby liberate themselves from the realness of being. Also, these teachings, as they went through the period of Nikaya Buddhism and abhidharmas, unfolded and were made into more sophisticated theories with doctrinal development and establishment. These are the very Basic Buddhism.

However, this teaching of Basic Buddhism had a stance to interpret and explain life and the world. That is, Basic Buddhism awakened us to how to see the world, but it did not explain how to change and transform the world and what world we should make.

The teachings of impermanence, non-self, and dependent arising are based on a relativistic worldview, and thus it does not establish any real beings. No being or value of this world is absolute, and they are all transient and groundless. In contrast, the Indian society of the Buddha's time had Brahmanism, of which the central doctrine is based on a universal real being 'Brahman.' Brahmanism taught that all values originate from Brahman. Besides Brahmanism, there were at that time many other prevalent teachings that professed a variety of realisms such as objective realism, subjective realism, monistic realism, pluralistic realism, etc.

However, as Buddhism appeared, the Indian society was dichotomized mainly by many religions that put up various realisms and Buddhism that did not recognize any real being. All the other religions and teachings besides Buddhism were based on realism. Naturally, there emerged heated debates between non-realist Buddhism and many realist religions.

'If the world is impermanent and devoid of self [atman], it means, after all, that the world is groundless. Then, why should we live lives?'

'Does life need to be extended at all?'

'How should we live our household lives?'

'If the world is untrue and groundless, do we need to reconstruct our society?'

'Can the theory that the world is untrue and groundless suggest the direction and method to change the world?'

These questions must have been poured on Buddhists. Is the world that does not presuppose real beings possible at all? It must not have been something imaginable or understandable. If there exists no real being like God or the nature of being, where does the value of our lives originate and where should the motive of our actions be based? Buddhists themselves as well as the followers of other religions could not but naturally raise these questions.

The task to find doctrinal solutions from the inside of Buddhism was the dilemma produced by these points. And this issue was naturally raised in the Indian society of the time amid the process of numerous debates conducted with other religions and systems of thoughts than Buddhism.

However, it must have been difficult for Buddhists to explain and make understood the worldview of impermanence and non-self in the process of debates done with those who had the realist worldview. Further, it must have been even more difficult to explain how to live a life with the stance that everything is transient and groundless.

Many sutras describe such situations. For instance, *The Prajnaparamita Sutra* (*The Diamond Sutra, The Shorter Version of the Mahaprajnaparamita Sutra, The Mahaprajnaparamita Sutra*, etc.), which is an early Mahayana sutra, has quite a few descriptions with the following import: "If one did not get surprised or fearful when he or she hears the teaching that there exists no real being whatsoever, it would be a very rare event."

Most people live their lives necessarily with the presupposition of the existence of real beings, whatever kinds of real beings they might be. For this reason, it would be quite difficult [for them] to accept the teaching that such real beings do not exist. Also, in the case of the life that does not presuppose any real beings, one would find the issue of how to live too vague and obscure. This is where Buddhism, which supports impermanence, non-self and emptiness, found it difficult to persuade the general public. The editors of Mahayana sutras like *The Prajnaparamita Sutra* were fully aware of this problem, and they expressed its difficulties.

In other words, some real beings (for instance, God, Brahman, good, reason, honor, wealth, pleasure, etc.) are generally presupposed at the bottom of people's lives and actions. And they receive the motives and goals of their actions from those real beings. If they accept the Buddhist teachings of impermanence, non-self and emptiness, they will come to lose the ground of realness. For this reason, they cannot understand how the motives of lives and the rightfulness and necessity of actions are established, and this is why they 'become surprised, fearful and at a loss.'

This situation has made Buddhism require 'an active and positive view of history based on dependent arising' with which to resist other religions and systems of ideas grounded on realism. Also, internally, Buddhism needed to unfold more advanced Buddhist theories that could let Buddhists, who understood the truth of dependent arising, live their lives enthusiastically. The teachings of Basic Buddhism came to develop into 'the Buddhism that includes new contents' in the process of responding to those doctrinal challenges. This is the very 'Mahayana Buddhism.'

Then, what are the new contents?

Buddhism requires the stance of life that we can liberate ourselves from the realness of being and the world through the non-realist worldview of impermanence, non-self, dependent arising and emptiness, and that we can eliminate all sufferings from their origins. The new contents of Mahayana Buddhism are about a certain stance and method that enable us to proceed one more step and live practical and active lives while keeping such a non-realist worldview.

Buddhists have the worldview based on the truth of dependent arising that does not presuppose the existence of real beings. Can they really live actively and passionately while they keep the view that the world is transient and groundless?

A solution based on calm judgment appeared here. 'It's transient, groundless, like a dream' is a fact judgment, not a value judgment. To say that the world is transient, like a dream and groundless is to say that reality is such and such, which belongs to the domain of fact judgment. That something is beautiful or ugly, that I am happy or I am suffering, or that I will do something or I will do nothing – these belong to the domain of value judgment.

It might conventionally be thought that 'It's transient, groundless, like a dream' is connected to 'I should stop it, I must not do anything, Oh, it's sad, etc.,' but these two groups cannot have any logical correlations. That is, fact judgment and value judgement belong to areas of two completely different logical levels. Mahayana Buddhism believed that there should be no problem in combining fact judgment and value judgment, and it actively tried their combination.

Whiteness and hardness are the contents of different levels, but they form a stone in Go game. Likewise, we presuppose the fact judgment that the world is untrue and groundless but we still act with a certain goal which is a specific value judgment. This is to combine the two logical domains of different characteristics and open a new horizon of life.

Mahayana Buddhism teaches us that we should be based on the fact judgment that this world is untrue and groundless but that we must put up a transparent value judgment like 'compassion' and 'vow' and live active and passionate lives through various upaya-paramitas.

Let us take an example. Movies function through the phenomena of our optical illusions created by the continuous movements of segmented frames of films. Movies made of these optical illusions are untrue and groundless, transient, and they are like dreams and illusions. This is the case from the perspective of fact judgment. However, people did not discard or eliminate these motion pictures in their early stages by criticizing that they are untrue and groundless illusions. To the contrary, people have continuously developed movies as they have incorporated, into the moving illusory films, humans' dreams, love, sadness, courage, and so on. That is, movies are illusory, but people have embodied [realized] their zeal and passion on this illusoriness. They have done so, but they know that movies are illusory. However, since they know the illusoriness, they have a great fondness for the features of life and dreams embodied in the movies.

Mahayana Buddhists have also tried, in the same context, to put, into the illusory life and world, their zeal and enthusiastic practices based on transparent 'compassion' and 'vow.' However, this would not be possible if we turned our backs on the worldview based on the theory of dependent arising that views the world with impermanence, non-self, emptiness, and prajna. To the contrary, it is possible because it is based on such a worldview of dependent arising, and this is the very subtle point of Mahayana Buddhism – as movies are possible through the property of groundlessness and illusoriness of motion pictures.

This is how Mahayana Buddhism was born.

Why *The Diamond Sutra* is a Mahayana sutra

The Diamond Sutra, which is an early Mahayana sutra composed of questions and answers, starts with the following famous question.

"If people have made a vow to achieve anuttara-samyak-sambodhi [supreme correct enlightenment], how should they keep and control their minds in their everyday lives?"

This is a question on how those who have the worldview of impermanence, non-self and emptiness should live. This question represents the common question shared by both the followers of religions based on realism and the Buddhists of non-realism.

The Buddha answered the question as follows: "Save all sentient beings, but you should not think that you are saving or have saved them." If you give a careful thought on this teaching, you will come to know that it means "Save them without the thought of saving them." This does not mean 'not conducting any actions of saving.' If any actions of saving, etc. were meaningless or unnecessary, the Buddha would have answered "Everything is meaningless, so you had better not do anything."

So, *The Diamond Sutra* encourages men and women to practice numerous good deeds and compassion but at the same time emphasizes the important caveats that they should know the illusoriness of beings, lives, and the world and should not be attached to or keep any of them in their minds. This is the practice of compassion that is not kept in or attached to anything, which is the first teaching of Mahayana, and this is why *The Diamond Sutra* is a Mahayana sutra. Buddhism calls this kind of compassion 'illusory compassion (compassion like an illusion)' and 'unconditioned compassion (compassion without any logical or actual connections),' and this is distinguished from the love or desires based on realism.

"A bodhisattva should produce a mind without dwelling on anything" – this representative phrase of *The Diamond Sutra* has contextually the same meaning. It means that 'the four marks of self, person, sentient beings and life are illusory. So, we should not be attached to any of them. Nevertheless, however, we must produce a mind to act.'

The gist of the message that this phrase purports to convey is that what is important is to produce a mind and act without dwelling, and that this becomes, in the end, the core cardinal point of Mahayana. Accordingly, if we wish to show better the very meaning of Mahayana, we should read the phrase "A bodhisattva should produce a mind without dwelling on anything" as having an emphasis not in 'A bodhisattva should produce a mind' but in 'without dwelling on anything.' Not dwelling on any mark or concept, but still producing a mind and acting – this is the pure mind and subtle practices taught in Mahayana.

The expression of 'pure,' which appears in Buddhist sutras or the collections of Zen masters' dialogues, often means the features of the dependently arising world rather than 'clean.' It will be correct to understand this 'pure' as describing a certain transparent state of 'being revealed in the relations with other things and changing without substantiality.' And it will be appropriate to think of 'the pure mind' as a mind that understands such a state well.

For instance, it means the same when Zen Buddhism teaches "Examine the mind and see purity,' and when *The Nirvana Sutra* and others say 'permanence, bliss, self, and purity,' this 'purity' is not about something clean, but it instead refers to the world of dependent arising and prajna. When we come across the phrases with the word "purity" in the sutras or the collections of Zen masters' dialogues, it will be mostly correct if we understand it as meaning 'the world of dependent arising.'

Anyhow, 'producing a mind and acting without dwelling on anything,' that is, the practice of compassion conducted with a pure mind may well be said to be the very character of Mahayana Buddhism. Referring to the paragraphs of *The Diamond Sutra* that emphasize these contents, Crown Prince Zhaoming of Liang gave these paragraphs subtitles such as 'Subtle actions without dwelling' and 'Magnificent decoration of the Pure Land.'

Most people believe that the message of *The Diamond Sutra* and other sutras on the prajnaparamita traditions is 'no dwelling,' 'losing the marks or concepts' or 'illuminating emptiness.' However, the truth is that the Mahayanist teaching lies in 'how to act without dwelling' and *The Diamond Sutra* is substantially dedicated to it.

Does *The Heart Sutra* express the teaching of Mahayana Buddhism?

However, if *The Diamond Sutra* shows the teaching of Mahayana Buddhism well, what about *The Mahaprajnaparamitahrdaya Sutra* (in short, *The Heart Sutra*)? Although *The Heart Sutra*, which Korean Buddhism loves to recite in various rituals, belongs to the prajna lineage, we need to see it as emphasizing Basic Buddhism rather than as addressing the issues of Mahayana Buddhism. For *The*

Heart Sutra has 'the illumination of emptiness' as its main contents.

In *The Heart Sutra*, to illuminate and understand that all five aggregates (aggregates of matter and four kinds of mental states) are emptiness is prajnaparamita, and it clarifies the teaching that we overcome all sufferings and achieve enlightenment through this prajnaparamita.

Emptiness means none other than dependent arising, and it is about the phenomena revealed by dependent arising. These phenomena change incessantly without stopping for any moment and they inter-penetrate into all domains mutually relying on one another. These beings, if understood as real beings, do not exist, but it is not the case at all that there are no beings themselves, either. This is why Nagarjuna of ancient India said in his *Mulamadhyamakakarika* that this mode of being might be described as empty, provisional or the middle. Many Mahayana sutras use, in order to describe the world of dependent arising, the concepts of dependent arising, emptiness, dharma, Buddha-Nature, etc., and all these expressions mean the same.

Accordingly, if the teachings of impermanence, non-self, dependent arising, emptiness, etc. are Basic Buddhism, we may well say that *The Heart Sutra* substantially conforms to Basic Buddhism. Unlike *The Heart Sutra*, although such prajnaparamita sutras as *The Diamond Sutra, The Shorter Version of the Mahaprajnaparamita Sutra, The Mahaprajnaparamita Sutra*, etc. basically explain prajna or emptiness, they emphasize, in addition, compassionate actions of various paramitas and the rescue of sentient beings. So, we call them Mahayana Buddhism.

Does the world of Consciousness-Only, the Womb of the Tathagata [Thus Come One, the Buddha] and True Suchness belong to Mahayana Buddhism?

If the teachings of dependent arising, impermanence, non-self and emptiness are Basic Buddhism, then, are the teachings of Consciousness-Only, the Womb of the Tathagata, Dharmadhatu [dharma realm], Dharma-Body, True Suchness, etc. Mahayana Buddhism or Basic Buddhism?

The answer is Basic Buddhism. The expressions of dharma-ness, empty-ness, dependent-arising-ness, and Dharma Body are all synonyms that describe the world of dependent arising. Likewise, Consciousness-Only-ness, dharmadhatu-ness, True-Suchness-ness, and the-Womb-of-the-Tathagata-ness mean the same and they are all synonymous words that show the true features of dependently arising beings. Therefore, if they are to explain the category of dependent arising and emptiness, even if they explain the world using the terminology of emptiness, the Womb of the Tathagata, True Suchness, etc., we must regard them as Basic Buddhism. But, of course, if they have as their basis the teachings of Consciousness-Only, the Womb of the Tathagata, True Suchness, etc. and talk about 'various paramitas and acts of compassion with the stance of no dwelling,' they naturally make Mahayana Buddhism.

If one mentions *The Awakening of Faith*, *The Suramgama Sutra* and *The Flower Garland Sutra* and emphasizes only the mind, the Womb of the Tathagata, True Suchness and the dependent arising of the dharma realm, it is to talk about Basic Buddhism. If someone discusses various paramitas and the acts of compassion in connection to such Basic Buddhism, he or she is teaching Mahayana Buddhism. In light of this point, we must examine well and see clearly if current Korean Buddhism interprets and accepts Mahayana sutras only as Basic Buddhism, or if it accepts and uses these sutras as Mahayana Buddhism.

Is Chinese Zen Buddhism Mahayana Buddhism?

Let us have a look at the case of Chinese Zen Buddhism as well. Is Zen Buddhism Mahayana Buddhism or Basic Buddhism?

Zen Buddhism is a trend of Buddhism that appeared during the Tang and Song Dynasties in China, which was quite some time after Mahayana Buddhism unfolded in India. So, we may naturally think of it quickly as Mahayana Buddhism, but it is in fact not the case. Zen Buddhism can be said to be a special genre in which Indian prajna thoughts, that is, the ideas of emptiness were transformed and expressed in a Chinese way. Many Zen masters have expressed Buddhism through dharma talks, the recitations of verses and various gestures, but most of them handled as the main contents, except for a small number of occasions, the issues of showing the world or prajna and emptiness. Then, we should naturally regard Zen Buddhism as Basic Buddhism rather than as Mahayana Buddhism.

Zen Buddhism especially emphasizes 'enlightenment.' Since the enlightenment in this tradition is an understanding and enlightenment of prajna and emptiness (dependent arising), Zen

Buddhism is actually a Chinese variation of Basic Buddhism.

Could Zen Buddhism then include compassion and paramitas? It must of course include them so that Zen Buddhism should not remain only as Basic Buddhism and instead unfold the style of their Zen traditions in the Mahayanist way. This is to have both wisdom (enlightenment) and compassion, and it is also to combine prajna and upaya. If Zen Buddhism reveals only prajna and emptiness and does nothing else, this is to emphasize only the basic aspect of Buddhism and exclude the aspect of Mahayana Buddhism which is the evolutionary consequence of Buddhism.

If we read the records on Japan's Dr. D. Suzuki about the lecture tours he made in Europe and America in the early 20th Century, we can see that he could give only poor and limited responses when he was often asked questions on whether Zen Buddhism also had concerns about the problems of society and history. Zen Buddhism has a cultural tradition 'to respect and take as important only one's correct eyes [perspective], but not to question his or her behaviors.' Due to this culture, it took a serious view only of enlightenment (on prajna and emptiness), and it came to be replete with the trend to neglect ethical and practical issues. That is, it lacked the reflection and expression of the problems of ethics, society and history.

Of course the teaching of dependent arising, emptiness and prajna is the ground of Buddhism, and it is definitely great and praiseworthy that Zen Buddhism is substantially dedicated to them. However, this is not good enough as it is. Ever since Early Buddhism, Buddhism has come to have Mahayana, which is the wings of historical imagination unique to Buddhism, in addition to its basic worldview. However, Zen Buddhism that appeared a thousand years after the Buddha's passing, although it has expressed the world of prajna and emptiness in a new, Chinese style, has remained in the scope of Basic Buddhism. It is only natural that Zen Buddhism may come to be called Mahayana Buddhism only if Zen Buddhism gets the wings of 'history.'

The Flower Garland Sutra – the quintessence of Mahayana Buddhism

I believe the sutra that best describes the true character of Mahayana Buddhism is *The Flower Garland Sutra.*

The genuinely true character of Mahayana Buddhism is that Mahayana Buddhism has as its basic ground the understanding of dependently arising world with impermanence, non-self, emptiness and True Suchness, but Mahayana Buddhism emphasizes, on top of all this, the practices of enthusiastic and zealous paramitas.

The chapter on the 'ten grounds' in *The Flower Garland Sutra,* which is an early Mahayana sutra, introduces ten-paramitas, and their contents speak well for Mahayana's theory of historical practices. As is widely known, ten-paramitas are six-paramitas of generosity, maintaining precepts, patience under insult, exertion, meditation and prajna combined with additional four-paramitas of upaya, vow, power and wisdom. These four-paramitas added in have the most Mahayanist characteristics.

The following is the explanation of these four-paramitas with a slightly changed order.

The tenth wisdom-paramita means to grasp well, comprehensively and in detail, the life of concrete and specific reality, the world and history. It means very realistic knowledge, wisdom and insight, and it is distinguished from prajna-paramita which means the insights based on dependent arising (emptiness).

The eighth vow-paramita is to establish a specific goal, personally or socially, based on the given time's situations and meaning that are grasped through the tenth wisdom-paramita.

The seventh upaya-paramita means to realize the goal, which is set through the eighth vow-paramita, with a various and appropriate methodology.

The ninth power-paramita means the power to drive upaya-paramita forward powerfully, and this might be seen as a paramita that goes along with upaya-paramita when it is implemented. No matter how accurate cognition we might have on reality (wisdom), goal (vow) and method (upaya), we will not succeed unless we have strong power and conditions to push ahead.

These four-paramitas that continue from six-paramitas are the satisfying historical imagination of Mahayana Buddhism, and they combine with the enlightenment of dependent arising and help manage our exciting historical lives. This is the very magnificent decoration of history and the Pure Land. That is, the basic six-paramitas starting with prajna-paramita, combined with these four-paramitas, finally come to have the world of dependent arising and emptiness obtain the concrete and specific property of history (sattva).

Six-paramitas are personal virtues and they mean the basic Buddhist worldview, and the rest of four-paramitas mean that those

Buddhists who have such virtues and worldview proceed to act, personally and socially, in a specific reality. This is why we can say that these ten-paramitas best express the teachings of Mahayana Buddhism. So, the chapter on the 'ten ground' that emphasizes these ten-paramitas is the core of *The Flower Garland Sutra*, and for this reason, *The Flower Garland Sutra* is the quintessence of Mahayana Buddhism. Accordingly, if *The Flower Garland Sutra* is to be described in a contemporary way, it is the Buddhist theory of social practices, of historical practices.

Mahayana sutras such as *The Pure Land Sutra, The Nirvana Sutra, The Lotus Sutra*, etc. have the same purports. That is, Mahayana sutras do not accept as their purposes an illumination of the mind, an interpretation and an explanation of the world. They are rather filled with the teachings on the prospect about the ideal society (the Pure Land) which is their goal, the stance of practices and the various methodologies to reach the goal.

On the other hand, these ten-paramitas are completely reflected in the chapters on the ten stages of faith, the ten abodes, the ten practices and the ten dedications in *The Flower Garland Sutra,* which seem to be modified forms of chapters of *The Ten Grounds Sutra*. And such Mahayana sutras and sastras as *The Vimalakirti Sutra, The Sutra on Understanding Profound and Esoteric Doctrine, The Yogacarabhumi Sastra*, etc. emphasize ten-paramitas as their main contents. So, ten-paramitas have truly become the basis of the theory of Mahayana Buddhism.

The Chinese Flower Garland School's misunderstanding of *The Flower Garland Sutra*

On the other hand, although 'the worldview and theory of historical practices of Buddhism' with ten-paramitas at its center is the most basic and core theory of *The Flower Garland Sutra*, the Chinese Flower Garland School in the Tang Dynastic thought that the main core of *The Flower Garland Sutra* was the theory of dependent arising such as the dependent arising of dharma realm, the complete interpenetration of the six characteristics of conditioned phenomena, the ten mysterious aspects of dependent arising, and so on. Also, they emphasized that the appreciation and reflection on such a theory of dependent arising, which was called the Flower Garland scriptural study and meditation practice, was a very important method of contemplation. The Chinese Flower Garland School interpreted *The Flower Garland Sutra*, the representative sutra in Mahayana Buddhism, within the frame of Basic Buddhism, which I believe was a mistake.

Due to this mistake, Korea, China and Japan, all of which were influenced by the Chinese Flower Garland School, came to have a tendency of understanding *The Flower Garland Sutra* as a sutra that teaches the theory of dependent arising. The theory of dependent arising had already been doctrinally systematized through the periods of Madhyamaka, Consciousness-Only and Abhidharmas. The Chinese Flower Garland School's theory of the dependent arising of dharma realm does not seem to be a theory that has made progress from their Indian predecessors'. Even if it has made progress in its own way, the theory of dependent arising still belongs to the category of Basic Buddhism.

The birth of bodhisattvas, and their dream and practices

It is very interesting to notice that the ideal model of life at the time of Basic Buddhism was 'arhat,' but it was replaced by 'bodhisattva' as Mahayana Buddhism appeared. Let us compare the worlds of arhats and bodhisattvas.

Basic Buddhism is a teaching that takes as its primary goal 'the interpretation (enlightenment)' of life and the world. So, as a consequence of this teaching, it was to realize the non-realness of life and the world, liberate ourselves from their constraint and suppression, and achieve the free realm of mind. And those who have achieved this realm were called 'arhats.'

This realm may be described as 'freedom from life, being and history.'

Mahayana Buddhism is based on the realm of Basic Buddhism but it refers to 'the task to make and change life and the world (history) through practice.' And they began to call those who live this kind of life 'bodhisattvas.'

This practice may well be expressed as 'freedom to life, being and history.'

Mahayana Buddhism puts up bodhisattva as the model of practical life. "Bodhisattva" is made by the combination of "bodhi" and "sattva" and it was used from the sutras of Early Buddhism. However, it came to be used with a new meaning in the time of Mahayana Buddhism. That is, 'bodhi' means the enlightenment of dependent arising, and 'sattva' is about the life and history of all sentient beings' world. And the combination of bodhi and sattva shows most appropriately the stance of Mahayana Buddhism where enlightenment and history are united.

There have been various interpretations on the concept of 'bodhisattva,' but it is difficult to find cases in which it is understood as a combination of 'enlightenment' and 'history.' However, I believe that the true mission of Mahayana will come to be realized with a new interpretation of the term 'bodhisattva.'

This stance of Mahayana Buddhism also generates a task of combining relativism and absolutism both of which may not look reconcilable at all from a certain perspective. Of course this absolutism here means a peculiar absolutism that has the features of being provisional, hypothetical and intentional.

Buddhism is usually regarded as an extreme version of relativistic worldview. However, Mahayana connects the intentional, imaginary and hypothetical stance of realism to this extremely relativistic stance. This was also possible as Early Buddhism's theory of dependent arising went through the 'Empty Self Real Dharmas' of the Abhidharma School, developed into the ideas of Emptiness Contemplation of Mahayana, and formed a unique perspective of ontology that views the world as empty, imaginary/hypothetical and in between. To graft the historical practices of intentional vow and upaya onto the thus developed ontological view based on dependent arising – this is the most satisfying theory of history that Mahayana Buddhism presents.

Several points to ponder on in relation to Mahayana Buddhism

Consciousness-Only Buddhism is not meant to address the issues of epistemology or psychology

Most people believe that Consciousness-Only Buddhism

belongs to the areas of epistemology and psychology. However, Consciousness-Only Buddhism actually aims to address the domain of the theory of dependent arising and further emphasize Mahayanist practices such as bodhisattva practices.

Consciousness-Only means 'the world, things, cognition, concepts, etc. – all these are the images reflected in the mind.' This means that cognition (the subject) and things (the object) mutually determine and penetrate each other, and they are related to each other in such a way that they can never be divided. The study of Consciousness-Only collects specifically 'the world, things, cognition, concepts, etc.' with the five groups of a hundred dharmas. That is, it says that these five groups of a hundred dharmas are the genuine features of dependent arising such that they are related to one another by inter-determining and inter-penetrating one another.

The Consciousness-Only School classifies the domain of being in this world mainly in five groups and then makes them classified again in fine-grained 100 kinds. They are, in general terms, material realm, mental realm and conceptual realm (The conceptual realm is the domain of concepts, which do not belong to the material or mental realm. Space, time, language, letters, numbers, laws, etc. belong to the conceptual realm).

One of the core teachings and main messages of the Consciousness-Only studies is that we should understand that these five groups of the hundred dharmas, that is, the material, mental and conceptual realms, or the subjective and objective realms are the beings of mutually dependent arising.

Early Buddhism teaches the theory of dependent arising with

'When this is, that is; this arising, that arises' and 'the dependent arising of life that functions in terms of 12 kinds of cycles.' This theory of dependent arising went through the stage that 'body, sensation, mind, dharma' and 'five aggregates, 12 sense fields and 18 compositional elements of cognition' and others exist with the mode of mutually dependent arising. When it reached the time of Abhidharmas and Mahayana Buddhism, it unfolded into the fine-grained and specific theory of dependent arising that the five groups of the hundred dharmas arise in terms of mutual dependence, which is the very Consciousness-Only Buddhism.

In a nutshell, the Consciousness-Only studies did not attempt to develop a fine-grained theory on the level of epistemology or psychology; it tried to emphasize that the material, mental and conceptual realms arise in the mode of mutual dependence.

Also, *The Sutra on Understanding Profound and Esoteric Doctrine* and *The Yogacarabhumi Sastra*, which make the bases of Consciousness-Only Buddhism, explain cognitive processes and the mode of being of material realm in terms of dependent arising, and recommends the method of cessation and observation to learn all this well. And, based on this theory of dependent arising, it explains extensively and emphasizes the 11 grounds and ten-paramitas. This is why we can say that Consciousness-Only Buddhism is Mahayana Buddhism that emphasizes wisdom and the practice of compassion. That is, Consciousness-Only Buddhism is neither epistemology nor psychology; it is the quintessence of Mahayana Buddhism that includes all of epistemology, ontology and the practice theory.

However, the reality is that when people explain

Consciousness-Only Buddhism, which is formed with the teachings of *The Sutra on Understanding Profound and Esoteric Doctrine* and *The Yogacarabhumi Sastra,* etc., they are confined in the areas of psychology and epistemology. This is very frustrating. In particular, the book title of *The Yogacarabhumi Sastra* has the following meaning: 'the stage of practice (bhumi)' of 'yoga practitioner (yogacara).' This book is a treatise that cites the entire text of *The Sutra on Understanding Profound and Esoteric Doctrine* and gives commentaries, and it explains various paramitas and other numerous methods of practice. Then, why do those who address Consciousness-Only Buddhism these days turn their eyes away from this point and instead talk about it only as psychology and epistemology?

It seems that this might also be the harmful effects of the Chinese Dharma-Character School. German Buddhism, which is said to be leading the studies of Consciousness-Only Buddhism these days, might not be able to escape this tendency, either. Now, Consciousness-Only Buddhism should justly make a proper Buddhology that advances and advocates the Mahayanist theory of practice based on the theory of dependent arising that harmonizes epistemology and ontology.

A critique of vipassana practice

It has been a while since the fever of vipassana practice, which was regarded as a critical alternative to Korean Zen Buddhism that practices the Chinese style of Phrase-Observing Meditation, started sweeping through Korea. I believe that this vipassana training, which is based on the understanding of the doctrines of Early Buddhism, is very encouraging for Korean Buddhism.

However, what I feel lacking is that when the practitioners of vipassana practice the mindfulness and observation on the four bases (body, sensation, mind, dharma), which is the central practice of vipassana, the practitioners exercise the mindfulness and observation on the body, sensation and mind but they do not use their mindfulness and observation for dharmas (the realm of beings, especially conceptual dharmas and material dharmas among the five groups of the hundred dharmas), and thereby their efforts result in the consequences that they cannot appropriately understand the world of dependent arising.

It is questionable if we must necessarily sit up straight or go to a training center for mindfulness and observation (Korean Buddhism, which tries to follow and reproduce Chinese Zen Buddhism, has the same issue), and what is important is the following problem: If the purpose of the meditation practice of the four bases of mindfulness is to realize that the material realm, mental realm, conceptual realm, etc. are all dependently arising phenomena (emptiness), can the feature of dependent arising of the entire lives and the world reveal itself if they leave out the mindfulness and observation on dharmas (beings)?

The issues of politics, society, economics, laws and nation, and the areas of physics, chemistry, biology and astronomy are related to one another in terms of dependent arising and they crucially influence our lives. All these belong to what the Consciousness-Only studies call 'the material realm and conceptual realm.' Then, why doesn't the current vipassana practice do mindfulness and observation for all of them?

In particular, the material and conceptual realms cannot be known to us simply through straight sitting up and meditative examination. To the contrary, it will be possible through a lot of reading, experiments, observations, dialogues, discussions and lectures. The abstract theories established in the Indian Buddhist Philosophy 2,000 years ago would not help us understand and observe these areas of material dharmas and conceptual dharmas. It is rather our current physics, bioscience (genetic engineering), chemistry, astronomy, politics, sociology, law, ethics, etc., which have been researched and collected through developed cognition and civilization, that will be more helpful.

Our realizing dependent arising and emptiness does not mean grasping the minute aspects of all areas of beings; it is knowing the structural correlation and changeability of beings. Accordingly, it does not demand knowledge about the subtle difference and distinctness of beings (dharmas) such as material dharmas, conceptual dharmas, etc. What this means is that we come to know the dependent arising of beings only when we know the structural correlations between material and conceptual dharmas and us ourselves (mental dharmas, etc.).

However, when we examine the contents of today's vipassana practices, the objects of observation through sitting meditation are confined to the problems of ourselves (breathing, body and the stream of mind). This is why I am saying that it is questionable if the practice of this vipassana can help make certain professional and appropriate judgments on the problems of life, society and the world.

We have exerted our efforts to accurately analyze and examine the body, breathing, mind and psychological phenomena. If we had made the same efforts for our lives, society and the world as well, Buddhists would truly have known the world and history comprehensively and become excellent teachers who help people.

Of course the goal of vipassana is not obtaining the specific and realistic (historical) understanding of life, society, etc. It is not like the tenth wisdom-paramita in bodhisattva' ten-paramitas. Its goal is to realize the dependent arising of all beings, which of course includes our bodies and minds, by understanding their correlations and changeability. That is, vipassana aims to obtain prajna wisdom, which is to realize dependent arising and emptiness, by properly practicing the four bases of mindfulness.

Then, vipassana's doctrinal status in Buddhism fits straightly in Basic Buddhism. Therefore, although Buddhists need to be basically awakened to dependent arising and emptiness by properly practicing vipassana, they should not think of their efforts for vipassana as everything there is in Buddhism. Genuine Buddhist practices consist, after all, in raising compassion and vow based on basic enlightenment (dependent arising, emptiness) and then cultivating various historical paramitas.

'Practice' is 'to cultivate bodhisattva practice'

Korean Buddhism has recently come to emphasize practice much. Slogans like 'Korean Buddhism practicing,' 'research and development of the practice theory,' 'boost of practice tradition,' etc. prove this.

The Korean and Chinese word for 'practice' is made of the words meaning 'cultivate' and 'act (or action).' So, 'cultivate' reminds us of the famous Chinese Zen Master Matsu's 'tile dharma talk' (It is said that a senior monk was grinding a tile while Matsu was in sitting meditation. The senior monk told the embarrassed Matsu that one could not obtain enlightenment by sitting or concentrating his mind as no one could make a mirror by grinding a tile).

We generally think of 'practice' as 'controlling the mind and body well,' but, in the Korean Buddhist order (Jogye Order), 'meditating (Phrase-Observing Meditation) to achieve enlightenment' is practice. And they might also regard as practice 'vipassana,' 'meditation,' etc. that have recently attracted much attention.

In early sutras, we can see that the term 'bhavana,' which means 'general practice,' appears numerously many times apart from the other terms like vipassana (observation), samatha (cessation) and dhyana (meditation) that require special efforts. This 'bhavana' means 'becoming, trying' and it is translated to 'diligent action, practice,' etc., and this 'bhavana' became the origin of the word "practice." However, the actual word for practice used in Korea these days must be the term "practice" that has been translated and used from Mahayana sutras like *The Flower Garland Sutra,* but this "practice" is a term that is interpreted as meaning 'to cultivate action/practice,' not 'to cultivate and practice.' This 'cultivate' in 'to cultivate action/practice' is a transitive verb like 'cultivate' in 'to cultivate the Way.'

Then, what is this 'action/practice' in 'to cultivate action/ practice' that Mahayana sutras address? It is the very 'bodhisattva practice.' Words like 'to cultivate practices,' 'to cultivate bodhisattva practices,' 'to cultivate bodhisattvas' all wholesome practices,' 'to cultivate wholesome roots,' 'to cultivate merits,' etc. are numerously repeated in Mahayana sutras like *The Flower Garland Sutra* and others. All of 'to cultivate bodhisattva practices,' 'to cultivate bodhisattvas' all wholesome practices,' 'to cultivate wholesome roots' and 'to cultivate merits' were abridged and abbreviated to make the word "practice," which means 'to cultivate practice.'

However, since bodhisattva practice means ten-paramitas, it includes meditation-paramita and prajna-paramita. Therefore, to cultivate cessation and observation practice, to cultivate vipassana, and to cultivate Phrase-Observing Meditation are naturally all practices. But the realm of Mahayana demands that meditation and prajna should accompany and cling to all thoughts and actions. Prajna-paramita is the correct perspective and wisdom that cannot be deserted even for a moment in all social practices and fields of historical life. Therefore, since the cultivation of bodhisattva practices in the Mahayanist sense means the practices that unfold basically grounded on prajna (the perspective of dependent arising), we need to regard both prajna and meditation as already achieved.

The issue of the worldview of dependent arising was a difficult problem to understand 2,000 or 2,500 years ago, but I believe we can understand it very easily these days by dint of advanced civilization, research and studies (liberal arts, social and natural sciences, etc.). If we believe that it is a difficult problem, it is because we think of it as some mysterious realm of the mind and body.

It cannot be the case that we necessarily need to investigate Abhidharmas and various Buddhist sutras to understand well the meaning of dependent arising of life, society and the world. Since numerous terms and contents were inaccurately translated and modified in the process of translating sutras and sastras, written in Indian Sanskrit 1,500 years ago, to the different language system of Chinese, we cannot recommend contemporary people to meticulously translate and understand them.

Accordingly, I believe that we do not have to follow the study method of Buddhism used when civilization was in its undeveloped stage and education was not appropriate. On the contrary, understanding dependent arising and emptiness has become easier in our contemporary time. I believe the study of Buddhism may well be made of the standard contents that an average adult can understand if he or she has contemporary education, learns Buddhist doctrines for a certain period of time, appreciates and organizes their contents well. However, this presupposes that the leaders of Buddhism should not mislead people about Buddhism or enlightenment. I am saying this because there still are cases in which some leaders of Buddhism assume the enlightenment of this dependent arising and emptiness as 'some realm of the mind and body' and they mislead people into the belief that practice is to cultivate (?) the mind and body while sitting alone on a rock in the deep mountains or on a mountain peak.

The light and shade of 'the theory of Original Buddha'

Ever since Early Buddhism, Buddhism has emphasized that life and the world are impermanent, with no self [no atman], dependently arising and empty, and has maintained the relativistic worldview that does not presuppose any fixed or unchanging real beings. The basic messages have been "All appearances are untrue and groundless,' 'so, know their groundlessness well and free yourselves from them,' etc.

However, as Buddhism underwent the time of Abhidharmas and came to profess Mahayana Buddhism, there appeared a new, strange current that conflicted with this relativistic worldview. Such terms as 'Buddha-Nature,' 'True Suchness,' 'womb of the Tathagata,' 'the Eternal Buddha,' 'the Original Buddha,' etc. began to show up in a variety of Mahayana sutras and sastras. Ever since this new current, the Buddhism that puts up True Suchness, the womb of the Tathagata and the Eternal Buddha, all of which *prima facie* look like realist ideas, and the Buddhism that emphasizes impermanence and non-self were mixed and mingled, and this situation brought about a lot of doctrinal debates and confusion in India. All this transferred to China intact. In China, the Buddhism that professes True Suchness, the Womb of the Tathagata and the Eternal Buddha, rather than the Buddhism that focuses on impermanence and non-self, obtained a higher status and was highly thought of as *the* Mahayana Buddhism.

And in China, apart from this issue, Daoist terminologies at the time of the Wei and Jin Dynasties were introduced to Buddhism in the process of understanding Buddhism, and Chinese Buddhism took in such views of realist ontology as 'Way' and 'nature.' And they also interpreted and accepted universal and realist Daoist expressions like 'The heaven-earth and I are one body, all things and I have one root' in a Buddhist way.

And later on in Zen Buddhism of the Tang and Song Dynasties, such expressions as 'The entire world is all truth,' 'Green bamboos are the features of True Suchness, and blooming yellow chrysanthemums are prajna itself,' 'Everything is a Buddha,' 'The green mountain is the figure of the Buddha, and the sound of running water is the Buddha's dharma talk' and 'Mind is the Buddha' began to be used ordinarily.

This Buddhism, represented by 'the Original Buddha' and 'the Eternal Buddha,' is the Buddhism that is these days most naturally accepted in Korean Buddhism. However, the problem is precisely how this Buddhism understands and accepts such expressions as 'the Original Buddha,' etc.

Early Buddhism would find it doctrinally difficult to tolerate these expressions. *The Diamond Sutra*, an early Mahayana sutra, also teaches that atman as Indian Brahmanism's eternal self, pudgala as an eternal person that subsists separately from five aggregates, jiva as an eternal life and sattva as everything alive are all untrue and groundless. Then, in what course were the ideas of 'the Original Buddha,' 'the Eternal Buddha' and 'the Womb of the Tathagata' born?

Paradoxically, these ideas were already conceived in the ontology of dependent arising. Early sutras have an expression "The truth of dependent arising resides permanently in the dharma realm whether Thus Come One[107] comes to the secular world or not (*Miscellaneous Agamas*, Vol 12, 299)," and also have the contents "To see the 12 links of dependent arising is to see the Supreme Way and possess the Dharma Body (*The Salastamba Sutra*)." These contents regarding the permanent existence of the truth of dependent arising in dharma realm gave significant influence on Nikaya Buddhism as well and were also connected to the debates on whether the truth of dependent arising is an unconditioned dharma or conditioned dharma.

These passages, related to dependent arising, might have been added or modified later in the process in which sutras were edited and made. Also, the worldview of dependent arising that denies the existence of any fixed and unchanging real beings might have been modified on the defense level to present counter arguments against the various realisms (Samkhya, Vaisesika, etc.) of Indian society.

Anyhow, I guess Buddhists have always needed ways to enable them to live active historical lives even with the theory of non-self and dependent arising. So, it is believed that they examined the teaching of dependent arising carefully and arrived at the following conclusion.

We came to realize, through impermanence, non-self and dependent arising, that the world is untrue and groundless, transient and just like a dream. We are liberated from everything in the world by dint of this understanding. This is the first lesson we earned through the teaching of dependent arising.

---

107 One of the names of the Buddha.

However, that the world arises dependently (changeability, relatedness) means 'Beings do not exist in the forms of fixed and unchanging real beings,' but not 'There exists no being at all.'

Then, the teaching that things are dependently arising beings does not mean that beings do not exist, but that they exist in special ways. And this means that beings are closely connected to other beings, they interpenetrate one another, and they constantly change with no dwelling even for an instant.

If we understand dependent arising this way, we can derive the consequence that we can have an active ontology that sees beings positively and dynamically. This is the second lesson.

As we saw above, two different meanings of lessons have been drawn from the teaching of dependent arising. These ideas were systemized through the movements of Abhidharmas and Mahayana Buddhism.

In particular, the Sarvastivada School developed the second lesson and presented their view of 'Empty Self Real Dharmas,' and it was responsible for such Madhyamaka expressions for beings as 'empty,' 'hypothetical/provisional' and 'in between.'

Buddha-Nature, True Suchness and the Womb of the Tathagata seem to be the names that were created in the process that such neutral expressions like 'Real Dharmas,' 'provisional/hypothetical' and 'in between' were religiously embellished. And we may well see in this context Chinese Zen Buddhism's expressions like 'Mind is the Buddha' and 'Everything is the Buddha.'

The Buddhist ontology has thus made various transitions through the following stages with terms of slightly different

nuances: impermanence, non-self and dependent arising →
emptiness → provisional/hypothetical → in between → Buddha-
Nature, True Suchness and the Womb of the Tathagata → Mind is
the Buddha → Everything is a Buddha.

The problem is whether the ontology of dependent arising is
appropriately reflected when the terms of 'Buddha-Nature,' 'True
Suchness' and 'the Buddha' are used. However, when readers come
across dharma talks and writings that use these terms, it is not easy
for them to tell whether it is being done or not.

When we use the terms of 'the Eternal Buddha' and 'the
Original Buddha,' unless we always heed this issue carefully, we
might inadvertently bring about the consequences of mistaking
Buddhism for Brahmanism or Daoism with only different
expressions.

After all, these terms have been used in accordance with the
situations and demands, and they will be continuously used. So, we
should use them always reminding ourselves of the two aspects of
the lesson that the Buddhist ontology of dependent arising gives us.

Therefore, when we use terms like True Suchness, the Womb
of the Tathagata and the Original Buddha, we need to have the
Mahayanist meaning of 'Produce a mind with no dwelling' in *The
Diamond Sutra* recalled to mind. Even this should be based on
the basic Buddhist perspective that the world is an illusion and
empty, and we need to use the terms of the Original Buddha, True
Suchness and the Womb of the Tathagata only if we know that they
are provisionally hypothesized and are only temporary names of
the characteristics of dependent arising.

This twofold aspect needs to be applied and used in the Mahayanist stance, and thus this is a cautious stance that is not always easy to understand. This difficulty is illustrated in the following episode of *The Lotus Sutra* that appears at the beginning part of the Buddha's dharma talk: the Buddha refuses to give dharma talks three times, 5,000 disgruntled audience left, and only after these twists and turns did the Buddha begin to talk about 'the Eternal Buddha.'

In the chapter on the ten grounds in *The Flower Garland Sutra* as well, Bodhisattva Vajragarbha gives dharma talks on bodhisattvas' ten-paramitas and the ten grounds (the ten stages of practices) only after he turns down the request for teaching three times but the audience still asks him for dharma talks repeatedly. These examples show us that it is not easy to explain the subtle twofold stance of Mahayana.

I believe the greatest attraction Buddhism gives people is that Buddhism awakens them to the truth of 'Everything is a dream, an illusion and transient,' has them put down at once all the heavy burdens that history and life give them, and liberate and free them.

As there is a title of a novel, 'The Unbearable Lightness of Being,' the stance to take a 'light' attitude in living a life may easily attract criticisms from those who accept life seriously and gravely. However, there is nothing we can do about it [the lightness] because this is the way that life, being and history are. Life is untrue and groundless, and it is an illusion, but while we live and exist, we must pursue happiness and solve the problem of suffering. Isn't this why the Mahayanist stance of 'Producing a mind with no dwelling' was put up?

However, when Buddhists talk about 'the Eternal Buddha,' 'the

Original Buddha' and 'All things are Buddhas,' they must always remember the following story in *The Vimalakirti Sutra*: 'The realm of sentient beings is an illusion. However, although bodhisattvas should raise illusory compassion, practice various paramitas and aim for the Pure Land, the Pure Land that bodhisattvas wish to achieve is also an illusion.' – this is the basic stance of Mahayana Buddhism. That is, we must think about the light and shade of 'the theory of the Original Buddha.'

The slogan of 'the Original Buddha' may approach people as a delightful teaching, but we must also consider the point that it may become a heavy burden and causes us fatigue when we face beings. And we should also be prepared to answer the following question: If we are all originally Buddhas for eternity, why do we need to make any efforts to improve ourselves and why should we set a new goal to achieve?

Only by doing so, people would not mistakenly understand the world and life in terms of Brahmanism and Christian realism when they hear expressions like 'the Original Buddha' and 'All things are Buddhas,' and they can take off the heavy burden about life that the proposition 'Everything is a Buddha' gives. And, finally, they should live lives of harmonizing the 'lightness' and 'heaviness' of life and history like music.

Conclusion

I have recently read a philosophy book written for the general public and come across a passage "The philosophy of our time has been known to virtually no one but philosophers." The author deplored that philosophy had been distanced from the interest of the general public.

What is the meaning of Buddhism for present day contemporary people and the Korean society, and how well is it known and how much attention does it attract? If Buddhism has no special meaning to most people these days, if it is almost unknown and if it is not receiving any good attention from people, all this must be because of the following reasons.

Firstly, it is because we explain Buddhism as a practice method to train the mind in a person's life, or as some method to realize a certain profound thing in mind and achieve a mysterious realm.

As there is a famous proposition that humans are social animals, no problem of life can be solved self-sufficiently on the level of person. The personal problem itself is also produced in the context of social relations. Love, money (economy), work, recreation and cultural life, and also freedom, equality, justice, etc. that are required to live social lives – none of these are possible separately from other people and social problems.

All these are the urgent and necessary issues of the contemporary people. But the problem is that Buddhism cannot address these issues at all. Instead, it only emphasizes the effects of the mind cultivation and psychotherapy, or it recommends a mysterious realm of enlightenment that has nothing to do with ordinary life.

Secondly, we are explaining Buddhism in a difficult way, and we have much tendency to use professional Buddhist terminologies which only Buddhists can comprehend.

It is a problem that monastics, missionary workers and

Buddhologists do not explain Buddhism with the terminologies of contemporary life but instead use for their explanation only Buddhist sutras and literature that reflect the civilizational level of the Indian society 2,000 years ago. Furthermore, we are using the terms and predicates translated in ancient Chinese letters 1,500 years ago for contemporary Koreans who cannot even interpret the Korean letters of the 15th Century. This is quite frustrating.

We should provide a new, fresh and contemporary style of stories on Buddhism if society and the economy come to have more flexibility and a higher level of education. For this purpose, we need to create Abhidharmas[108] of our time. If we simply introduce yet again the doctrinal issues of the time of Nikaya Buddhism by analyzing and researching the literature of their time, we will not be able to attract contemporary people's attention and understanding.

Thirdly, Buddhism is not being able to meet the expectations and aspirations that the general public has about Buddhism' socio-historical utility.

Of course, Buddhism is actively engaged in fortune-seeking religious activities like prayers, Buddhist services, ancestral rites, etc., and the image and refutation formed through these activities are representing Korean Buddhism. However, we cannot say that these activities embody the teachings of Buddhism, can we?

Be it the East or West, what Buddhism lacks most is its social, historical and ethical characteristics. Mahayana Buddhism, which

---

108 In this context, 'Abhidharmas' mean discussion, debates, discourse or philosophical arguments.

claims to combine enlightenment and history, should be ashamed.

The sophisticated doctrinal system of Early Buddhism, the expansive worldview and rich and symbolic theory of practices in Mahayana Buddhism, Zen Buddhism's world of prajna full of metaphors… However, if all these have nothing to do with the language and contents of the life of our time, what value do they have?

This article is not a story about 'What is Buddhism.' It is about an idea on 'What is it like to live a Buddhist way of life, how should Buddhists live?' Its conclusion is that we need to understand and practice Buddhism in the Mahayanist way. For this goal, it suggests that we should fundamentally have, as the base, Basic Buddhism – that is, the perspective of dependent arising, emptiness and prajna –, raise compassion and vow on that ground, and live the history that practices various paramitas.

With 'various paramitas' I mean nothing symbolic or abstract but something as very specific and realistic as the four-paramitas of upaya, vow, power and wisdom among ten-paramitas. And we should begin to create a theory of paramitas related to history, the theory that has not been able to attract any attention and has remained stagnant for almost a thousand years.

Newly created paramitas must have specificity in everything from the problems of ethics and morals to the issues that lead society and history. We do not have to find the contents of all these in the sutras, treatises or Zen masters' dialogues. For they do not exist in there.

These contents exist in the studies and theories, which our contemporary society is replete with, and also on the field of history that progresses in complicated ways. We must find the contents in there.

For this is the very meaning of the tenth wisdom-paramita that tells us "Bodhisattvas, raise enormous compassion, enter the densely-packed forest of sentient beings and realize the distinctive characteristics of the world!"

Glossary

Most entries in this glossary are based on the corresponding entries in A. Charles Muller's *A Korean-English Dictionary of Buddhism* (Unju Books, 2014) and Park Young-eui's *The Practical Dictionary of Korean-English Buddhist Terms* (Joheun Inyeon, 2012).

arhat ⏐ The highest type or saint in Hinayana.

bodhi ⏐ Enlightenment.

bodhicitta ⏐ "Bodhicitta" is a combination of "bodhi(enlightenment)" and "citta(mind)." The idea of bodhicitta is that one should wish (or, 'mind') to achieve enlightenment to save suffering beings of the world. According to the Korean Buddhist tradition, having bodhicitta is as good as achieving enlightenment because the great compassion of practitioners helps make their enlightenment easier and faster.

dharma ⏐ This word has a wide range of meaning such as the Buddha's teaching, truth and ontological entity.

five evil activities ⏐ They are killing, stealing, adultery, lying and drinking intoxicants.

five gates of mindfulness ⏐ They are (1) worship of the image of Amitabha, (2) invoking the name of Amitabha, (3) vowing to be reborn in the Pure Land, (4) meditating on the glories of the Pure Land and (5) transferring one's own accumulated merit to all sentient beings.

four immeasurable states of mind ı They are (1) the immeasurable loving-kindness, (2) the immeasurable compassion, (3) the immeasurable mind of joy at the happiness of others and (4) the immeasurable equanimity.

four marks ı *The Diamond Sutra* and other scriptures address the four types of attachments that most people have. (1) The mark of self is about the attachment on the part of self when there is a relation between self and others. (2) The mark of personality addresses the state in which one, being a member of human race, is immersed in the narrow and limited, very human perception. (3) The mark of sentient being is about the way we get used to the phenomenon of life and mistake it for a self although life itself comes into and passes out of existence only in terms of relations and changes. This mark also refers to the stance that one might assume when he or she comes to have some inferiority complex when his or her life is compared with the good lives of others. (4) The mark of soul is a misconception that life is a substance and subsists for a period of time.

four noble truth ı The Buddha's teaching of suffering, craving, elimination and the way: life is full of suffering, its cause is craving, we can eliminate suffering by removing its cause, and there is a way to accomplish this.

four winning methods ı The four leading methods that bodhisattvas employ to approach and save people and other sentient beings: generosity, kind words or speech, beneficial conduct and amicable association.

noble eightfold path ı The Buddha's teaching of right view, right thought, right speech, right action, right livelihood, right effort, right mindfulness and right meditation.

paramita ∣ 'Paramita' literally means 'to cross over from this shore (this world of suffering) to the other shore (world) of enlightenment and nirvana.' It also means 'practice' and 'perfection.'

sangha ∣ The Buddhist order or community.

sixteen meditations of Amitabha ∣ They are (1) meditation on the setting sun, (2) meditation on the waters, (3) meditation on the land, (4) meditation on its jeweled trees, (5) meditation on its jeweled pond, (6) meditation on its jeweled palace, (7) meditation on its flower-adorned throne, (8) meditation on Amitabha's true form, (9) meditation on Amitabha's true body, (10) meditation on Avalokitesvara's true form, (11) meditation on Mahasthamaprapta, (12) meditation on one's universal body after rebirth in the Pure Land, (13) meditation on complex concepts, (14) meditation by superior practitioners, (15) meditation by middling practitioners and (16) meditation by inferior practitioners.

Sunim ∣ A transliteration of the Korean word for 'Buddhist monastic.'

sutra ∣ A scripture, book. The recorded words of a sage.

ten abodes ∣ What it means is that the mind dwells peacefully in the principle of emptiness. They are (1) the abode of awakening operation, (2) the abode of nurturing, (3) the abode of practice, (4) the abode of producing virtues, (5) the abode of being replete with skillful means, (6) the abode of correct mind, (7) the abode of no-backsliding, (8) the abode of the true child, (9) the abode of the dharma-prince and (10) the abode of lustration.

ten dedications (ten kinds of directing) । They are (1) dedication to saving all sentient beings without any mental image of sentient beings, (2) indestructible dedication, (3) dedication equal to all Buddhas, (4) dedication reaching all places, (5) dedication of inexhaustible treasuries of merit, (6) dedication causing all roots of goodness to endure, (7) dedication equally adapting to all sentient beings, (8) dedication with the character of true thusness, (9) unbound liberated dedication and (10) boundless dedication equal to the cosmos.

ten good actions (ten wholesome behaviors) । They are (1) not killing, (2) not stealing, (3) not committing adultery, (4) not lying; (5) not speaking harshly, (6) not speaking divisively, (7) not speaking idly, (8) not being greedy, (9) not being angry and (10) not having wrong views.

ten grounds । The ten grounds of bodhisattva development in the Flower Garland system are (1) the ground of joy, (2) the ground of freedom from defilement, (3) the ground of emission of light, (4) the ground of glowing wisdom, (5) the ground of overcoming the difficult, (6) the ground of manifestation of reality, (7) the ground of far-reaching, (8) the ground of being unperturbed, (9) the ground of wondrous wisdom and (10) the ground of the dharma-cloud.

ten kinds of mindfulness । They are (1) mindfulness of the Buddha, (2) mindfulness of the dharma, (3) mindfulness of the sangha, (4) mindfulness of the precepts, (5) mindfulness of giving, (6) mindfulness of the gods, (7) mindfulness of cessation of thoughts, (8) mindfulness of breath-counting, (9) mindfulness of the fact that the body is not eternal and (10) mindfulness of death.

ten practices ⏐ They are (1) the practice of giving joy, (2) the practice of benefit, (3) the practice of non-opposition, (4) the practice of indomitability, (5) the practice of non-confusion, (6) the practice of skillful manifestation, (7) the practice of non-attachment, (8) the practice of that which is difficult to attain, (9) the practice of good teachings and (10) the practice of truth.

ten stages of faith ⏐ Faith is the entry of Buddhist practice. They are (1) the stage of faith, (2) the stage of mindfulness, (3) the stage of making efforts, (4) the state of mental stability, (5) the stage of the wisdom, (6) the stage of self-restraint, (7) the stage of directing to goals, (8) the stage of maintaining the dharma, (9) the stage of detachment and (10) the stage of aspiration.

thirty seven aids to enlightenment ⏐ They are the four bases of mindfulness, the four right efforts, the four magical powers, the five faculties of goodness, the five powers, the seven factors of enlightenment and the holy eightfold path.

upaya ⏐ A skillful mean or convenient tool. The Buddha and bodhisattvas use a variety of (innumerably many!) different methods to teach and save suffering beings depending on their aptitudes, temperaments, capabilities, etc.

upaya-paramita ⏐ One of ten-paramitas. It is the practice and/or perfection of (the virtue of) skillful means to lead suffering beings to the other shore and save them.

• The cover design is a contemporary graphic symbolization of the relations among the core elements of Buddhism such as impermanence, Non-Self, dependent arising, emptiness, and compassion.

Enlightenment and History
Theory and Praxis in Contemporary Buddhism

First Edition June 1, 2017
Written by Ven. Hyun-Eung
Translated by Chang-Seong Hong & Sun Kyeong Yu
Cover design by Koodamm
Published by Bulkwang Publishing
3F, 45-13, Ujeongguk-ro, Jongno-gu, Seoul, Korea
Tel: +82-2-420-3200
www.bulkwang.co.kr

Copyright © Ven. Hyun-Eung All Rights Reserved

ISBN 978-89-7479-347-0 (03220)

Printed in the Republic of South Korea